£25.00

D1477008

C905036964

Keith Kyle, Reporting the World

Keith Kyle, Reporting the World

Keith Kyle

I.B. TAURIS
LONDON · NEW YORK

Published in 2009 by I.B.Tauris & Co. Ltd
6 Salem Road, London W2 4BU
175 Fifth Avenue, New York, NY 10010
www.ibtauris.com

Distributed in the United States and Canada Exclusively by Palgrave Macmillan
175 Fifth Avenue, NY 10010

ISBN: 978 1 84885 000 2

A full CIP record for this book is available from the British Library
A full CIP record for this book is available from the Library of Congress

Library of Congress catalog card: available

Typeset in Perpetua by A. & D. Worthington, Newmarket, Suffolk
Printed and bound in Great Britain by CPI Antony Rowe, Chippenham

FSC
Mixed Sources
Product group from well-managed
forests and other controlled sources
Cert no. SGS-COC-2953
www.fsc.org
© 1996 Forest Stewardship Council

Contents

Illustrations

Preface

The late Ruthenian-American celebrity Andy Warhol was responsible for the view that everyone had in him 15 minutes of fame. I doubt it. On many occasions I was led to question it in the course of noting down these reflections on my life and times. My work for *The Economist* does not count since it was anonymous. Perhaps a few of my television reports for the BBC would rate a few minutes, especially the two controversial ones from Israel and Northern Ireland. Could these be knitted together with my book about Suez and the crisis of 1956 (and another about Kenya) to make up the 15 minutes? I was a political correspondent and an international reporter and I failed four times to get into Parliament.

I started this account as a private hobby after I had retired as Visiting Professor of History at the University of Ulster, my last (part-time) appointment, and added to it off and on over a number of years. Finally I was persuaded – or was it that I persuaded myself? – that, for all my doubts, I should go for publication. It will be for you, the readers, to decide whether that was a good idea.

I feel that I must apologise in advance to two classes of people. The first are those sometimes close personal friends and professional associates who could reasonably have expected that I should have mentioned them but find that I have not. I have not forgotten them. My only defence is that I did not want to drift into what would amount to making lists of my favourite people, and I hope that except on a very few occasions I have succeeded in not doing so. Absence of mention does not in any way reflect lack of appreciation of the warmth and comfort I have drawn and still draw from a great variety of individuals.

The second class deserving of apology consists of those who find inaccuracies in the text or, having been present, take a different view of an episode that I have described. I did not keep a diary but I have my own articles and television scripts to act as guides and I have several boxes of letters to my parents and, later, my wife. I have done my best to check publicly verifiable facts. But when all is said and done the book is held together by my memory, rather good in its long-term form, as opposed to my short-term memory which those who know me recognise as being somewhat deficient. But as a historian I fully accept that no long-term memory is perfect and mistakes (I hope not too many) will undoubtedly have crept in.

One other thing I should explain. Readers will find only a few scattered references to my dear wife Suzy and even fewer to my two sons. When I first mentioned to my wife the idea of writing memoirs she said that it would be fine if I wrote a history of myself but she would not like a history of the family. I have kept to this but it ought not to obscure the immense debt I owe to Suzy and my sense of pride in our two sons, with whom I enjoy a degree of companionship unthinkable with my own father. My elder son Tarquin has a lovely wife, Mary, and they have presented us with a heavenly four-year-old grandson, Patrick, whom I dare to hope will one day want to read this book. I am doubly fortunate because my younger son Crispin and his wife Edith are expecting my granddaughter this year. And without Crispin's constant guidance I should never have been able to function in the world of computers.

My wife's indispensable contribution to this book has been the hours of time she has spent with the sub-editing of the material and its preparation for the publisher. It is, of course, dedicated to her.

Keith Kyle
1 February 2007

CHAPTER 1

Foundations

I was born in Sturminster Newton in Dorset, the 'Stourcastle' of Thomas Hardy's *Tess of the D'Urbervilles*, where on the brow of the hill overlooking the ancient bridge stood the thatched-roofed cottage hospital. It was and is a pretty building, now converted into a number of professional offices, and at the time of my birth was flanked by two palm trees. They were not large palm trees, mighty symbols of an 'empire on which the sun never sets', which in 1925, with George V on the throne, Stanley Baldwin in Number Ten and Calvin Coolidge in the White House, seemed set for ages; they were in truth rather puny palm trees and since then, like the Empire, have disappeared. 'Is his nose straight?' asked my mother anxiously. 'Is he cross-eyed?' my father wanted to know. 'You are a strange pair of parents,' said the midwife.

My father was a Cornishman by birth but of Scots-Irish descent. He had started off in Penzance in a solicitor's office, where he had picked up shorthand and was taught to write the magnificent old-fashioned legal script with which he always used to dress up important documents. From there he managed – how, I have no idea – to escape from his Cornish background by becoming assistant agent to Lord Bolton at his Hackwood estate near Old Basing, a post which put him in close contact with Lord Bolton's overweening tenant, the Marquess Curzon of Kedleston, former Viceroy of India and future Foreign Secretary. Lord Curzon's style can be gauged by his mode of address to employees, such as, 'Housemaid, throw wide the casements.' It used to be left to my father, who must have been a rather self-confident young man, to clear up the wreckage left behind by the former Viceroy's passage. The servant who was told 'Gatekeeper, I applaud your absence of presumption' would require repeated reassurance that he had not caused serious offence.

My parents were married in 1922 and my wholly metropolitan mother was abruptly translated, somewhat to her dismay, into a country dweller at the bottom of a lane. Electricity had not arrived; I can remember the gaslights being trimmed of an evening. The villa bordered a farm and I clearly recall my distress at not being allowed to recover a precious chain which had fallen through the gate lest I be interfered with by snuffling pigs. There was a sizeable vegetable garden, which I improved by planting sweet peas among the carrots and potatoes, and there was an outhouse which provided a home for our seven cats, who followed me in single file when I crossed a field with my mother to the shops. They were all stray and some, as the result of inbreeding, lacked one limb or another.

About the interior of the house I can remember little, except that the rafters came down very low in my nursery. I recall only one item in its furnishing, a picture showing a tug of war between, on the one side, 13 dogs of various shapes and sizes each labelled by the name of a European country, with 'the little Portuguese' falling off the end, and, on the other side, a single resplendent and clearly victorious bulldog wrapped in a Union Jack. The accompanying rhyme declared that John Bull was 'equal to all these'. Thus early was my introduction to the proper study of international affairs.

I did not go to school immediately. This was because my parents had social ambitions for me. My mother in particular was determined that I should be the first member of my family to go to a public school and university, while the local school, with boys and girls of the village in attendance, might mark me for life with an accent. As a qualified schoolmistress she was allowed to teach me at home. Since I did not go to school until I was nine, I should say straightaway that she gave me an excellent start in all subjects except Latin (which she did not know herself) and maths (in regard to which I was unteachable). She had a lovely reading voice and I could listen to her reading to me for hours at a stretch. To her great frustration, I was a late reader until, one day, I picked up *Alice in Wonderland* and read it through without the slightest difficulty.

I cannot remember having any friends, except for children I met on holidays. I was and remained an only child. This did not worry me in the least, though grown-ups were forever saying in my presence either that I must be spoilt or that I must be lonely. Later on my mother used to ask me whether I would like a little brother or sister. I displayed perfect indifference. To this day, I do not know how seriously the question was asked or whether a different reply would have had consequences. My mother did, however, once give me a reason for my being alone. She said that since it was impossible to guarantee that the next child would be a girl, who would not need money spent on her education, the danger was that two boys would have to split the meagre funds available.

Summer holidays were spent in Cornwall, which for me ever since has been a very special place. The devil, I was taught at the time, never crossed the river Tamar into the duchy because he had been warned that if he did he would be chopped up like everything else to be put into a Cornish pasty. The earlier stages of the annual pilgrimage to the paternal homestead were very tense since we had to travel on a local railway line to join the Penzance train at the junction of Templecombe. My father invested the switching from one train to another with an atmosphere of high drama as our large trunks had to be deposited in the luggage van of the Cornish Riviera (as the Penzance train was optimistically described). The rushing up and down the platform, the bawling of orders, the bullying of family and porters made such a scene out of Hades that several halts would have to pass before I had recovered the poise to enjoy the simple pleasures of the journey.

Sunday was a very special occasion in the little semi-detached house in Cornwall. It was the day both of the weekly bath and the Sunday roast. I would be led by my mother (when I was older I would go alone) up to the nearby farm for the milk. This was dispensed by an immensely fat young woman called Miss Roach, whose face was covered with huge clumps of bristling hair and who passed locally for an intellectual ever since a Cornish dialect play of hers had been accepted by the BBC. Morning was spent going to and from the village well, so that 'the copper', a huge receptacle that was dragged out from under everything else in the kitchen, could be filled for the bath. We then set forth, grandfather, mother, father and I on the long walk across the fields and over the stiles to the nearest church. My grandfather, dressed in a Panama hat, frock coat and high winged collar and perspiring mightily on the journey, stopped at each stile to take off the hat and wipe its band with much vigour. My aunt Omy, staying behind to prepare the roast, used to equip me with a milk can for picking enough blackberries 'to stain a tart'.

My mother, for as long as I could remember, spent much time dreaming of going abroad. She never succeeded in leaving the country. For some reason she had a special wish to see the Dolomites. Every year the brochures would come round and she would debate first with me and then with my father where we should go. Father never exactly vetoed foreign travel, but somehow the booking was never made and my parents would ultimately pronounce, 'We had better go to Cornwall again this year.'

Until the age of about seven I had a butterfly mind, with no steady hobbies, little enthusiasm for anything in particular and much restless moving about. One day I asked my father who was king before the present monarch, George V. I was told Edward VII. Who before him? Answer: Victoria. Who before her? My father, tired of this game and possibly not knowing the answer, called in at Beach's, a brand new bookshop in Salisbury's High Street, now replaced by an

1. Aged nine.

Italian eatery, and came back brandishing a thick volume, Haydn's *Dictionary of Dates*, for whose many pages he was delighted to be able to report that he had only to pay sixpence. From that moment 'all changed, changed utterly'. Greedily I hoovered up the dates of kings; then I zeroed in on one of them: King Hardicanute or, as he is normally spelled, Harthacnut, son of Canute the Dane. Every scrap of information about him had to be pursued. His burning down of Worcester showed to me that he was not a man to be trifled with; his dropping down dead after saying 'If I lie may this bread kill me' was the chastisement of an implacable God.

How was I to learn more history? Help was at hand in the shape of my father's next employer, William Pleydell-Bouverie, seventh Earl of Radnor, a descendant of Laurens des Bouverie who was a Huguenot immigrant from Frankfurt in 1536. Fairly soon after we had come to Longford Castle (near Salisbury) I had been invited by Helena, Lord Radnor's highly attractive wife, to play with her elder children – Jane, who was older than I was, Belinda, who was about the same age, and Jake, the heir to the peerage, who was a couple of years younger. Through the endless woods and paths of the estate with its seasonal cycle of snowdrops, daffodils and bluebells, through the formal gardens and the informal ones, in happy concourse with my new companions, I felt gloriously liberated. With the countess I was something of a favourite, so that I was included in all manner of castle pursuits, such as Christmas parties with such guests as Humphrey Lyttelton and Edward Montagu (Lord Montagu of Beaulieu), amateur theatricals, pony riding and brilliant pageants on major historical themes (such as, one year, the Canterbury Tales, as explicated by Lord David Cecil).

One day I was allowed to accompany a group of foreign visitors being shown round the castle's impressive collection of pictures. Lord Radnor was himself the guide and my father was present. 'And this,' the Earl said, 'is Mary Queen of Scots with her son James I.' 'Oh no, that's quite impossible,' I piped up. 'That boy is at least seven and Mary never saw James after he was ten months old.' My father's face fell open. 'Quite right,' said Lord Radnor, 'only we must allow the artist a little licence.' My father, much out of countenance, mumbled incoherently. As soon as his guests had gone Lord Radnor asked, 'How did the boy know that?' 'Oh, some silly craze he's got. He'll soon get over it.' 'You encourage him. You tell him that he's to have complete access to the Muniment Room. It's full of history books. I've tried to interest my family but none of them goes near the place.'[1] My life was transformed.

From then on I either worked on the books in the castle or, some time later, was allowed to take home the many volumes of the famous 11th edition of the *Encyclopedia Britannica*, with its leather binding and rice paper. Toys, with which I had hitherto played in a rather desultory manner because it was expected of me, were abandoned, outside interests were neglected. For hour after hour I read history in a state of great exaltation. 'There's that boy,' my father would roar, 'rumped over a book,' and then I was locked out, with orders to go and climb a tree. There was a tree stump in our rose garden right beneath the kitchen window, which I had sometimes used to enable me to toss mown grass into the salad when my mother wasn't looking; it now enabled me to climb back into my books. The little kitchen maid would be my ally, so much so that I once impulsively kissed her hand and, this being seen by my mother, I was in deep disgrace for three days, my parents being too embarrassed to explain why.

It must not be thought that I was entirely without childhood interests. I became, for instance, hooked on Richmal Crompton's Just William books, though I arrived at them by the unusual route of acquiring *William the Fourth* under the impression that it was a biography of the King.

At about the same time that I went to prep school, Chafyn Grove near Salisbury, a new development took place in my intellectual life. My father, who was always glued to the six o'clock news on the radio and was anxious to stop me fidgeting and dashing about, cried out that today's news would be tomorrow's history. This struck me with the force of a great revelation. Instantly I addressed myself to our daily paper – Beaverbrook's *Express* – and followed the radio bulletins with rapt attention. The abdication of King Prajdhipok of Siam in 1934 was the first contemporary event that thus came to my attention; by the time I was ten I was keeping a current affairs notebook in which I made entries daily. The lesson had been learned: the Prajdhipoks of today would be the Hardicanutes of tomorrow.

Starting on 1 January 1936 that diary soon had to take account of the death of a king. All I knew of his successor was that in the Empire he was gratifyingly popular and that, according to the *Express*, he was always falling off his horse. I remember listening to the new King's first broadcast and feeling uncomfortable at my father's reaction to it, which was, 'He didn't indicate what changes he was going to make.' I thought that this was constitutionally unsound but kept my counsel – I was after all only ten; it was not my place to comment out loud.

What was more exciting was the arrival of the King in person at Longford Castle. Lord Radnor was Warden of the Stannaries, which gave him an important role in the Duchy of Cornwall, of which King Edward VIII, having no direct heir, was still Duke. The King therefore came to discuss Duchy business and my father took the minutes. He found this monarch a disappointing individual with minimal attention span. He reported that he fidgeted constantly, forever adjusting his tie and finding it difficult to concentrate on the business at hand. However, the meeting promised to advance my father's career. The King talked of his frustration at the archaic way in which George V had run Sandringham. Lord Radnor volunteered that his agent had had hands-on experience of modernising estates. As a result, a few weeks later my father was requested to make an assessment of Sandringham and to submit a report. He was hard at work on it during the summer and autumn and it was with no little pride that I saw him enclose the typed result within a folder on which was written in large letters in his Old English calligraphy, 'Your Majesty'.

Three days later the Bishop of Bradford preached a sermon and the balloon labelled Mrs Simpson went up. Having been at school all day and knowing nothing, I was startled to be asked by my mother, 'What do you think of your King, now, then?' At class next day the boys were invited to write their impressions of the crisis. Since I had just learned (either from a book or from a master) that a good essay should begin with a short arresting declaratory statement, which later could be qualified or enlarged upon, I wrote, 'All royal politics are basically sexual politics'. After a few apposite references to Henry VIII, Charles II and George IV, I concluded that it was the present King's duty, in return for the unique privileges he enjoyed, to marry a 'sensible princess' to ensure the succession. By 'sensible' I think I meant that no question of love need enter into it. Several essays were read out at school assembly. Mine was not. I was given to understand that the less said about it the better.

The *Express* did not satisfy me for long, except for the cartoons by Strube, which taught me how political life would appear to his ubiquitous 'Little Man', small, bespectacled with a perpetually puzzled frown. My father began bringing *The Times* home from the castle at the end of the working day. I read its news pages avidly and, mimicking the pompous 'distinguished invalids' column, issued regular communiqués about our family and friends, who were 'comfortable' or 'enjoying indifferent health'. Having read about 'famous last words' I was also much concerned about the timing and content of my own. Should they be solemn as in the younger Pitt's supposed, 'O my country! How I leave my country!', or facetious, as with Pitt's alternative version, 'I think I could eat one of Bellamy's veal pies'? And then there was a question of timing. If my (carefully prepared) adieu was uttered too soon, I might be condemning myself to an unnecessary period of silence; if too late, I might find myself unable to utter the words intelligibly at all. These were grave questions to occupy the immature mind.[2]

During the 1930s my father displayed very definite political views. He was ferociously anti-Hitler and viciously anti-Semitic. He was raring to go to war with the Germans over the Saar in 1935, let alone over the Rhineland in 1936. His opinion of politicians could and often was summed up as follows: 'There is only one man: Winston Churchill. The others – Baldwin, Chamberlain, Simon, Hoare – should be lined up against a wall – and shot.' As for the Pope, nothing could exceed the excoriating scorn which greeted every papal appeal for peace. From the very outset my father was certain that Hitler meant us harm. Britain should rearm and make a stand at the first ditch; unhappily her leaders were 'as weak as water'. He would end these long tirades with, 'Of course, the one thing I agree with Hitler about is the Jews.' He continued to make anti-Semitic remarks throughout the war, and after it when he served in the Control Commission in Germany. I became more and more repulsed in spirit over an issue on which I was absolutely certain that he was not only wrong but wickedly so.

My relations with my mother were friendly enough, even affectionate, but over the years increasingly cautious and reserved. We spent much time together, during which I must have bored her horribly with my incessant chatter about political affairs, outlining, for instance, cabinet reshuffles of my own devising and commenting on speeches in *Hansard* (also supplied from the castle). It is still with a sense of shame that I recall the walks on which she amiably endured being subjected to multiple-answer questions from me on world affairs, in the manner of a modern TV quiz show. (I cringe at the recollection of my shouts of triumph when, for example, the unfortunate lady, asked who was the Soviet head of state, had answered 'Stalin', instead of that truly unmemorable peasant with a goat's beard, Mikhail Kalinin.) With my mother indeed there was often a climate of cosy complicity in our relationship. There were the bicycle expeditions into Salisbury when we would go to the pictures to see my mother's latest heart-throb and then visit the bookshop and a tea-place called the House of Steps.

When I first came to Chafyn Grove I had thought that I would enjoy football, as in my first term I seemed rather good at it. I then became afflicted with one of the nameless physical conditions which have haunted me all my life. Whenever I ran I acquired almost at once a very acute stitch, and when I persisted my body became drained of all energy so that I had trouble in standing erect. Doctors were useless. Every games period was for me a Calvary as I staggered about the field, permanently offside, crouching with pain and being blown by the wind as my strength ebbed. When teams had to be picked it was the general opinion that it was better to play one short than to have me on side.

Cricket was little better as I was too clumsy to catch a ball and too uncoordinated to hit one.

But the real problem was other. In my ointment there exists a fly that at times has loomed Kafka-like threatening to absorb all else. I am and have been since birth absentminded. This defect, which to be sure can lend itself to humorous treatment, has been for me a constant and at times agonising source of frustration. Allied to it has been the operation of what Paul Jennings once described in the *Observer* as 'the loss force' – an abnormal propensity to lose objects. In the Boy Scouts it was beyond my capacity to assemble all items of the uniform – the woggle, the tassels, the penknife and everything else – at one and the same time. In a way I learned to deal with these misfortunes by practising a 'stiff upper lip', which could be mistaken for fecklessness but was in reality a determination to escape being dragged down into a state of anxiety and depression. The trouble, I think now, must be due to some minor physical malfunction in that part of the brain that deals with short-term memory. I have compared it to a faulty electrical connection which spasmodically works but is always liable to put a light on the blink. When I was a teenager it complicated all my relations, but particularly those with my father, whose treatment of me was in part excusable in that he was unable to reconcile my alarming lapses with my scholastic reputation for an excellent memory. Several times I began shyly to explain the problem to my mother. She, normally so sympathetic, brushed it aside with, 'Of course you could remember if you wanted to. You just need to apply a little self-discipline.' Or, even worse, she would repeat, 'You only forget the things you want to forget.' This was so manifestly untrue that once or twice I tried to reason with her. She said the same thing the next time, so that one more channel of communication was closed.

Hitler struck at Poland as the Kyle family was halfway up Mount Snowdon. Since my grandfather's death we had at last broken the pattern of summer holidays in Cornwall – 1938 was Ventnor in the Isle of Wight and 1939 was Wales. We must have set out at the crack of dawn on 1 September to climb Snowdon without first listening to the radio. Presumably my father felt that, with the despised Chamberlain in Downing Street, Britain could not be serious in defying Hitler. We reached a little workman's hut with the workman not working but glued to his tiny set. He gave us the news: the Germans were across the Polish border and it meant that we were going to war. It was nearly dusk before we could check out of the hotel and hit the road for home. Blackout had already been ordered but we had not been prepared for it; once darkness had fallen we encountered angry shouts of 'What about it?', since our lights remained undimmed.

War was now to govern all. The Earl of Radnor raised his own artillery battery which was housed in tents that appeared in the park. The agent for the outside farms wore uniform as the second-in-command and my father, with that deficiency in tact I had already noted in him, hailed the new captain as he drilled his squad with remarks about 'pips sprouting like mushrooms' on his shoulders.

The initial knot of tension, the expectations of immediate *blitz* and a great clash of continental armies gave way to unnatural calm. Children were evacuated, petrol, food and clothing were rationed, the blackout was strictly enforced, spy stories rapidly spread. Meanwhile, having won a national prize – the Townsend Warner – for history, I attained that grand object of my parents' ambition: a private (known as public) school. As they could not afford to pay the fees the choice of school had depended on who would accept a history paper in a scholarship exam in which I might shine instead of a maths one which I could not but fail. Of those willing, Bromsgrove in Worcestershire was selected. I had visited the school before the war, had sat the papers and had gone on a long walk with the history master, who asked one question about Sir Robert Walpole and had to listen for upwards of an hour while, scarcely drawing breath, I dilated upon the career and personality of our first prime minister. They gave me the scholarship.

As a scholarship boy I was cordoned off with half a dozen others, all bright except for one, to be in the classical stream; that is, to spend certain periods doing extra Latin and classical Greek instead of science. We were referred to by the rest of the school as 'ints' (for intellectuals), as if it were assumed that physics and chemistry (in both of which I have never, to my loss, had a single day's instruction) were intended for lesser but more earth-bound mortals. With the ruthlessness for which public schoolboys are famous, the one classicist who could not be described as bright was assigned the nickname of 'Dimmer'. 'Dimmer', he was asked one day, 'Why do you read classics when you are so dim?' 'Because I am going into the Church. My father was also dim and he seems to manage a parish perfectly well.' A glance at Crockford's shows that my former classmate has achieved his ambition.

I found myself placed, to my dismay, in the advanced maths stream, addressed, if that is the word, by Major Harold Gray, who ran the Cadet Training Corps with Tacky Tom, the sergeant-major. Partly it was his odd intonation which meant that I never understood a word he said. But it also was the subject he taught, which was called 'statics and dynamics'. Not having mastered elementary arithmetic this might well have been Chinese and Japanese. But I desperately needed, to meet the requirement for entering Oxford, at least four credits in School Certificate of which at least one had to be a science. I did not doubt the four credits (I actually got six, of which three were distinctions) but I was offering no science except maths, and time wasted on statics and dynamics would mean that I would fail elementary mathematics as well and all would be lost. I organised my demotion to a lower class in mathematics. It was run by a Mr Merriman. I instantly dropped like a stone to the bottom of this lower class. As a good schoolmaster Mr Merriman's curiosity was aroused. He visited the school library and noted what books I was taking out. I was concentrating at the time on playwrights (especially Ibsen, whose complete works I reached by way of Bernard Shaw's *Quintessence of Ibsenism*) and philosophers, leaping for joy over Descartes, wide-eyed with wonder over Nietzsche and striving to get my mind round Kant and Hegel.

Mr Merriman, who was a housemaster of one of the smaller houses, invited me to tea. I attended nervously, as the previous day I had tried to deliver his house's breakfast by hand-cart and in my clumsy way had distributed the eggs over the roadway. Gently, as I tasted his wife's scones and sipped her tea (she was very beautiful but had a voice like a corncrake), he explained in his slow ruminating style that many mathematicians were not particularly good at mental arithmetic. Algebra and geometry, he said, were not to be thought of as advanced forms of arithmetic. Rather, they should be treated as branches of philosophy; he spoke of Euclid and Bertrand Russell. At the next classroom test I leaped from bottom to second top and I got my credit in maths.

I spent much time in the school library. Besides playwrights and philosophers I remember being immensely excited by E.H. Carr's *The Twenty Years' Crisis*, which set me aflame about international relations. Then there were Karl Marx and Sigmund Freud. The first did not detain me long: for a few weeks I practised standing every proposition on its head and determining what it meant objectively, which was usually the reverse of what it would appear to mean to the ordinary mind. This was fun and sounded profound, and I was for a little while much taken with a book called *The Scientific Method of Thinking*, which encouraged this form of intellectual contortion. But soon I wearied of it. And, more profoundly, I could not forget the Moscow trials. Towards them I had a simple attitude. The confessions of all these senior Communists were either true or false. If true, they meant that every one in the hierarchy except Stalin was willing to betray the cause, which did not say much for betrayers or cause. If false, they meant that the top Communist had wilfully destroyed all his colleagues. Neither explanation struck me as an advertisement for an ideal society.

I was for much longer intrigued by Freud, whose confident style held me despite reservations about his central oedipal proposition (I did not think that my own difficulties with my father had anything to do with my love for my mother, which in any case was not very profound) and I greedily absorbed every book of his that I could get my hands on. I also took a great interest in written constitutions and wrote to many ambassadors on school writing paper requesting information about their arrangements. I tried to word the letters as if from an elderly pedagogue, down to the sob in the voice with which I made reference to 'this terrible war'. I received a great deal of material, some of it addressed to the Rev. J.K. Kyle, which I felt was only my due. I thus at an early stage met up with the problems of the distinction between federalism and confederalism and of power-sharing among distinct communities which I subsequently encountered in my career as a journalist. I also made a firm resolve never to acquire any habits which would constrain me in later life, never to smoke or drink alcohol, never to swear or be influenced by women. I had a rather Jezebel view of women. I had read in Sir Maurice Powicke's *The Fall of Normandy* his explanation for King John's sudden alternations between remarkable vigour and damaging languor. Powicke correlates these changes with the known presence of his Queen, Isabella of Angoulême, whom he describes as 'a magnificent animal'. No animal, I held, however magnificent, would ever divert me from my purposes. Women threatened marriage, children, mortgage; these must never tie me down. But I regarded these choices as strictly personal; I passed no judgement whatsoever about others who did not share them.

One day my father received a letter from the New York manager of Thomas Cook, the original tourist agency. They had been to the same school in Penzance and, as so many generous Americans did, he made an offer of a safe haven for the son of his old friend. I was asked my opinion and allowed for once to reply without interruption. I made a little speech, declining to leave my parents and my country in their hour of peril. The second half of that assertion was perhaps more genuine than the first. But my parents were, I think, quite touched, which was my intention, and nothing more was spoken of the idea.

Lord Radnor had by now been posted away and, following Dunkirk, Longford had been requisitioned by General Claude Auchinleck, the head of Southern Command. My father, left in charge, busied himself with preparing a kind of Domesday Book of the estate which after the war was held up by the compensation authorities as a model of how all estate owners expecting to be paid for damages should have proceeded. The Auk then installed in the castle the man who was to prove his most insubordinate corps commander, General Bernard Montgomery. My father was in his element. Sensing at once the massive ego with whom he had to deal, he massaged it with a will, ensuring that in the castle and on the estate nothing short of royal treatment should be 'Monty's' lot.

For Montgomery's staff, as for the rest of his command, physical fitness was the general's watchword; once a week during school holidays I watched the desk-bound warriors assemble outside our house ready to begin the seven-mile run which was to tone them up. Those over 50 were allowed to walk. When Winston Churchill heard of this he was not impressed. 'Who is the General of this division and does he run the seven miles himself?' he asked his War Minister. 'If so, he may be more useful for football than war. Could Napoleon have run seven miles across country at Austerlitz? ... In my experience, based on many years' observation, officers with high athletic qualifications are not usually successful in the higher ranks.' Churchill was to learn much more about General Montgomery.

While the nation waited to be invaded a sense of solidarity gripped us all. Its focus was the radio. Our school Matron, Miss Lonsdale, was very kind: because of my weak chest I had to receive a large dollop of a sweet, glutinous mixture called Bynol every day. Knowing the intensity of my interest in the news she arranged for me to receive my daily slug at exactly nine o'clock, after which I was allowed to stay for the bulletin. It being wartime, interest was widespread and as I possessed then the ability, long since gone, to memorise long passages, I used nightly to reproduce in almost complete imitation the rotund banalities of the bulletins to a crowd gathered in my 'bedder'.

My schooldays were coming to an end and I continued to get good reports. 'I have nothing but the highest praise for his industry, his zeal for his work and his promise,' wrote the headmaster, adding, 'I feel very strongly that he should cultivate some hobby or relaxation.' But at the close of an earlier term my housemaster had written, 'We suffer his forgetfulness with cheerful resignation but I doubt if the outer and unfeeling world would be so lenient. Some find him difficult to understand, but I am glad to think that I know him well. And what I know I like.' There my master, while being gentle and kind to me, had touched upon my inner torment. The more confident I became of my own powers, the more limitless my ambitions to be the torchbearer of a new generation that should abolish the curse of war, the more determined to be in control of myself in all circumstances, the more gnawing was the anxiety about the flaw in the crystal of my nature. Try as I might, I could not overcome my absentmindedness, with its attendant unpunctuality, loss of possessions and minimal sense of direction. Time and time again I let myself down by my own lights. Determined not to become a depressive, I practised an outward indifference to the consequences and confided my agonies to no one.

The most searing instance of this came at a time when I was rehearsing the part of Lavinia in *Androcles and the Lion*. I had been given this large role when my voice had not yet completely broken because Bernard Shaw had provided the lady with a two-and-a-half-page speech and no one else was thought capable of memorising it. One day it was my turn to put up the blackout screens in part of the school. I forgot them and was summoned before the master on duty. I assumed this would mean a beating. It meant something much, much worse. The master, a scientist who did not teach me, wounded me deeply by referring to the duties of a Roman citizen and declaring that I should not suppose that just because I was clever I could contract out of responsibilities owed by all. I was moved by this more than by anything else in my schooldays, and left the room an intensely unhappy boy. Feeling myself to be innocent of the charge of intellectual arrogance, I saw the impossibility of refuting it. The thought that my high-minded ambitions might be fatally flawed overwhelmed me. I remained in the deepest gloom for 24 hours, with the result that the next night I again forgot the blackout screens.

My last history master was Basil Hills. He was half-deaf and half-blind and a dedicated mountaineer. He could not see further than the front two rows of a classroom and, unlike many deaf people, did not shout but tended to drop his voice below audible level. His was a great influence on me and more than anyone he was responsible for my gaining admittance to Oxford. He decided at once that I knew enough history for a scholarship and that what I needed to concentrate on was preparing for the general paper, in which I should be asked such abstract questions as 'What is justice?' He set about with a will to coach me in this respect. Being himself very interested in psychoanalysis, it was he who introduced me to the writings of Sigmund Freud, which I absorbed in large dollops. The headmaster, on discovering the direction of my reading, persuaded me to sample some John Macmurray, who much later was to emerge as Tony Blair's guru, by way of balance.

Above all, Basil Hills saw that Bromsgrove's usefulness to me was coming to an end and he offered a solution. Because of wartime conditions, Oxford colleges were allowing scholarship examinations in Modern Studies to take place at schools with applicants only being called for interview if they were likely to be successful. Suspecting that my parents would think that at 17 I was too young, I did not inform them (and I am uncertain whether even the headmaster knew in advance). Hills himself invigilated at the tests and handled the correspondence. The history papers I found easy; unfortunately I needed to take a second modern subject, and although I had received enthusiastic school reports for my French I knew very well that it was not up to the same standard as my history. For one paper I was required to translate into French a piece involving architectural terms whose meaning I did not understand in English. The dreaded general paper, I felt, did not go at all badly. I went home on vacation willing myself to hope. In due course I received a letter inviting me to come for an interview and was obliged to confess my lack of candour to my parents. My mother was in her seventh heaven to such an extent that my father was for once deprived of words. I went and was awarded an Open Exhibition at Magdalen College. (Later I was told by the college president, Sir Henry Tizard, that on history alone I should have won a demyship, which is the top award, but that my French had been the spoiler.)

At 17 I was to go up for the Hilary term and to start my adult life.

CHAPTER 2

Oxford at War

Wartime Oxford was surprisingly alive, considering that the entire undergraduate body was theoretically away at the wars. Some like myself were under age, others unfit for service, there were foreigners like the son of the Greek Ambassador, many were on short-term courses connected with the services. There were even some mature gentlemen, not dons, such as E.M.W. Meyerson, author of a study of Chatterton in addition to a shelf full of other volumes that proved on inspection to have been privately printed, who had taken up residence for the duration. The Oxford Union still held debates, though just after I went down the president was dramatically arrested *in situ* for failing to report for military duty, and the political parties were still recruiting new members. Peter Brook was making a film of *The Sentimental Journey*, *Twelfth Night* was produced on Worcester College lawn and Anthony Besch was plotting elaborate operatic productions.

When I arrived at Magdalen College in January 1943, at the start of Hilary term, I was assigned rooms in the New Building, new in the sense of having been built only in 1733, as opposed to the famous Tower, which had been opened in 1509, and to the cloisters, which date from the fifteenth century but which have had a lot done to them since. Magdalen was founded by the second Provost of Eton, William of Waynflete, after he had become Henry VI's Lord Chancellor; the lilies from his crest nowadays supply the pattern on the college tie. The royal charter is dated 1458 and stipulates that the new college's name is 'commonly called Maudaleyne'. At one end of the college there is a deer park (after the war a member of the peerage would be sent down for slaughtering a beast with his bow and arrow), while at the other end there is the entrance to a beautiful riverside stroll, called Addison's Walk after the superb essayist and negligible Secretary of State who was a Magdalen man. From there at the right season one can look back at the college buildings through a meadow of fritillaries.

To become a member of Magdalen, especially if one is historically minded, is to enter a world of magic. On a corner staircase of the great Georgian sweep of the New Building I had my own rooms, with a manservant ('scout') called Ing, impeccably dressed with hair tightly brushed back. He used to wake me in the morning with a cup of tea, polish my shoes and light my fire. When I had struggled up, I crossed over to the cloisters and made for the college hall for breakfast carrying my wartime rations (a pinch of sugar, a tiny square of butter). Then, off to one of the several libraries – College, Bodleian, Codrington or the Oxford Union – to hoover up material for my weekly essay.

C.S. Lewis was my air raid warden and A.J.P. Taylor my tutor. The former, florid, bucolic, his rubicund face surmounted by a tin hat and with a pail of sand in either hand, was a reminder that we were at war. The latter, stumpy, bow-tied, in a corduroy suit, was audience and critic of the weekly essay, read to him in the house with a mill race just off Addison's Walk.

At the very beginning of our relationship Alan Taylor taught me an important lesson. I had been set an essay relating to the first years of the French Third Republic when the National Assembly had had a monarchist majority and serious thought was therefore given to the restoration of the Pretender, the Comte de Chambord. However, the Comte had blown his chances by stubbornly refusing to accept as his own the Tricolour, the flag of the Revolution, and by insisting in bringing back the white flag of the House of Capet. Without much thought I voiced the conventional wisdom that this showed an absurd lack of proportion on the part of the claimant; Henri IV, after all, had thought that Paris was worth a mass. Alan Taylor hitherto had appeared to be totally absorbed in two preoccupations: stroking a large white cat on his lap with one hand and with the other worrying with the stem of his pipe a prominent wart at the dead centre of his ample forehead. Suddenly he let fly with an almighty 'Why?' My timbers shivered, I floundered desperately for words. None very impressive formed themselves. Then Taylor launched on a tremendous oration to the effect that the Pretender understood perfectly well that if he were to be a constitutional monarch he must rise above the parties which had bitterly divided France since the Revolution, that the Tricolour was the symbol of one of those parties and that only by use of his personal flag could he demonstrate his neutrality. My temporary amazement at hearing this from a man notoriously on the left was of less significance than the lesson it taught me, which was not to go in for automatic writing. When in 1972 I was to tell this story to Jean-François Deniau, a French member of the European Commission, while we were waiting around for the final word to be pronounced on British entry into the European Community, he said that his great-uncle had written editorials on precisely those lines.

Alan Taylor was a strong supporter of the Soviet Union, not only in the general sense that most of Britain was applauding the great achievements of the Red Army and echoing the reproachful slogan 'Russia bleeds while Britain blancos', but specifically in backing Moscow's territorial claims in the post-war settlement. Yet, his packed-out public war commentaries in the town hall, bravura performances without a trace of notes, were, though lively and pointed, admirably balanced and immensely popular. The government brought them to a premature end following Communist objections that the strategy of the Red Army had been too coolly assessed, while the Americans had earlier disliked candid criticism of their initial performance in North Africa. At the time Taylor was being profiled in the *Oxford Mail* as part of a series by Stanley Parker called 'Drawn and Quoted'. In a boyish gesture of defiance, Alan placed a strip of paper marked 'Censored' across the middle of the sketch that accompanied the interview. The very day on which he was being banned at the insistence of local Communists, the *Manchester Guardian* carried a letter from Moscow with fawning praise of him from Communist stooges from the three Baltic states.

It was not necessary to agree with Alan politically – indeed, as a Liberal, I belonged to the party he most despised – to enjoy his company. I became one of his favourite pupils and was often invited socially to his house, where one might meet Lord David Cecil, as immobile as a waxwork with curls tastefully in place, or Frank Pakenham, the future Lord Longford, who was the prospective Labour candidate for Oxford and used Taylor's house to change into his proletarian canvassing outfit. Alan's first rather mannered wife, Margaret, who had been taught music in Vienna by the last pupil of Liszt, was an ardent patron of cultural events and cultural people; at a reception for Benjamin Britten and Peter Pears one would be recruited by Alan 'if', as he said, 'you want to avoid drinking my wife's mint tea', to dodge into the study and play such intellectual games as guessing with what clichés the eminent historian Dr G.P. Gooch would round off successive paragraphs of his latest work.

Taylor spoke very warmly about my work to the college president, Sir Henry Tizard, who was one of the government's leading scientific advisers. In appearance Tizard reminded me of Strube's 'Little Man', an impression reinforced by a story he told against himself. In wartime Britain oranges were extremely rare, so that it was a kindly thought of General Arnold, the American Chief of the Air Staff, to present Sir Henry with a huge crate of them at the conclusion of a conference they were both attending. Unfortunately Tizard had not been provided with a car to take him to the station, taxis were scarce and this distinguished but diminutive scientist was to be seen staggering down a nearly empty Whitehall balancing in his arms the weight of his colleague's generosity.

Alan cleared the way for me to work in peace and frequently alone in the uncluttered atmosphere of the Codrington, the huge library of All Souls College, where, except for the gentle padding of the librarian, a state prevailed of total erudition and repose. One day this peace was shattered by a very noisy commotion. A very old man, with a white moustache resembling that of Marshal Pétain, in a frock coat and high winged collar, tall, a little bent and with an immense booming voice, advanced in full cry with quick though uncertain steps up the central aisle. This was the Chichele Professor of History, Sir Charles Oman, author of a multi-volume history of the Peninsular War, who was 87 and irremovable so long as he could manage two lectures a week. His unfortunate heir presumptive in what was then one of only two chairs in history in the whole university had been waiting for decades and was now, at 63, within two years of the new compulsory age of retirement (which did not affect his predecessor). On this occasion Sir Charles was accompanied by a sidekick with a satchel who looked up at him silently and nervously and whom I immediately dubbed Alice's dormouse. As they passed my reading desk, the dormouse hurried up to me to apologise profusely for the noise that 'we' were making. That was my first encounter with the egomaniac Dr A.L. Rowse.

College life was stimulating. Peter Brook, a man who moved so softly that his feet seemed to float above the ground, would tell of his eccentric aunt, the theosophist Madame Blavatsky, and of his consultation with Aleister Crowley, the self-proclaimed wickedest man in the world, whom he had enlisted for a college production as his adviser on magic. Rather banally, I thought, Crowley, who was staying at the Randolph Hotel, had replied to a request for his room number with a pat '666, the number of the Beast of the Book of Revelation'. Then there was John Simopoulos, the Greek Ambassador's son, who produced for me the most creative salad I have ever enjoyed; and, since we were allowed to stay up free in vacation if we firewatched at the top of the Tower, there were the fellow members of C.S. Lewis's firewatching team. They included Max Hayward, who learned a fresh language every year but who eventually settled down to translating and writing about Russian authors under Communism, and a refugee from Vienna called Guggenheim. One night in the Tower Max was persuaded to do his celebrated imitation of a Hitler speech which sounded eerily authentic and was certified by Guggenheim to be accurate 'right down to Hitler's bad Linz accent'. But my best friend among undergraduate historians was Michael Thompson, who was not at Magdalen but at The Queen's College next door. He was later to serve with me in the Royal Artillery and to become Professor of History at the University of London and Director of the Institute of Historical Research. He and I would engage in fervent discussion on historical problems long into the night.

I was advised by A.J.P. Taylor not to bother about going to lectures, which he said were no use, but having been issued with a schedule I was determined to sample them. The impression I gained was that there could be few professions for which the most elementary vocational requirements were so totally neglected. I felt that if I heard one more strangulated voice start by saying, 'It is one of the most extraordinary paradoxes of the sixteenth/seventeenth/ eighteenth/nineteenth century that …', I should scream. It was 40 years before I felt able to make a restrained use myself of the sometimes worthwhile concept of the historical paradox. Once, on the way to a lecture for which I was late, I spun round a corridor to come face to face with Adolf Hitler. There was the slick of hair, the tooth-brush moustache, the transfixing resemblance. Adolf had passed out of my sight before I had sufficiently recovered my wits to ask someone else who this could possibly be. The answer was Alan Bullock, a man whose regular war commentaries I had followed with great respect in *The Spectator* and who was to become for many years the leading authority on the Führer.

Scarcely had I first occupied my rooms in the New Building when notes appeared under the door advertising the merits of the different political clubs. In retrospect this appears surprising since over much of the country there was little party activity during the war. I promptly joined up as a Liberal. I disbelieved in socialism, which I thought high-minded but unreal, but I wanted passionately to ensure that the immense let-down of those who had served in the First World War would not happen a second time round. In this I was much influenced by a book by Sir Philip Gibbs called *Since Then*, which recorded the betrayal of the wartime generation both at home and in foreign affairs.

Since I had enjoyed taking part in the school debating society at Bromsgrove I joined the Oxford Union – the subscription to it was the only money I ever asked for in my life from my father. The Union had a great reputation as a nursery for statesmen, derived in part from the example of Mr Gladstone, who passed from his debating triumphs there by almost imperceptible stages into the House of Commons for a pocket borough owned by the father of an Oxford pal. (To do him justice, Mr G. did show some faint signs of remorse for the drastic reprisals, including removals, that were taken against those electors who, in the days before the secret ballot, had failed to vote for him.) For the rest of the nineteenth century and the first half of the twentieth the long list of ex-officers of the Union in public life was enough to inspire the undergraduate politician. For some, it is true, election to be president, the ultimate Union accolade, turned out to be the high spot of a man's career; from then on it was downhill all the way and once in a while one saw the pathetic haunting of the scene of unrepeatable triumphs by an ex-president forever reciting to any willing ear his proudest quip. But for many it was an early mark of the high flyer, though in the twenty-first century William Hague, a member of my college with a First (class degree) and the presidency of the Union behind him, whose debating style in the Commons was the Oxford Union at its best, spectacularly failed to come across to the country as a convincing Tory leader. I am thus forced to admit that this era may now finally have passed.

The attitude of the wartime Union to party politics was rather uncertain. True, one Union orator who defiantly cried, 'I glawwy in the name of Tawy' was elected president, but in general party politics was at a discount, not simply because there was a war on but because the party system was held to have failed. Two regular participants in debate, Geoffrey Rippon (the future Tory cabinet minister and Common Market negotiator) and Frank Berendt, were invariably greeted whenever they rose with a susurration of 'party stooge, party stooge, party stooge'.

The Beveridge Plan was immensely popular. One guest speaker, a right-wing publicist called S.W. Alexander, had the difficult task of attacking it and he did not make the task any easier by speaking unmemorably for as long as 40 minutes. His opponent, Emanuel Shinwell, the socialist goad of Churchill in the Commons, had little difficulty with a riposte. 'The Tories say they know all about social security,' he said. 'Of course they do. They've never known anything else.'

High drama came when Victor Gollancz spoke on a motion condemning the government for its inadequate response to the terrible information that was becoming available about the Holocaust. Members entering the chamber took their places as usual on either side of the House, according to whether they initially supported or opposed the motion. On this occasion once the leading undergraduate speakers had spoken for and against, Gollancz, in the most moving and effective oration I have ever heard, presented the facts that had so far emerged with a deft combination of restraint and emotion. When he sat down all the occupants of the opposition benches silently rose and crossed to the other side. The motion was carried unanimously. I left feeling utterly drained. It was an experience never to be forgotten.

Oxford would not be Oxford, nor the Union the Union, if all debates and all speeches were of this order of solemnity. At least one of the weekly motions each term was of a facetious or teasing nature. Also Union reputations are often made by the ice-breaking mirth that precedes or accompanies a serious point. I have forgotten most of the jokes, many well prepared but tossed off with an assumed air of negligence; in any case many of them do not survive being reduced to print, divorced from their occasion. But I recall, from a 1943 debate on a motion condemning modern styles of architecture, the pronouncement of a smooth and polished West Indian called Cameron Tudor that, 'Those who live in glass houses cannot even turn their pictures to the wall.' And a guest speaker was told that his college, All Souls, which has high talent, a fine cellar and no undergraduates, was 'where the best brains in Oxford are preserved in alcohol'.

I attended the Union debates regularly every Thursday evening and took a modest part in them. Among the most accomplished participants was a hand-some 17-year-old who spoke with the utmost self-confidence. This was Tony Benn, then known as The Hon. Anthony Wedgwood Benn. Many came to the Union to acquire the art of public speaking, but Tony arrived fully equipped, which was the less surprising in that the parliamentary ancestors on both sides of his family added up to an impressive total.

There was, however, another activity which I was obliged to undertake, namely two days a week of military training, at which I did not feel so much at ease. This was my introduction to the life I was to lead for the next four years. Since the war showed no sign of concluding and I was within eight months of my 18th birthday I was expecting to be called up and it seemed only fair that in return for my university education I should make an effort to prepare myself for that day. Yet, the truth was that I was no natural soldier. For one thing, in four years I never learned to march in step. For another, I could not run except for very short distances. And for a third, my natural clumsiness with physical objects made the handling of even elementary mechanisms very problematic. I was in a way repeating my school experience – alternating between doing things at which I excelled and doing things at which I was lamentably bad.

There were times as I staggered around Christ Church meadow on an organised run, aching all over and sustained only by the sparkling conversation of Anthony Besch, when I felt hopelessly outclassed. The first term's training was in infantry work, at the end of which came a test called Cert A, which enabled one to abandon the infantry, if one so wished, and aim at Cert B in another arm. I decided that I wanted to go for the artillery because, though it involved maths, it meant less running and therefore less total humiliation. With both certificates under the belt, I could enter the army as a potential officer (PO).

After assembling the kit, daubing the blanco and shining up the brass,

I presented myself for drill, under regular sergeants who would shout such encouraging messages as, 'Open out your legs, nothing will drop out' or 'Hurry up, Mr Kyle, my bread and butter's getting cold.' One of our officers was the poet Edmund Blunden. Addressing the man next to me he said, 'You must not look like Byron when an NCO tells you off.' Then turning to me, who had been feeling relieved that for once I was not being singled out, he added, 'And *you* should not look like Shelley when somebody's been rude to him.' On one afternoon we did an exercise across the houses and gardens of north Oxford. My companions had vaulted nimbly over a wall. I followed and hit the brickwork with a crash, at which the entire wall fell down. A youngish couple, both of them dons, dashed out of the house with broad smiles and compensation claim forms at the ready. I readily accepted their invitation to tea. No one who knew me would have expected me to pass Cert A but, towards the end of term, I decided that I would not accept defeat; in a mood of intense concentration I passed with surprisingly high marks.

Next term I was on to gunnery. I did not find this easy, though mercifully there was no running and, as I managed to master the slide-rule, I found some temporary relief from my mathematical anxieties. The chief instructor, Captain Hall of the Royal Horse Artillery – the snobbish cousins of the simple gunner – did not see me as officer material. He accustomed all of us to the menace of the RTU –'returned to unit' – which would be the fate of any officer cadet at OCTU (Officer Cadet Training Unit) who failed to make the grade. 'When you are RTU-ed from your OCTU, Mr Karl,' he would drawl, slapping his leggings with his riding crop, 'I advise you to become a latrine orderly. It's a very good job, latrine orderly.'

With another huge effort I passed Cert B. I remember only the motorcycle test, for which, rather implausibly, I scored 77 per cent. By memorising the instructions and carrying them out by rote I successfully coped with the tricky tests in a muddy field; I lost points only on elementary road discipline. In truth I never succeeded in mastering the motorbike, which was usually able to master me, and once I had left the army I resolved never to ride one again. But once again I was through – ill-fitted to be a soldier perhaps but a gunner I would be and a potential officer to boot.

With great sadness I went down from Oxford though fortified by two starred sections (marks of distinction in a wartime exam on two terms' work), a promise of a place whenever I should be free to return and the prospect, held out to me by my tutor, that I should then consider myself a candidate for a First and, with it, the chance of an academic career. I was myself still thinking of the diplomatic service, but either way the future seemed promising enough provided I could survive the intervening period as a soldier. Yet, as I believed the war was just and I was the right age, I must serve. The next event was to be my medical. To prepare for this I was brainwashed by my father, who was anxious for the welfare of his only child. His psychology was unsound, since it took no account of the possibility that I might have patriotic emotions. Day after day, night after night he drilled me with the excuses I should make to the board for my utter unfitness for military action. I was to emphasise my chronic cough, my agonising breathlessness, my supposed bad nerves.

The continual nagging about my forthcoming interview lowered me to the point at which I at last weakly answered 'Yes' to the endlessly repeated demands that I should promise to speak the required words. It was a promise that immediately afterwards I very much regretted but, having made it, I was clear that I must keep it.

The day of the interview arrived. My father drove me to the address I had been given. I had decided what to do and was quite calm. When I was invited to say whether there were any medical facts that the board should know about I repeated the required answer in a low, toneless, trance-like voice. The brisk chairman of the board said, 'I expect your mother instructed you to say just that, didn't she?' I nodded wordlessly, not bothering to switch my parents. The interview was over. I returned to my father, who had been waiting outside in the car. 'Did you say what I told you to say?' he said eagerly. 'Yes'. 'What grade did they give you?' 'A1'. With infinite sadness my father drove me home, shaking his head but not uttering another word.

My 18th birthday passed and the authorities did not seem to be in any hurry for my services. I began to think I should have returned to Oxford for a third term. Then at the end of November 1943 I was summoned to go to Northampton, a town much used in the Middle Ages for the convening of royal courts and parliaments as being in the approximate centre of England. It was a town I was not to visit again until 40 years later, when I entered it as a parliamentary candidate.

CHAPTER 3

To Be a Soldier

O ne day in November 1943 in Northampton barracks a mob of miscellaneous civilians shambled into line to be received into the army.
Whether or not we had already been kitted out with uniforms by
then I do not remember. What sticks in my mind was that we were addressed
by a very old colonel who looked as if he had been plucked out from a cupboard
without having been sufficiently dusted. I noticed that his puttees were on
upside down and that in place of a swagger cane he was carrying a garden
hoe. He gave us what was intended to be a stirring address, one calculated to
remove any fatal trace of idealism stirring in our breasts. 'You get poets and
chaps like that with long hair saying that warfare is bad,' he intoned. 'But it
says in the Old Testament that a nation needs to go to war every 40 years.
Otherwise it gets soft and things fall apart.'

For me life in a Northampton barrack room was a new but not upsetting
experience. As with boarding school, I found it relatively easy to accommodate to a fresh environment. It was true that sleeping between blankets without sheets was a novel and not altogether pleasant experience. But I did not
really mind. Nor did I find the company unpleasing, though it was undoubtedly strange. My new comrades were almost all from the working class, whose
conversation displayed the full range of the single f-word, used as a noun, verb,
adjective and adverb, and in every tone and pitch of voice. After lights out I
used to listen with awe to an entire vocabulary being dispensed with in the
manner, I used to think, of the clicks used by some South African tribes.

There was one other public school boy in this particular billet who had had
a short run as a schoolmaster before being called up. I did not take to him and
noticed that, by attempting to outdo in crudity the language of his fellows, he
rapidly forfeited their respect, since they expected better things of him. My
fellow recruits seemed to me a goodhearted lot who stood in dire need of my
services on their being confronted with the novel challenge of having to write
letters to their parents or lovers. One tough, broad-shouldered giant, virtually

illiterate, was sufficiently grateful for my efforts in rendering into plausible stanzas the sentiments which he felt could not properly be expressed in prose that he promised in a loud voice that if anyone gave me any trouble I should just let him know and he would work him over. No one gave me any trouble.

I was able to square the corporal in charge of the barrack room by lending him my copy of Machiavelli's *The Prince* which I had brought with me as a suitable guide to my conduct as a soldier. We were put through basic infantry drills and weapons instruction, with such injunctions as, 'Grasp firmly with the thumb and forefinger of the right hand', 'Screw the male part inside the female part', 'You aren't paid to think', and 'The proof is in the pudding'. We were taught the basic infantryman's skills, charging straw men with bayonet and war whoop, the better to disembowel the Hun. I was not bad at the war whoop but got into trouble with the straw men. Any brownie points gained by making myself useful in the barrack room were badly needed to offset my undistinguished performance on parade. I was rather uneasy about being labelled from the start as a PO (potential officer), since any dispassionate observer would surely have placed me in the bottom quartile of the squad.

After a few weeks of basic infantry training, I was sent to an artillery training unit in Newtown in Wales, where I was joined by my Oxford friend Michael Thompson and two other soulmates, Denys Reid, who subsequently went into the Church, and Charles Regan, a German Jewish refugee who went on to have a successful career in the Civil Service. Denys, Michael and I signed on to a correspondence course in Russian to keep our brains ticking over and I also took an elementary course in economics. When 14 years later I became the political correspondent of *The Economist* I found myself in the next office to the hitherto unseen lady who had been my exacting economics tutor.

Advanced gunnery work was no great problem; for me the devil was in the detail of elementary military living. There was the old difficulty about marching in step, there was the acute problem of managing to keep all parts of my equipment clean, polished, mended (in the case of socks) and above all together. And there was the forgetting. In consequence, Newtown was marked by the regularity with which I appeared on weekly punishment parades, staying in barracks to peel potatoes while others were on the town.

Every few weeks a party of potential officers was dispatched for a weekend to attend a 'Wozbee'. This was a War Office Selection Board (WOSB) which, being ensconced in a country house with ample grounds, chose from the POs offered to it the cream of the litter. Out of a group of 12 that had most recently been sent, only two were selected. When it came to my turn, my pessimism was intense. I had had serious misgivings as to whether it was right to allow my name to go forward at all. But I decided that I was now not my own master and should go with the flow. I might think I would never make a soldier, let alone an officer, but this was no longer for me to decide. There were all these rigorous tests, WOSB, then pre-OCTU, then OCTU, at any one of which the unsuitable would be sifted out by competent judges from the others. Why should I pre-empt their verdict? Yet as the train carrying the latest batch of POs approached Hereford station I had really no doubt in my own mind what the verdict in my case would be: to fall at the first hurdle. As we pulled into the station, there was just time for Charles Regan, always a precise man, to observe that Hereford was the town which had the highest *per capita* ratio of insanity in the United Kingdom, to which he added a mention of the next two frontrunners before we were lined up with our kit-bags on the platform.

It was time for the pep-talk. I started to listen with a calm bordering on indifference. We were told we were not going to be judged by whether we could march in step (What was that? I pricked up), nor by whether we ate peas off a knife. This last point must have been a standard one because it featured also in an account of the 'Wozbee' published half a century later in the *Oldie* by a post-war National Serviceman. No, what the DS (Directing Staff) wanted to know was whether we were possessed of certain abstract qualities – courage, drive, initiative, leadership. This for me complicated matters. Sleepwalking to rejection, which had been my preferred course of action, no longer seemed so attractive if it could be taken as implying acquiescence in the absence of such qualities. I therefore perked up as we were swept through the drive of the estate up to the big house and decided that I would after all compete. Disillusion soon followed. We were instructed to go to our rooms, change into sports gear and adjourn to the football field. I knew at once that this meant instant death to the prospect of a commission. Miserably I drifted down with the others. The DS were poised, clipboards at the ready. We were lined up opposite each other in two teams. An officer addressed us in clipped tones. 'In this game there are no rules except these: here is the ball, and there are the goals. Your job, once the whistle is blown, is to get the ball behind the goal. Every method is allowed, there are no fouls.' The whistle blew. The two sides rushed forward and, with a display of great drive and ruthless courage, engaged in a fierce, heaving, kicking, shoving, eye-gouging scramble in the middle of the field, each man eager to show that he bore no scruples. All hope abandoned, I tottered towards the edge of the action. Unseen by the contestants, the ball trickled out of the morass into the open. I sidled up to it, picked it up and loped over to the goal posts.

The clipboards shifted. Kyle it was who had showed D & I (drive and initiative). Thus encouraged, I went on to the next task. In full uniform now we were ordered one by one to leap across a series of obstacles of the kind that had always defeated me. Fortunately I had taught myself at school how to fall without doing myself an injury. With the clipboards in mind, I hurled myself at each obstacle, after first assuming a mien of stern determination, and collapsed in a crumpled heap. Immediately I rose, shook myself, jutted out my jaw, and tried another flying leap. Down I crashed, and yet again, without hesitation, prepared to try once more. 'Stop him,' yelled a clipboard, 'stop him or he'll kill himself.' I thought that 'courage' would be a suitable entry for this caper and walked round the remaining obstacles. My comrades, I found, were drawn up in front of a sheer cliff, at the bottom of which was some water. We were told to step off the edge and that, provided we remained rigidly erect, all would be well. A volunteer to lead the way was called for. Calculating that the army could not wish to kill or maim its potential officers, and on the principle that going with gravity was not beyond me, I instantly stepped forward and, holding myself as instructed, stepped into infinity. The water was deep enough.

I was by then feeling very tired. We were allowed just sufficient time to change our clothes and be shoved into a classroom. There was a large conference table, around which we were arranged, with the clipboards taking up their station behind us. We were told to discuss post-war development. No chairman was appointed and we were given the signal to start. The pattern of the football field reproduced itself. Everyone except me spoke at once, trying to impose his personality and his agenda on everyone else. I closed my eyes and remained wrapped in silence, sorting out my mind in the mêlée of views thrust forward. After a while everyone suddenly stopped simultaneously; I opened my eyes and, assuming the leadership which I trusted was being recorded on the clipboards, summed up the diverse strands that had emerged so far and allocated specific tasks to individual discussants. There were some other tests, but I was by now too exhausted to take any significant part. But it was enough. I was on my way.

Then I found myself part of a unit that was apparently taking ship for Europe since it was the summer of 1944 and the second front was about to open. My training as an officer and a gentleman seemed in the crush of great events to have been overlooked. But appearance was all. We were part of the decoy that was to make the Germans think we were to land at Calais instead of Normandy. By my 19th birthday I was at last at Wrotham, scene of the pre-OCTU. I remember the traumas of that birthday well. The post was distributed by a warrant officer and, in addition to my own birthday greetings, I was handed a letter to give to someone else who was not present. I put it in my pocket and, being me, forgot all about it. Mail in the Services is a very sensitive matter. At a later parade I was ordered to turn out my pockets and, of course, produced the letter. I was in the eyes of the NCO in deep trouble, though the man to whom the letter was addressed accepted my apology without any fuss. But for me that could not be the end of it. It was the school blackout screen all over again. I felt desperately that my integrity was in question. I was troubled in conscience as to whether I ought to go on: was I fit to be an officer when I was liable to such lapses? After an agonising debate for most of the day, I lurked outside the NCO's mess until the warrant officer appeared and confessed to him my unfortunate failing. He looked startled but said at last that he found what I said very strange but that he felt I was being honest. I thought it probable that he would report the conversation and that my officer training would be at an end. So be it, I said to myself. I had at least told the truth. Nothing happened.

My inability to run having become too apparent, my passage to a commission was further delayed while I was sent on a remedial course to toughen me up. It was hell, but I made faces to show I was determined to overcome, and at long last was delivered up to the 123 OCTU (Officer Cadet Training Unit) at Catterick in Yorkshire. A 28-week course lay ahead and it was understood that one could be RTUed (returned to unit) at any time up to the halfway point. How could I last that long? If bluff had got me so far, what hope was there of sustaining it under so much rigorous inspection?

Much of our work consisted of TEWTs (Tactical Exercises Without Troops) – a practice strongly recommended by Machiavelli – stressing the making of decisions and the giving of commands. Broadly speaking, the more senior the simulated rank I was assigned in these scenarios (and therefore the more implausible that I would ever fill the role in reality) the better I performed. I was at my best standing at a sand-table disposing of guns on a grand scale. Dealing with a troop, which was the largest unit I was likely ever to command in action, was more of a problem. But whatever the size of the unit I tried to sound decisive even when, as was often the case, I did not really know what I was being decisive about.

In the course of these exercises, we were always liable to be jumped upon by the Directing Staff with odd questions and contingencies. I remember once an officer, correctly deducing that I was helpless without my slide-rule, leaped out of the shadows and told me that a shell had just shattered my instrument. Instantly I whipped a spare slide-rule out of my hip pocket. Then again, when I was in the middle of planning an all-night operation, I was told that a Parsee member of my staff had been killed. What, I was asked, was to be done? As it happened, I knew the answer (build a Temple of Silence, place the remains on top and let the birds dispose of them) but it seemed a bizarre test.

In my spare time I was recruited by a thrusting, forceful, ambitious colleague, some years my senior, who wanted to produce a unit magazine. I learned much from him but one day he disappeared, a victim to RTU. Presently, my comrades were going down like flies, by no very obvious principles. Of two Australian cadets, both ex-sergeants who had served in the Western Desert, the robust commanding personality went down and his shy, nervous compatriot survived. There was much speculation that they had got the two mixed up but surely that could not be so. Our culled ranks soldiered on.

Then I got a lucky break. How it came about I have no idea. We were to simulate a regimental dinner, to accustom ourselves, I suppose, to being gentlemen as well as officers. A toast was to be given to the Directing Staff and the person who was asked to propose it was myself. I spoke as I had done at the Oxford Union, without notes, and prepared a few sentences but not the whole speech. It came off. The high point was when I exploited the ill-concealed fact that the Directing Staff largely consisted of ex-Desert Rats, proud of their war record and depressed at being relegated to an OCTU. So I said of them, 'They have fought well in the Desert. Now they have had their reward (longish pause): they have been sent to Catterick.' I did not think, after hearing the great roar of laughter and applause, that I was going to be RTUed.

There was, however, one big obstacle still to overcome and one, moreover, that would test me at my most vulnerable point. For the two weeks before the mid-course break after which we would be safe we were dispatched to the Lake District. Here we would be subjected to survival tests. We were, for example, taken in sealed lorries and dropped off, one at a time, at remote spots, from which we would have to get back to some central point. For the purposes of camouflage our faces and hands were blacked up. I liked the Lake District and had had some experience of tramping moors, but I had no map and there were no houses or traffic in sight. I looked for the sun but could not find it. I have very little sense of direction at the best of times (another reason perhaps why I ought not to have been an officer). I usually turn instinctively in the wrong direction, unless I have subconsciously corrected for this; the difficulty lies in deciding on any given occasion which of those two is the case.

I tramped off glumly down a track, then saw a wisp of smoke coming from behind some rocks. As I moved nearer there appeared a cottage and a small hill farm. I knocked on the door, a woman opened, screamed and fell backwards in a faint. I thought this reaction to me rather excessive until I remembered my camouflage. Ladies often fainted at moments of stress in Victorian novels, but I had never seen it happen before. I was wondering where to look for the smelling salts when the lady's brother appeared and she herself regained her poise and her sense of all that she owed to a soldier in uniform. After I had swallowed the hot tea and good farm fare that I was offered, the brother volunteered to take me in his truck to where I wanted to go, which in view of petrol rationing was very good of him. I got out just before the town and walked cheerfully into the camp, one of the first little pigs to find his way home.

We carried out an assault crossing of Ullswater and an ascent of Helvellyn. In those days I was fairly fit for hill-climbing, or perhaps I should say less unfit than for anything else. I was carrying a rifle and pack but I sauntered up at a reasonable pace. There was no one on the top when I arrived except a member of the Directing Staff. 'Magnificent view from up here today, sir,' I said cheerily. 'Better than when I was here last.' 'You are not supposed to be a tourist. You should be thinking of how to defend the position against a counter-attack.' This, I must confess, had not occurred to me. Would I never react like a soldier? I sloped off, resolving to lower my profile for the immediate future.

Next day we had a very long march indeed. I was dropping before the end and only got through because for the last two miles an incredibly strong and generous French-Canadian cadet half carried, half frog-marched me along. When I arrived at the camp site for the night I was truly on my knees and my mind was quite switched off. I flopped down by the fire on which supper was being brewed. At that moment the Directing Staff chose to switch functions and put me in charge of the whole operation. I tried to pull myself together, as the dead tired men now under my command ate their meal and turned into their tents for the night. Something told me not to follow suit. 'A little touch of Harry in the night', I muttered to myself as I promenaded among the tents, seeking to recall the other lines of that speech. I saw a bright light at one end of the camp. An NCO belonging to the staff was crouched over a fire. I sidled up to him. For some reason he chose to reveal that his officer's intention was shortly to order an emergency move to test our resilience and my power of leadership. I went from tent to tent warning the men not to undress and to be ready at a moment's notice to strike camp. Fortunately for my reputation the order was not long in coming. The exhausted cadets responded with commendable speed and under my command (as Monty would have put it) we set off over the hills.

The second half of the OCTU course went by with much less tension because now it was assumed that the band that remained were certain to be

2. To be a soldier – the first pip.

officers and that as such we would be off to war, commanding men and guns in action. The war in Europe was now clearly coming to an end and, while the country was preparing itself to rejoice, our thoughts were turning towards engaging with the Japanese, probably on their own main islands. Much of the talk, however, was not about that but about the future of Britain. I remember with great clarity how shaken I was by the grim but realistic assessment that was made one night by a thoughtful Canadian who was, I suppose, about ten years my senior. He laid out, accurately enough as it turned out, the facts about Britain's crippling poverty after five years of war. He sliced into assumptions about the British Empire's world role that stemmed simply from the fact that we would be one of the victors. He doubted that the Empire would long survive. And he said that he saw no future even for these islands, unless we exported 20 million of our population. It was a sobering thought.

Meanwhile, there were still some most important military secrets to be imparted to us, on, for example, correct behaviour in an officers' mess. 'You must be punk-chilous about etiquette', a breathy little major whom I had not seen before insisted. He pronounced the word 'punk-chilous' several times for emphasis. Then we were measured for uniforms and passing-out day arrived. We were actually translated into officers and gentlemen by Sir Alan Cunningham, the general who had gloriously conquered the Italians in East Africa and had then gone on to be humiliatingly out-generalled and vanquished by Rommel in North Africa. Churchill had decreed that he should never be employed again in any capacity, but Field-Marshal Jan Smuts, attaching more importance to his victories than to his defeats, had intervened to rescue his career. He had received various home postings and was shortly to go out to Palestine as the last High Commissioner. My one impression of him, as I was trying desperately to keep in step, was of a bulbous, purple nose ripe for the plucking.

On leave afterwards, I accompanied my mother to the London theatre, wearing proudly my brand-new uniform with the single pip of a second lieutenant. My mother glowed. As we entered, she pointed disparagingly to another military figure just ahead and said, not particularly softly, 'Look at that colonel, he's wearing a very rumpled uniform.' I had recognised the officer in question. It was the Chief of the Imperial General Staff, General Sir Alan Brooke.

CHAPTER 4

Officer and Gentleman

T he words Officer and Gentleman have a conceptual affinity that was still in common usage in the Second World War but was often expressed in different tones by professionals and temporaries. By the former, ancient customs, traditions and above all hierarchies were implied. By the latter, the usage would often be tinged with irony, bordering at times on sarcasm. Nevertheless the difference in an officer's lifestyle from that of the ranks, even the ranks of officer cadets, was marked. As an officer one had, for example, a manservant, known as a batman or orderly (or in India as a bearer). And, in place of the Naafi with its humble 'char and wad' (tea and bun) one had the facilities, as well as the obligations, of membership of the officers' mess. Still, a second lieutenant is the lowest form of such life and it is as well that he shows he knows it.

I was told that victory in the West meant that no more Russian speakers were needed but that if I was still interested in the 'I' Corps I should learn Japanese. I thought not and was posted at the end of my leave to a training unit at Alnwick in Northumberland. On my first day word came from my battery commander that I should take a staff car, pick up some documents and then drive over to where a test-firing of 25-pounders had been aborted because the shells had failed to go off. Eager to please, I jumped into the driver's seat before remembering that I did not know how to drive. There had been driving lessons at pre-OCTU but I had missed them through illness. The major was waiting in the field and I must not fail him in my first task. I had been watching my father drive for a number of years and it did not look too difficult. So the car screamed off and halted with a jolt outside the battery office where, since I did not know how to reverse, I jumped out and strode purposefully to the office door, tossing the keys to the first OR (other rank) that I saw and ordering him to turn the car round. Saluting smartly he did so. There, I reflected with relief, was the power of a single pip. I was off again. On sighting the major I contrived this time to bring the staff car to a dignified halt. 'Would you like to

drive or shall I?' he asked. 'Why don't you drive, sir?' Considering the circumstances I thought I had done rather well; it was just a pity that throughout life,
apart from learning how to reverse, I never managed to drive any better.

VE Day found me at Alnwick and so did the ensuing general election. Since
I had been a Liberal at Oxford I was excited at finding myself in the constituency of the great Liberal hero Sir William Beveridge, who had been returned
unopposed at a by-election and was seeking re-election. He had an attractive
poster showing the figure of the kindly old gentleman, who was now famous as
the author of the report which called for welfare from the cradle to the grave,
standing in the road thumbing a lift. The caption was 'Going my way?' I did
not realise at the time what an impossible egocentric the man was, rivalling
even Dr A.L. Rowse. At the time everyone imagined that Winston Churchill
would go on as Prime Minister and some Liberals at least were thinking in
terms of a new coalition; one heard (and knowing him later I can well believe
it) that Sir William had indicated that the National Insurance portfolio was not
good enough for him – Chancellor of the Exchequer was more in his line. Some
years later, on joining the Reform Club, I was awed to find Beveridge seated
alone in the library and willingly sat at his feet while he as willingly discoursed
about his greatness. Whenever he spotted me subsequently he made as if to
repeat the performance but after a while the sense of privilege diminished and
avoidance became the rule. But this was for the future. In Alnwick, not knowing him, he was my hero.

I could, however, not vote for him. In the khaki election of 1918 serving
men of 18 and over were allowed to vote. In 1945 no one's opinion counted
unless he or she was at least 21. As a junior officer, it became my duty to
lecture the men on the importance of the ballot without having a vote myself.
I felt this keenly.

After the voting occurred on 5 July there was then a delay while the serv-
icemen's votes were being collected and counted, so that Churchill's defeat
and Labour's victory were not announced until 26 July. On that day my
colonel came into the battery mess and sat down heavily next to the battery
commander. 'I feel now,' he said solemnly, 'as I felt on 3 September 1939
– [pregnant pause] – as if anything might happen.' Gloomily the major took
up the theme: 'Now I suppose they will send me down to work in the mines.'
The colonel looked around the room, fixed his glare on me and said savagely,
'I suppose *you* will be very happy.' As a matter of fact my joy was not unabated:
Beveridge had lost his seat and so had my party leader, Sir Archibald Sinclair.

Given leave before embarkation for the Far East, the amazing news broke
of the atom bomb on Hiroshima. By the time I had taken ship Nagasaki had

followed and the Emperor had ordered surrender. Thus, as I set out for the seat of war, the war vanished; my military skills were not to be tested in battle. I found myself among a miscellaneous group of subalterns ready, after several false starts, to board the troopship for India. We had two briefings, medical and intelligence. Apart from telling us about mepacrine, which would turn the whites of our eyes yellow but save us from malaria, the medical briefing concentrated on exercise. We should devote every spare minute to some sporting activity; otherwise the fell climate in the East would get us. It was to be with some slight satisfaction that subsequently I watched my brother officers who were so vigorous at tennis, squash, polo and other activities go down one after another while I, who took no exercise at all that could possibly be avoided, remained immune. Next there was the intelligence briefing. I do not remember its formal content but I remember the shock of hearing one throwaway remark by the briefing officer, a major, at the end. Speaking of the two atom bombs dropped he said, 'I hope they've kept one back to drop on Moscow.'

On board the officers were segregated from the men, but the women, either WAAFS or ATS, of whom there were quite a number, were not segregated from anyone. Most of them soon paired off and remained locked on the deck in voyage-long horizontal embrace, so that they had to be delicately stepped around when taking a promenade. Several of the junior subalterns resolved to play bridge, an option which I declined; they would be bidding and quarrelling (as in Chekhov's *Ivanov*) when I would drop off to sleep each night and were still bidding and quarrelling when I woke up in the morning. I divided my time between Macaulay (which A.J.P. Taylor had advised me to read while I was in the Services) and an elementary Hindustani textbook and noted with pleasure that we were off Cape Trafalgar on Trafalgar Day. We pulled into Port Said and I saw for the first time the Suez Canal which later was to mean so much to me. I remember witnessing with a feeling of repugnance the demeaning antics by which the Egyptians in the tiny boats which had surrounded our vessels attempted to win our patronage.

Just before dawn we steamed into Bombay harbour next to the pompous Gateway to India and alongside docks whose surface appeared to be entirely covered by an expanse of multicoloured cloth. Suddenly as dawn broke the cloth rose like a cloud and broke up into innumerable fragments as the sleeping labour force of coolies awoke to a new day. India is a very special place, some of whose scenes, sounds and smells may not be for the fastidious, but there is something about the multiple varieties of its ways of life, its art, its philosophies, its religions that has got under the skin of many generations of its visitors. It was so with me. Despite discouraging aspects, I was caught up with the thrill of being in India and of being there, moreover, when the country was alive with portents of great political change.

We were to go to Kalyan, a great dumping camp for spare officers until somebody could think what to do with them. We travelled there by train, a very underpowered train, which crawled slowly for miles out of Bombay before picking up any speed. This was fortunate for the more enterprising of the young beggars, thieves and salesmen who perched themselves like Simeon Stylites on poles, from which point of vantage they could thrust their goods or persons through the open glassless carriage windows. Sometimes a hand would reach in to snatch the spectacles off an unwary face; occasionally a knife thrust would remove the watch from an unwary wrist. But more normally they were simply trying to sell; it was, however, advisable to face the window frame. A stiff, buttoned-up fellow officer, who had confided to me in a rare moment of disclosure that he could not wait to get back to wearing a stiff collar every day in a City office, was sitting with his back to the window. 'There's a gentleman just behind you who would like to have a word with you,' I remarked. As he turned round, the Indian on the pole adjacent to him pressed the button on the knife he was holding, so flashing a blade to within an inch of my companion's throat. He did not recover his composure until we reached Kalyan.

Since no one knew what to do with me at Kalyan I plunged into as much Indian life as I could manage, practising my still very elementary Hindustani and reading anything about India that was written by Indians. Since the war was no longer on I vowed that the army should be my tourist agency and when I was offered a chance of being attached to the Indian Army I eagerly accepted. For quite a while nothing happened and I was given permission to visit Bombay. Then I was sent to Vizagapatam, on the southeast coast. It had a large beach which was empty when I first set eyes on it, but I had only to don swimming trunks for it to be filled instantly with small boys fighting each other for the honour and above all the reward of being able to wash the sand from my toes when I emerged from the sea. I took ship from there to Rangoon, where I was again left suspended in a transit camp.

Rangoon in 1945, freshly liberated from the Japanese, was on the move, with busty women stripped to the waist pushing heavy carts of furniture through the streets while smoking immense cheroots wrapped in pages of the *Rangoon Liberator*. This last was a lively enough journal with candid copy, describing, for instance, a press conference held by a leading *dacoit* (gangster), so designated, in which he announced his intention to retire from that profession. I visited Insein jail, a shocking spectacle of row above row of men caged in open structures like animals in a zoo without space or privacy. And I marvelled at the magnificent Shwedagon Pagoda. I even made a flying visit to Saigon at the invitation of an RAF pilot. Finally I got my posting to Lamaign in the southeastern province of Tenasserim. I was to belong to the 1st Indian Field regiment and, within it, to Scindia's Field Battery. The battery belonged to the Maharajah of Gwalior, whose ancestor Ranoji Scindia and his natural son Mahadaji, both Maratha generals, had established the state in the eighteenth century; their descendants, unlike many other Marathas, were prudent enough always to side with the British. For the duration of the war Scindia's Battery had been incorporated in the 1st Indian Field as its third battery. But there was a special feel about a state unit. While a majority of its *jawan* (young men) were Hindus, many of the specialists were Muslims or Sikhs. The unit song was *Hindu, Mussulman, Sikhs, Isai / Ham tum to mil ke bhai bhai* (Hindus, Muslims, Sikhs, Christians, when we are together we are all brothers). The battery CO and second-in-command were white; the other officers except for me, who was the most junior, were Indians. The officers' mess served only Indian food, of which I became rather fond. Being a teetotaller and in any case far more interested in Indians than in Englishmen, I spent all my evenings with my Indian colleagues while the two senior officers, the major with his fluent command of Hindustani and the captain with his fluent command of the major, departed for the regimental mess which, to the colonel's evident displeasure, I scarcely ever favoured with a visit.

We were billeted under canvas in a jungle clearing and our functions were military government and administering Japanese prison camps. More immediately we were supposed to deter *dacoits* from battening on the people and raiding the camps. When I arrived nothing much in practice seemed to be happening and I spent fruitless hours in 'supervising maintenance', which meant hanging around the guns appearing to be in charge while the Indian NCOs got on with the job. But there was a more agreeable and rewarding task, that of establishing friendly relations with neighbouring Burmese families. These lived in small, neat, highly polished houses built on stilts, to avoid the monsoon flooding, comfortably furnished usually with a grandfather clock in a corner, not of course telling the time, which in any case seemed of little interest to the owners. The village had its community of Indians. They did most of the heavy work, rather after the fashion of Irish navvies in the nineteenth century, and were consequently treated with disdain. In contrast to the solid Burmese houses, Indians made do with the kinds of lean-to slums to be seen in the suburbs of Bombay which were swept away with each monsoon. In addition there were some Chinese gentlemen who owned quite extensive gardens and made the point rather often that they relied on us for their physical protection.

My first proper job was to collect a Japanese officer from prison camp and deliver him for a war-crimes trial. I was frankly nervous because of the Japanese propensity for committing suicide. Since no one actually told me to mention to him the object of his journey I refrained from doing so. With relief I handed him over: if he were to kill himself now it would be on someone else's watch. With a guard of 14 *jawan* I was then sent to take charge of two Japanese camps, one of 200 and the other of 300 men. I was told that I would have the services of an English-speaking *havildar* (sergeant). Shortly before leaving I was summoned to the CO's office. My *havildar* was sick – the major wrote 'VD' on his note pad – and I was to have a replacement. I knew him. He did not speak English. Or, to be accurate, he spoke only one phrase in English – 'Good night, sahib' – which he used incorrectly. He meant 'Good evening' and it was an introduction to a long list of outstanding business.

The isolated camp to which I repaired looked to me rather dismal, and the officer from another unit who handed over the command did so with evident relief, expressing the opinion that I could not expect a happy time. The first task was to tidy the place up, which I did at first with my own men, but for more ambitious projects I brought in Japanese labour. By the time a general came round to inspect he was openly impressed. The second task was to cram myself with Hindustani. Fortunately there was an ambitious *naik* (bombardier/corporal) who was trying to learn English. We made a pact and spent hours together in the evenings. As I disliked having to deal with my senior NCO through one who was junior to him, I had every incentive to learn.

It had been explained to me in advance that the Japanese in the two camps were not POWs. They were SPs – Surrendered Personnel. They had not suffered the disgrace of being captured in battle; they had obeyed the orders of their emperor to surrender. Most of them were not fighting men but headquarters staff and support troops. The British had assigned them the task of building an all-weather road from Moulmein (our nearest town) to Ye. A sapper officer set them a weekly target and once a week checked up on performance. I told the interpreter to fetch his commanding officer. The Japanese colonel was small and very fat. I received him seated and, sweating profusely, he placed his forehead at my feet. It emerged that his men were mainly interested in being allowed to have a concert on a Saturday night. I told him that permission depended each week on the work quota being met; if it was, permission would be granted. If not, not.

I had no trouble of any kind from the Japanese during the weeks I was in charge. (I even volunteered to do a second tour, to postpone the boredom of 'supervising maintenance'.) The main anxiety was over the Burmese *dacoits*. It was reported that they were harassing the Japanese camps and stealing from them. I spoke to a man who was supposed to carry weight with the Burmese gangs and told him that I would not hesitate to give the Japanese weapons to defend themselves if there was any more trouble. Though I had been given the authority to do this, I was privately most reluctant to put it into effect. To my great relief, for one reason or another the contingency did not arise. For the next few weeks, during which I was the local manifestation of military government, I exercised more executive power, being still under age, than I was ever to have again. I will not pretend that I did not enjoy the sensation.

On return to base I decided to study Hindustani up to interpreters' level, especially as there was a cash incentive and in any case going to classes was better than supervising maintenance. The language class, which was attended by officers from various units in the neighbourhood, was held in the open air and was presided over by the Munshi Sahib. He was a man of that rather special status that goes in India with being *parha likha*, or educated. Although he dressed scruffily and walked barefoot (not unlike a *sadhu* or wandering holy man) he was always to be treated with respect. He called you 'sahib' but you also called him 'sahib'.

At our first session the *munshi* started talking in Hindustani to each of the officers in turn. I noticed that they managed little more than a grunt or a *tee khai, sahib* (OK, sir) in reply and was awaiting my turn with some anticipation, ready to show off. Eventually he came to me and I replied with a fair degree of fluency. He drew himself up to his full height and speaking with great deliberation in English he declared, '*Sahib*, THAT is the language of sweepers' – the last word uttered in a tone of withering contempt. '*Sahib*', I replied, 'it is the language of the men I command.' Unfortunately I did not stay in Burma long enough to complete the course.

Scindia's battery left Lamaign for Gwalior and, after the delays inseparable from military life, we pulled in by train at the state capital, Lashkar. The officers were most comfortably accommodated and were, to say the least, not stretched during a leisurely period of handing over. One of a number of parties to which we were invited sticks in my memory. The host was the Agent (as HMG's diplomatic representative in an Indian state was called) and, when I arrived, I noted with disfavour that only the three white officers from the battery were present. The other guests, clearly from Gwalior's European community, were gathered around a *chaise-longue* on which our hostess, the Agent's wife, was draped in eviscerated fashion. Presently she addressed me in a faded voice. 'What's it like now in the UK?' she asked. 'I've not been in the UK recently. I've been in Burma.' 'They tell me there aren't any servants any more.' 'That's right. They're all making munitions.' 'I simply wouldn't survi-i-i-ve.'

Finding this intolerable, I left the neighbourhood of the *chaise-longue* and sought refuge in the far corner of the room. There, seated alone on a settee, totally ignored by all present, was a well-dressed Indian in a smart *pagri* (turban). Apart from the waiters, he was the only Indian in the room. I sat down beside him. He was the Prime Minister. He explained his present difficulties. The Maharajah, wishing to be modern, had initiated a Question Time in the state's Parliament. The original questions were not so bad: one had notice of them and could look up the answers. But, most unfairly, opposition members were then allowed to ask supplementaries with no notice whatsoever. I tried to calm the Prime Minister by giving examples, drawn from my childhood memories of *Hansard*, of ways in which such supplementaries could be either anticipated or neatly turned aside. I doubt if he was much comforted.

Before the three white officers left the state we were received in the palace by our prince. The palace was a strange medley of authentic Indian art and decoration and cheap European junk. Its most original feature was a railway which ran through the principal rooms and duly conveyed tea, sandwiches and cakes to the Maharajah and his guests. While the two others, who had seen action in Burma, then left for England, I temporarily rejoined my regiment which had moved into permanent barracks at Trimulgherry near Hyderabad. All I can remember of this interlude is the acting commanding officer, a Major Edge, making a determined effort to restore soldiering to what it was supposed to be in peacetime India. All the officers were summoned to a meeting in the mess during which the major, who was not an eloquent man, spelled out with many pauses and in excruciating detail what would be involved in our keeping a polo team. He was a chain-smoker and at every pause the smoke billowed through his ample moustaches like smoke from an artillery round rising through a clump of trees, first slight and wispy, then opening out laterally to create a critical mass, then bursting out of the foliage into the open air. As the talk of 'hundred chippers' (a chipper is a rupee), of the need to retain grooms and of sundry other details entered the dead air, I became more and more absorbed by slight variations in the behaviour of the smoke. At last the major had finished. 'Who', he asked wearily, 'would like to come in on this?' Not a hand, not a voice stirred. 'Well, put it another way, who wants to be left out?' Everybody's hand went up. There was a long pause, much pulling at the cigarette, much smoke filtering through the undergrowth. Then, very faintly,

'Well, that's that, gentlemen.' He never addressed us collectively again.

As I had no proper function I thought that it was travel agency time. I applied for a surveyor's course and was sent off to the foothills of the Himalayas. When I reached Rawalpindi, I was stranded for a week by a rail strike. It was the week of my 21st birthday, the time when by the conventions of the day I had reached man's estate. Coincidentally this also proved to be true for two other officers, not of my regiment, who were also stranded. Our celebrations were modest because we were not carrying much money and the banks also were closed. But we did jointly celebrate. At the end of the week I pressed on to Murree, crossed into the Northwest Frontier and what is now Pakistan, and by a tortuous mountain track along which only one-way passage was allowed was delivered to Ghora Dhakka (Horse Leap). The scenery was astonishing, the air bracing, the atmosphere one of absolute isolation from India, from the world, from events of any kind.

I was assigned to a well-appointed hut and had just settled down to a large volume of Indian history when there was a knock at the door. My visitor was the most distinguished-looking Indian I ever met. With grave face, beautiful moustache, dazzling white robes and impressively intricate turban, he seated himself in the lotus position. He raised his large, sad eyes to my level and, speaking in a deep baritone voice, said, 'You want dirty pictures, sahib?'

We spent several weeks chasing around the tops of hills with theodolites. Not having any intention of becoming a surveyor, I took a fairly relaxed view of our tasks while enjoying the mountain air, and when it was over I got myself posted off to Poona on a course for education officers. Poona (Pune, as it is now) had before the war earned a very special place in the British mystique of empire. Among stand-up comedians at pier-ends and in old-fashioned music halls Poona was made to stand for all that could be made to sound pretentious and ridiculous about the 'empire on which the sun never sets'. There had been no cheaper way of striking at the soft underbelly of the governing class than by satirising the accents, attitudes and assumptions of the rulers, civil and military, of the Indian Empire. And within that Empire there was one town, one military cantonment, which offered an incomparable target. And Poona did not disappoint: there was plenty of silver in the regimental mess; the conversation revealed the underlying assumption that, come socialism or high water, there would always be an Empire. In one sense that was not far wrong, since when I returned to Poona after 30 years the old customs and the old accents were still there but even more over the top than I had remembered them. Only the skin colour of the officers had changed.

The education course was well run and practical and, on receiving a posting to a regiment in Quetta, I looked forward to being tutor to the civilians of the future. But first there was the inevitable stay in a transit camp (this time Deolali) and then an endless train journey by night and day through the hottest region in the world. This was the occasion when for the last time I tried to confront my private demons head on. I should explain that being a teetotaller my mess bills were so modest that I had been able to live in Burma off the field allowances which I was paid in cash. The money from it only ran out when I was ready to leave Deolali. My pay as a lieutenant had been accumulating untouched; I needed to draw from it for the first time for my journey to Quetta but, being me, I forgot. I entered the train with only a few *anas* (pence) in my pocket. Sick at heart at this grotesque set-back to my campaign for self-mastery I flagellated myself, as it were, by abstaining from borrowing cash for food, water or, most important of all, ice for the whole journey. The experience might, I desperately hoped, inflict on me such a drastic physical and mental jolt that I might finally break free of my maddening disability. I was alone in my compartment but there were other officers on the train who would surely have provided assistance. But I was determined to suffer. We stopped for a while at Jacobabad, which laid claim to being the world's hottest town, and, neglecting the cries at this and other stations of pedlars of ice, tea or chapattis, I stretched out on the seat and endured. Eventually when we pulled in at Quetta I lacked the strength to get up. Fortunately somebody found me and helped me out of the train. I was asked the name of my unit but with my swollen lips I could not articulate it in English, though oddly I was able to do so in Hindustani. Some kind individuals took me and my kit to the officers' mess. Everyone was out except the mess servants, who provided me with a meal and lashings of orange juice.

I sat regaining my strength on a sofa with my back to what would have been a window if the mess had run to such. Suddenly, without warning, an immense dog landed on my lap. Considerably discomposed, I struggled to regain my breath, at which point a second immense dog did the same. Before I could take evasive action it was followed by a third. Possession of such monsters was the permitted eccentricity of this regiment. The next two surprises were that my new unit felt no need for an education officer and that it was about to convert to a paratroop regiment. The CO was kind about my predicament and promised to try and get me another posting and then asked me whether, if that failed, I would be prepared to jump. I said 'Yes' – why, I am not quite sure but my answer was evidently the right one since I shortly thereafter was switched to the other end of India, to Coimbatore in the Madras Presidency.

About my experiment in self-mastery I have to report total and abject failure. The experience altered me in various subtle ways. I accepted that I had a burden for life and that I must learn to accommodate myself to it. This was at times, I fear, at the expense of my former dedication to absolute truth. People who knew me very well indeed had to be told about my chronic absence of mind. Everyone else was liable to get intricate and often invented explanations for otherwise inexplicable lapses.

As for myself I was confronted with the most severe challenge of my military career. Turkeys had arrived for Christmas and I was commanded to keep them alive until the appointed hour of their quietus. I was warned that it was in the nature of turkeys to die at the slightest provocation. But, as luck would have it, these particular specimens did not let me down. Otherwise I alleviated my own boredom by efforts to alleviate the still more pronounced boredom of the men by devices such as constructing a Piccadilly Club, starting a unit newspaper, running education classes, holding current affairs discussions and importing an Indian magician who divided his act into two parts, one labelled Sleight of Hand and the other Magic. I had by then been promoted to captain (or rather temporary captain, a reminder that this was a make-believe rank in a make-believe army).

Life trickled slowly and stickily by. To my huge disappointment, I discovered that I was not going to get early release to return to my studies at Oxford because only those whose demob number, an amalgam of age and length of service, was 55 or under were made eligible for this privilege and my number was 57. Mess life on the Madrassi plain was not exciting. There was an old-fashioned His Master's Voice gramophone of the kind which came with its picture of a dog listening faithfully to a protuberant horn. Along with this we had precisely one gramophone record. Pregnant pauses would be punctuated with 'Let's have some music', and the air would once more be filled with 'Drinking rum and co-ca-cola'. Once a visiting Cochinese princess gave an informal demonstration of the symbolic dances with which she had been nurtured. At last it became our battery's turn to have a spell up-country in the cool Nilgiri hills, at the fabulous hill station of Ooticamund, whose soubriquet 'Snooty Ooty' was not undeserved. Here chhota pegs were downed by pukka sahibs. Here also were a curious assortment of marooned English eccentrics, some of whom I recognised 20 years later when Mollie Panter-Downes (the *New Yorker* writer) made a television film about the place. Here an officers' mess was the proper focus of social life, not with Indians but with the British community, which included the official set – mainly wives and daughters of officials of the Madras Presidency seeking refuge from the summer heat. I have a memory of attempting conscientiously to discharge my functions as a host while odious women talked across me about the state of Lady Nye the Governor's wife's new hairstyle which was apparently dire. I remembered that episode when I subsequently read in the *National and English Review* Pennethorne Hughes's brilliant article on the Mem Sahib entitled 'The Women Weren't Wonderful', which attributed the decline of British prestige to the coming of marriageable women to India. Then there were the *pagal* (mad) planters, way-over-the-top characters who dropped in for a hearty breakfast, complete with pork chops, before tending their crops. Their view of the future of India seemed at no point to make contact with reality.

Suddenly I learned that I had been granted home leave, which meant that I went down to Madras to board a train for Bombay. But to say that I boarded it is to understate reality because it was a military train and, thanks to my recently acquired third pip, I was the senior officer aboard. I signed for the train – my permission was required for it to leave – and at each phase of the rather long journey a deputation of Indian railway officials would wait on me to learn at which station I would stop for a meal. For some reason food was not prepared on the train but was laid out on the platform under an awning. The Raj was visibly approaching its demise but its ceremonies were kept up to the end. I never actually signed off for the train at Bombay so that for all I know there may still be some rolling stock on the Indian track or in an Indian Railway Museum that is officially committed to my charge.

Rather the worse for wear after a cocktail of inoculations, I was determined nevertheless not to lose my berth through unfitness and was helped down to the dock by a brother officer. I just had time to reach into a barrow-load of pornography to pull out a copy of Bertrand Russell's *History of Western Philoso-phy* before staggering on board. Fortunately a little sea air soon blew away my fever and I was transported from the tropical heat of Bombay to the acute cold of the notorious winter of 1947 in bleak, rationed, post-war Britain.

For some reason I found myself stranded for two hours at Gloucester station. There was a waiting room slightly heated by a small fire. Pulling my army greatcoat tightly around me I hunched over it, seeking a limited relief from the arctic cold. I was the only person there. Presently a woman official entered and made as if to extinguish the fire, remarking to me casually that there was a fuel crisis and she could not keep a fire going for a single passenger. Fixing her with an intense stare, I said with fierce emphasis, 'I have just come from India. If you put that fire out, *I shall die.*' The lady fled.

CHAPTER 5

Oxford on a High

With Hitler, Mussolini and the Japs having been smashed and with the Raj heading for the ashcan, there were few more tricks for me to pull in the armed services. I was told I was not returning to India and so was obliged for several months to endure the various time-wasting activities of a peacetime conscript until, the full term of my service having expired, I was sent off with a stiff pork-pie hat and other civilian accoutrements into the nirvana that was Oxford. I straightaway immersed myself in academic life in the spirit of a novice entering a monastery, devoting body and soul to the study of history, all social life totally excluded. In the first year I hardly knew the names of more than half a dozen other undergraduates, including my old friend and fellow historian Michael Thompson, with whom I resumed discussion of problems of interpretation.

Unlike those ex-servicemen whose reason for eschewing the high life was their wish to graduate at top speed and make up for lost time in the 'real' world, I was a true believer in learning for its own sake, excluding from my mind for the next couple of years any impure thoughts of where my studies were going to lead. Except for lectures, I kept opening hours in the libraries, sometimes skipping lunch altogether and on one occasion being so transfixed by a book (*Le Compromis Austro-Hongrois* by Louis Eisenmann) that I did not shift position for the whole day and in consequence collapsed in the street when I left the building. (I was picked up by an ambulance and, on coming to, was cursed the whole way to hospital by the attendant for my filthy drunkenness at a time before the first alcohol had passed my lips.) The topic of my weekly essay I treated as if it were a PhD thesis, following up, insofar as was humanly possible, all the footnotes in the books and articles that I was expected to read. I was deliriously happy. All the frustrations and annoyances of the past four years were behind me. I revelled in total privacy so that the tides of history could engulf me utterly. I felt myself to be supremely fulfilled.

I attended rather more lectures than before. First and foremost there was

A.J.P. Taylor, displaying to the full his bag of technical tricks, albeit in the service of a most powerful intellect. He chose to lecture at nine o'clock on a Friday morning, to show off his pulling power at an unseasonable hour. A packed hall would see him stride in, a short stumpy figure in his corduroy suit. With studied delicacy he would lift up the lectern and place it on one side in a gesture which said 'Look, no hands' before launching into a subtly ordered but totally unscripted ventilation of the issues. At the end all strands were brought together in a climax that exactly coincided with the great clock towers of Oxford signalling the hour. Later, television viewers were able to experience this bravura performance in several series of compelling lectures.

I had a few other favourites, in particular C.A.J. Armstrong, best known as the editor of the works of Mancini, an Italian eyewitness to the usurpation of Richard III. Admittedly John Armstrong was an acquired taste and one which the bulk of his initial attendance did not care to acquire for long. But 13 of us persisted, complimenting ourselves on possession of a refined palate. He lectured on the Wars of the Roses and the Yorkist monarchy and gave his listeners a sense of participating with him in mining the evidence from the raw coalface. He was an Aristotelian perambulator who, as he strode up and down the lecture hall, would pause to emphasise the exact title of each noble character on every occasion on which he referred to him. On completing a pace, he would say, 'And thus the Battle of Wakefield was won by Henry Percy, third [long pause, turning on his heel and resuming his stride] Earl of Northumberland.'

There was also a woman lecturer, Dr Naomi Hurnard, grim, austere, flat-chested, dressed in severest black, who said things that were hilariously funny in such a mournful voice that laughter followed only at some remove. Her subject was medieval justice. Michael Thompson was one of her pupils and with a few other favourites was invited to her barely furnished rooms for a drink. Small talk not flowing easily, Michael finally referred to a scrambled sculpture above the mantelpiece and asked her what it represented. 'Oh,' she said in her usual toneless manner, 'don't you recognise it? It's a pair of breasts.'

For the first year I was again tutored by A.J.P. Taylor. Relations remained friendly. I was not thrown by his political views, which besides being pro-Russian at every turn were also specifically anti-Liberal. But I had not come to him for political views and, anyway, I was inclined to believe that dons were meant to be eccentric. I was, however, thrilled when, having been invited in 1948 as a supposed fellow traveller to the Congress of Intellectuals at the Polish town of Wroclaw (or Breslau as it was before its German inhabitants had been ethnically cleansed), Taylor reacted to the ritual garbage from a

Soviet cultural tsar by treating Moscow's literary establishment to a stinging critique. Kingsley Martin, the famous editor of the *New Statesman*, who was also there, referred in his published account to the wart at the dead centre of Taylor's ample brow as his 'devil's horn'. Alan to my surprise promptly had the horn cauterised.

Since I needed to do a paper on medieval history I went also to Magdalen's other celebrated historian, Bruce McFarlane. He was in many ways a contrast to his colleague. For one thing, while Taylor published a steady series of major academic works, McFarlane could not, with the exception of a small book on Wycliffe, bring himself to believe in his lifetime that any of his intensely researched labours was ready for publication. The four volumes now on my shelves – referred to by an acolyte as 'a respectable oeuvre' – were all assembled by his admirers after his early death. He was a quiet, tallish, rather shy man who swept through the college swiftly and silently with his fine episcopal head sharply tilted to one side. He made me think of the man in one of Dr Hurnard's lectures who had been half-hanged, his reprieve arriving at the last conceivable moment with the result that he bore the physical effect all his life.

McFarlane had an awesome reputation among medievalists and, as a known 'favourite son' of Alan Taylor's, I approached the prospect of my first tutorial with him in a mood of some trepidation. It was rumoured among some of those who looked up to 'the Master' (an appellation that, however highly his pupils regarded him, none would think of applying to Taylor) that he did not really regard those who specialised in the nineteenth and early twentieth centuries as historians at all. I took extra trouble with my first essay for him. I found Bruce stretched out, as if eviscerated, on a sofa. Tensely I read through my offering. There followed what seemed to me to be a very long silence. 'There is only one criticism I would wish to make,' McFarlane eventually said in a hollow voice. 'And that is that where you say *a* Pipe Roll of 1130, I would have said *the* Pipe Roll of 1130.' Such was the aura of the man, I was more proud of that one sentence than of anything else said to me at Oxford. Later, though some always found him monosyllabic, he became quite chatty, as if purveying fresh gossip from a medieval court. Once he said, 'You know that, according to Walter Map, when they took the chrisom off the forehead of Henry IV after his coronation, they discovered lice crawling underneath.'

The Oxford of the late 1940s was adjusting itself not without some embarrassment to a wide age-range of undergraduates. Some who had served from the start of the war were three years older than I was; others, straight from school, were three or four years younger. A bulldog, a member of the university police, raising his bowler as he did so, accosted an undergraduate in a pub

and charged him with consuming beer in public contrary to university regulations. The offender was an ex-lieutenant-colonel and, after some scenes from
the theatre of the absurd, the rule was changed. But the full weight of donnish
disapproval was brought to bear on *Cherwell*, an undergraduate weekly, when it
was cheeky enough to start running critical reviews, like brief theatre notices,
of university lectures.

My self-exclusion from extra-curricular activities was not quite absolute
because I could not entirely give up my interest in politics. The very first day
I was back in college, in high spirits because no longer in uniform, there was
a circular under my door from the British Union (the suffix 'of Fascists' tactfully omitted) commencing, 'How much you must miss the discipline and
companionship of the Army!' There were other more acceptable approaches
and, feeling myself radical by instinct but still not possessed of a sufficiently
saintly view of human nature to be a socialist, I once more identified myself
with the Liberals. I went to a few political meetings, at which I stayed strictly
in the background and afterwards scrupulously made up for lost time by working into the small hours. For a while I attended the Union debates on Thursday nights and, because the gates of the college were locked from midnight,
used to climb back over the eponymous Longwall, an easy task for a man of
my height which was greatly assisted by the way the spikes were fixed on the
neighbouring lamp-posts. But, being seldom called on to speak and then only
near midnight for three minutes (which did not suit my style) I presently abandoned attendance.

I would perhaps have completed the whole of my university life in this
cocoon of my own creation had it not been for Robin Day. That I began to live
a fuller life was due to the strong bond of friendship which, thanks solely to
his initiative, I formed with that remarkable man. One dark and stormy night
I trudged through the snow to attend a debate between the Oxford University
Conservative and Liberal Clubs. The motion concerned India. It was proposed
by the Tories, who argued that everything that had taken place since the
departure of the Raj one year before had shown that departure to be a terrible
mistake. I went with no expectation at all of speaking and with every intention
of escaping back to college the moment the debate was over.

As the evening progressed the Conservatives, some of whom were still in
military uniform, seemed to be having things far too much their own way,
arrogantly using their unmatched Indian experiences to override their opponents. Their Liberal rivals had scarcely time to shuffle their notes before one
of the sarcastic Tories would interrupt with, 'And what is your experience of
India?' Alas, credentials there were none. At last, unable to restrain myself

further, and in total violation of my anonymity, I leaped up, caught the eye of the evening's chairman, Robin Day (who, as secretary of the Union, was already something of a celebrity within Oxford's closed world) and launched into a counter-tirade. 'And what are your credentials for speaking on India?' came the Tory voice, bored yet assured. 'Scindia's Field Battery, 1st Indian Field.' From that moment I felt I had the audience in the palm of my hand and, filled with adrenalin, I poured out my convictions about the end of the Empire. The Liberals, immensely relieved, gave me a great round of applause. When I sat down I was both elated and horrified, horrified at being so elated and at my cover having been blown.

The instant the debate was over I dashed for the door to avoid any possibility of social intercourse. The snow outside was by now quite heavy. I ploughed through it as fast as I could. I heard Robin Day's voice behind me shouting my name. I pretended not to hear. Then I heard it again and realised he was following me. I tried to press on faster but he was overtaking me. At the third shout I turned round. Since I was trapped, I thought I would make the best of it and accept his invitation for a coffee. 'Why haven't I heard of you before?' Robin demanded, looking at me accusingly half-over and half-through what in the years of his national fame as a television interviewer came to be described as his cruel glasses. 'Because I have not chosen to be heard of,' was my reply. I was then subjected to a prolonged cross-examination on my motives and aspirations which I half resented and half enjoyed. He dismissed my explanations peremptorily and lectured me, rather I imagined like an elder brother, on the folly of my ways. I was not immediately convinced but, having discovered my reasons for abandoning the Union, he proceeded, a Mephistopheles accosting a Faust, with the query whether if offered a paper speech at the Union I would accept it. A momentary vanity, the recollection of that night's triumph, or perhaps a sense of politeness for once overcoming the borrowed boorishness with which I usually brushed off social contact, prompted me to say I would.

I sensed that nothing would come of it; the president after all, not the secretary, chooses paper speakers. I returned to my books, only to experience the tiger-like persistence that Robin could devote to a cause (and that cause, though sometimes his own, was just as often that of someone he had chosen as a friend). The president was harassed until he gave way and my name was up on the order paper for the 'committee debate' – on, so far as I can remember, Western European Union (the predecessor of NATO). The committee debate was an occasion on which unknowns were given their chance to make 'paper speeches', ten minutes in length, at the start of the debate and there were no visiting celebrities.

When the night arrived, another on the list who was also from my college suggested that we went together. When I joined him, he said we should first pick up two girls for the gallery. At that time the debating floor at the Union was a strictly male affair with women only admitted to the gallery so that they could watch the gladiatorial performances beneath like fair damsels at a medieval tournament. Several terms later there was to be a motion to allow them to become full members and take part in debates. It was moved by Michael Summerskill, the son of the feminist politician Dr Edith Summerskill who herself was in the gallery for the great occasion. The balance of argument, very calmly and responsibly put, seemed to be going Michael's way until a senior ex-president called Anthony Walton, a small, crusty lawyer with an unstoppable ability to recite *verbatim* the screenplay of any film he had recently attended, intervened with a rising intonation, 'We are not arguing with them. We are *telling* them. We just don't WANT them!' The immense wave of applause, as the inhibitions of a threatened breed were swept away, was all that was needed to bury female aspirations. Women remained in the gallery until another generation, the generation of Benazir Bhutto and a slimline Ann Widdecombe, was let in. We, on the other hand, were preserved from having to listen to such of our contemporaries as Margaret Roberts (later Margaret Thatcher).

Our two girls turned out to be scruffily dressed, winsome and (to my eyes) hopelessly young. They must, I condescendingly concluded, be waifs or orphans to whom my companion, a member of the Oxford University Labour Club, was out of charity giving a night out. What I did not grasp until several days later was that they were the two most famous women undergraduates in Oxford, Shirley Catlin (later Williams) and Val Mitchison (later Arnold-Foster) who were bracketed together as children of the book, Shirley being the daughter of Vera Brittain and Val the daughter of Naomi Mitchison. There was for a while a third member of this band, Bar Belloc, granddaughter of Hilaire Belloc, who was found in bed with the man who later became her husband and was promptly sent down. He, of course, was not. All this was hidden from me as I approached the President's chambers where we were to dine.

The officers of the Union were, as usual, accoutred in white tie and tails, the night's speakers being in plain black tie and evening dress. I ate my meal with some relish, not altogether shared, I noticed, by some of the other novices who spent most of the meal glancing surreptitiously at their prompt cards. We were just leaving for the debating hall when Robin Day approached me with some earnestness and said, 'I hope you've got your notes ready.' 'Notes?' I said. 'Why would I need notes? I'm speaking fifth and will reply to the other speakers.' 'I hope you realise,' Robin gravely riposted, 'that it is my reputation that is at stake as well as yours.'

The house was perhaps half full. It was not a major debate, though the topic was meaty enough. My fellow speakers produced thoughtful, meticulously prepared and scripted remarks while I listened and turned some phrases over in my mind. I think I was lucky in coming fifth since by then worthy ventilation of the issues had reached a point at which a change of pace was particularly welcome. I spoke without notes, which gave me a certain psychological ascendancy, of the kind that a twenty-first-century MP like John Bercow possesses in the Commons, and rebutted previous arguments. At any rate, Robin Day, seated as secretary next to the dispatch box from which I spoke, was able to feel that his reputation had been preserved.

This was enough, I felt. I had demonstrated that I could do what I always thought I could do. But I must never allow myself to get drawn into the hierarchy of committees and offices by which the Union is governed. Unlike the other speakers that night, I was not a candidate for either the Library or the Standing Committees. The exhilaration of a successful performance might be addictive. Robin, part of whose charm was that he never hesitated to abuse his friends, called me sanctimonious. I clung to my splendid isolation until at the end of term his viewpoint was reinforced from a most unexpected quarter.

It was the practice at Magdalen College at the end of each term for the undergraduate members to appear one at a time in gown and mortar board before the complete board of dons, whereupon the appropriate tutor would read out an assessment of that term's progress. I had been accustomed to listening to upbeat, appreciative remarks from Alan Taylor and I was gratified when Bruce McFarlane started off on much the same tack; but then in his toneless voice came the sucker-punch. 'He will become a better historian when he learns rather more about men and women.' I left the hall feeling numb and all the more moved by the observation in that it came from a man whom I had always thought of as the epitome of a withdrawn and cerebral don. I took some immediate steps. In the hope of overcoming my diffidence I decided to cease being a teetotaller and, in a first attempt to learn more about men and women, I accepted the editorship of the *Oxford Guardian*, organ of the Liberal Club.

My introduction to the demon drink was a modest one. I began to sip a single sherry and even a much diluted scotch; I could not abide the taste of beer and have never understood the blokish enthusiasm for it. Without making an issue of it I went to a few parties and made tentative steps towards joining the human race. I became, at any rate with men, a little less reticent. Why I was offered the editorship I shall never know. Perhaps someone heard that I edited a service newspaper. Probably Robin Day, himself at that time a

Liberal, though the Union rather than the Liberal Club was always the main focus of his interest, had something to do with it. The *Oxford Guardian* was in dire straits, losing money, lacking impact and seemingly heading for the chop. I suppose that is why they offered it to me.

I threw myself into the task of rescue. We went to a different printer, adopted a different format, recruited a fresh team of writers and tried our hardest to make this modest enough journal modestly significant. We broke even and managed to get national recognition – an article that I had commissioned about the relationship of words to music rated a *Times* leader, a powerful piece by George Bull on Bellocian corporatism provoked serious discussion in the political journals. A mischievous piece of reportage by myself about a round-table meeting of three Labour MPs was first taken up by Pendennis (Henry Fairlie) in the *Observer* and then reprinted in full with accompanying editorial in the *Daily Mail* under the heading, 'Uncertain Starlight Shines on Oxford'.

The occasion for this my first scoop had been a visit to Oxford by a left-wing brains trust of Ian Mikardo, Stephen Swingler and Harold Davies. The revolutionary idea, subsequently institutionalised as the Tribune Forum, was to have no speeches, only questions and answers. Ian Mikardo was the star. Sallow-skinned and heavy-jowelled, he practised a style of cauterising candour. He had evidently decided that these idealistic college socialists needed to be taught a thing or two about hard proletarian politics. Asked about public ownership, he explained that, 'To say that party conference after party conference has accepted a policy does not mean that the majority who voted for it believed in it. You can't say that people believed in a thing if they don't understand it.' The way to get people into the party was to talk about pensions, free health service and other social benefits. It speaks volumes about the shift in the language of politics between the age of Attlee and the age of Blair that such a statement should then have created a scandal or even surprise. 'You may call it bribery,' said candid Mick, 'but it's the way to get people into the party. If you want to convince people about nationalisation go ahead and try, but you won't get members and, if you want Socialism inside 30 years, you had better leave the job to crooks like me.' As for the Labour Chancellor Stafford Cripps, he was 'a clear example of what would happen if ever democracy was replaced by theocracy'. It was my first break into national journalism.

I was then visited in my rooms by 'men in suits' of the type who used to sack Conservative prime ministers. The burden of their tale was that, whereas it was usual for one term's secretary of the Liberal Club to be elected as the next term's president, the present secretary was widely felt to be unsuitable for such a position. Since my editorship was rated as a success, would I stand against him as an opposition candidate? This was a complete surprise. The unfortunate secretary was, I knew, a master of the *lapsus linguae*, though in other respects an admirable person. I swallowed hard, thought of Bruce McFarlane's admonition, and allowed my name to go forward. In those halcyon days, canvassing for any elected office was strictly forbidden; there were Star Chamber courts and cancelled elections if there was any hint of violation. But my opponent in effect canvassed for me whenever he read out the secretary's notices complete with such spoonerisms as 'the Guardian of the Editor'. I sensed the votes falling into my tray at every meeting.

I was elected president of the Liberal Club and, since Robin Day insisted that the holder of that office should have a presence in the Union, this time I allowed him to strongarm me into taking the necessary steps for election to the Library Committee. Its members were brought together once a week, together with our senior librarian, a lovable old bachelor called Canon Claude Jenkins, who bore the traces of more than one week's breakfasts on the front of his stock, to discuss what books to add to the collection.

Being on the committee also put me on the bottom rung of Union office, should I ever be tempted to embark on a Union career; it also meant that I could have lunch at the committee table in the Union dining room. Most importantly, I began to acquire a group of friends who have remained such throughout my life, men like Robin Day, Dick Taverne, Peter Blaker, Godfrey Smith, William Rees-Mogg, Uwe Kitzinger, Oleg Kerensky, David Wedgwood Benn (younger brother of Tony), Ivan Yates, Stanley Booth-Clibborn and the American Howard E. Shuman. Paul Johnson was also a close friend.

Dick Taverne, now a member of the House of Lords, who became one of my closest friends, was a Dutchman, born in the Netherlands' East Indies. His father was an important executive in Anglo-Dutch Shell. Dick's upbringing was largely English and he took British nationality as soon as he reached the age of 21; in a Union speech I was able to congratulate him, for he was then an ardent socialist, on himself achieving 'nationalisation'. To a remarkable degree Dick has all his life displayed the gift of infectious enthusiasm for whatever engages him; it is a most attractive trait and in the Oxford setting it was shown in respect of classical Greece and Rome and, in contemporary politics, in an ardent embrace of such principles as complete equality of all incomes from boardroom to office-boy. This last belief did not long survive departure from Oxford. But when he was up he was determined to get to know the working man at close quarters. At the end of a working day on a construction site he would drop into my rooms in dungarees and, with a smut tastefully adorning his handsome features, would give me a vivid account of the lives and adventures of his mates with the same immediacy and genuine feeling as in his talk of Pericles and Alcibiades.

While Dick was several years younger than me, Peter Blaker was as many years older. His father was chairman of the Hong Kong and Shanghai Bank and had been caught in Hong Kong by the Japanese invasion. The family had previously been evacuated to Canada, where Peter graduated with a First in classics before serving in the Canadian Army. Quite badly wounded after D-Day, he has had periodic trouble since. Thinking that the family would never regain its fortunes he qualified as a solicitor by a quick-entry scheme for ex-servicemen and settled down in a local firm in Lewes. It was only when his family fortunes were fully restored that he felt able to go up to Oxford, pick up another First, this time in law, and afterwards read for the Bar. He subsequently switched to diplomacy and finally to politics. Peter was in those days a Liberal like me (subsequently he was a Tory minister and peer) and when I became president was a pillar of strength and common sense on the committee.

William Rees-Mogg, like Dick Taverne, was one of a remarkably talented generation of men who came from Charterhouse singing the praises of that exceptional headmaster Robert Birley. I remember how impressed I was at discovering that William had contributed while still a schoolboy an article to a learned journal on seventeenth-century pamphlets and pamphleteers. Although he was more gifted as a writer than as a speaker, he eventually became president of the Union and at the time that I knew him seemed set on a political career.

Godfrey Smith was a genial figure with a lively and ever-fluent pen and a marked appreciation of the good things of life. As a speaker he excelled in literary pastiche and, taking part mainly in non-political debates, he would have occupants of both benches in stitches throughout his speeches. He was my president when I was secretary of the Union. Godfrey joined the *Sunday Times* from Oxford and remained with it, in various guises and under successive ownerships, for the whole of his career.

Ivan Yates, the only socialist of my acquaintance who regularly took snuff, was a delightful, rather old-fashioned figure, with an encyclopedic knowledge of the inner workings of the Church of England. 'I hear that Salisbury is being thought of for York', he would observe in his amiably pensive manner. He had made no great impact on the Union at the time when I became its secretary but yet was felt, through his position in the Labour Club, to be deserving of a paper speech. But how to fit him in? True, there was to be a debate deploring the decline of the middle classes but all the slots opposing the motion had been filled. Godfrey Smith, who was president, deputed me to raise with Ivan the delicate question of which unpromising opportunity he would prefer, should he really wish to speak. 'I think I would like to speak satirically in favour of the motion on the middle classes' was the measured but immediate answer. It was well judged. Ivan's speech was an unqualified triumph, one of those which in memory we like to savour. He went on to become president.

Then there was Stanley Booth-Clibborn, who had already set out on the road which took him to a mission station in Kenya and the bishopric of Manchester. There could be no more proof of his practical Christianity than his selfless but wholly abortive attempt to teach me how to play squash for the good of my health.

When I first came to the Union committee table its intellectual heavy-weight was Sir Edward Boyle. He had been one of the now-celebrated but then wrapped-in-secrecy codebreakers of Bletchley Park. His Union speeches were always on a high plane and invariably contained references to what I once described in print as his heavenly twins, Keynes and Mozart. He was podgy rather than stout and in appearance used to resemble a badly packed parcel. He had the power of investing even the most banal observation with the cloak of authority. Rotating his index finger rapidly he once told me, 'As my late father once said, "Honesty really *is* the best policy."' When he pronounced at the committee table, which he never did to excess, other conversations died down. With the young baronet one felt in the presence of a superior mind. At Schools (the final exam before graduation) he was awarded third-class honours. This inexplicable result did not stop him from becoming Minister of Education and Vice-Chancellor of Leeds University.

While speaking of the Oxford Union and indeed of the Oxford of my time I should perhaps say a word about its single most famous undergradu-ate, Kenneth Tynan. I did not know Ken Tynan personally but he was of my college. Magdalen had been the college of Oscar Wilde, and Tynan was clearly desirous of making the kind of extravagant impact that first made Wilde's renown. While his dress – which ran to purple suits and scented handkerchiefs – and some of his mannerisms might suggest the contrary, he was most asser-tively heterosexual. He was tall and dramatically thin and wore his hair some-what in the manner of Sir Andrew Aguecheek. His knowledge of the theatre was precocious and searching. He was the only undergraduate who would lead booksellers to place a large notice in the window reading 'Tynan: His First Book'. He was unquestionably both talented and a *poseur* in a well-established Oxford tradition. A typical spectacle on a hot summer afternoon would be of a punt containing a reclining Ken Tynan while one young lady handled the pole and another took down on a typewriter his sundry thoughts.

Although the Union had begun to take up more of my time, my immediate task was with the presidency of the Liberal Club. A vacation was almost wholly occupied in arranging a suitably varied programme of activities. My speakers included Lady Violet Bonham Carter, Asquith's gifted daughter, and the Marquess of Reading, who possessed to perfection a talent for dropping his monocle on to its string in precise harmony with his punctuation. On Sunday evenings we Liberals would earnestly go through drafts of conference resolutions, in one sense a singularly fruitless activity for an uninfluential part of an uninfluential party, yet in another sense admirable enough since it ensured that we were obliged to come to terms with the substance and not merely the glitter of politics. I specialised in foreign affairs including European policy and questions of civil rights and individual liberty but between us we covered the whole front.

I had made one condition before agreeing to stand for office. Trinity term being summertime, the political clubs used to arrange a variety of outdoor social activities but I had made it clear that this was not for me. A social secretary would need to be appointed to take this off my shoulders. One such was readily to hand. His name was Jeremy Thorpe – up from Eton after a very sharply foreshortened spell of military service. Jeremy was a man of great, even frenetic, energy though given on occasion to collapsing dramatically. He came from a political family with ancestors in public life on both sides, stretching back, we were given to understand, to the reign of Edward II. His father had been a highly promising barrister-politician who had died young, leaving prominent lawyers like the former Lord Chancellor Viscount Simon with a sense of obligation to take an interest in the son's well being. His formidable, monocle-wearing mother, prominent in local government, was a looming presence. Rather surprisingly for a man who appeared consumed with ambition for the glittering prizes, Jeremy was to remain wholly committed to a Liberal Party which had precious few such prizes on offer, and did so even when his godmother, Lady Megan Lloyd George, and his patron, Dingle Foot, deserted it for Labour.

I found that I was asked to speak and canvass in various parts of the country – in the Border country where Wilfred Roberts held a seat for the Liberals, in Plymouth where the prospective candidate enthused over my microphone technique when for the first time I spoke to a large outdoor audience, and in mid-Bucks where after hearing me speak the local Liberals promptly offered me the candidacy for the coming election. I would have followed in the footsteps of the bestselling thriller-writer Edgar Wallace. This was heady stuff after my previously cloistered existence and it must have been then that the possibility of a political career entered my mind. But I managed not to be carried away. I was firm about the priority of my university degree.

CHAPTER 6

Decline and Fall

My father's final job was as agent for Cornelia, Countess of Craven, at Hampstead Marshall, near Newbury on the Hants/Berks border. Lady Craven was an elderly American who had at 16 become one of the so-called Pilgrim Daughters, young daughters of very rich American families married off to impoverished members of the titled European nobility. According to a published account of New York's great parties of the nineteenth century, her family, the Bradley Martins, displayed their trophy at an exceptionally spectacular reception in New York's Waldorf Astoria Hotel, which for the occasion was remodelled as the Palace of Versailles. Guests arrived in chain mail and other suitable outfits. The New York papers devoted several pages to describe in words and pictures the glorious ostentation of the occasion. Unhappily the year was 1893, a year of economic depression in New York, and social critics were not slow to moralise about the contrast between excess and deprivation. Mrs Bradley Martin, greatly put out, issued a statement of pre-Keynesian enlightenment on the large amount of counter-cyclical employment her wedding party had created. It was in vain. Claiming to be much misunderstood, this branch of the Martins wiped the dust of an ungrateful America from off its feet and departed for Europe.

The lady's outlook was not to be bounded by the tightened horizons of post-war Britain. One of my father's first duties was to start a chicken farm so that she could serve her guests with chicken soup. Princess Marie-Louise, one of Queen Victoria's grandchildren who, now nearly 80, had been divorced since she was 28, was a frequent guest and used to swear that she never had at Kensington Palace the type of service available at Hampstead Marshall.

After the war but before my father came to work for her, the Countess had decided to revisit her relatives in the United States. She had instructed her lawyer to arrange all the necessary permissions and immunities to enable her to sail with her entourage and manifold possessions. The poor man rapidly ran into obstacles; the post-war government regulations respecting exports were not designed to accommodate Pilgrim Daughters. Accordingly Lady Craven transferred herself and ample staff to a whole corridor of Claridge's Hotel and obtained an interview with Harold Wilson, the new 31-year-old President of the Board of Trade. In the deep swooping diction she knew how to employ to maximum advantage, she acquainted the minister with the proposition that she, an American, had stood by Britain throughout the war. 'Do you expect me to go back to my family *in rags*?' Wilson explained that there were certain rules which would affect even her. The amount of jewellery she could take out of the country, for example, was strictly limited. Thrusting forward an ear to the lobe of which a large diamond was attached, she demanded with pathos, 'Do you expect me to undergo *a major surgical operation?*' After much more of the same, 'Lady Craven,' said Mr Wilson, 'take what you like.' She swept out, pausing only to remark to her lawyer, 'Why couldn't you have done that?'

At Oxford I made in 1949 one other tentative beginning to fill the gaps of my way of life. Bruce McFarlane had said, 'When he knows more about men *and women* he will make a better historian.' Ah, the woman question. I had not really spoken to a woman (I mean, spoken socially) since childhood games with Lady Jane and Lady Belinda at Longford until I met the Liberal Club committee. I did not know how to approach women and until I had to preside over the club I had seen no need to do so. Having rather complacently assumed that I was quite unattractive to women, I had up till then treated their occasional intrusion as a not very welcome development.

One evening this opinion was for the first time modified. I had gone to a rather large and incoherent party and, after exchanging a few words with a strikingly beautiful and animated young lady whom I had met before but who was usually surrounded by admiring young men, I had moved on and, feeling more bored by social life than usual, was about to leave. It had simply never occurred to me that this young lady, with whom I had exchanged words but nothing more, had paid me the least attention. Moreover, having read at one period rather a lot of Freud, I had idly speculated, though not particularly on this occasion, that the absence of women in my life might be due less to the reason I had ascribed to it, namely a determined resolution never to be swayed by them, and more to my being a repressed homosexual. But then, I thought, surely not, since I would have been bound to notice the tension between the strength of attraction and the effort of repression. Suddenly and impulsively with no particular object in mind I picked up a large brandy glass, filled it with martini and swallowed it in one go; I then refilled the glass and did it again. I was still not very used to strong drink and for the first – and only – time in my life I remembered not a thing that happened thereafter.

When I woke up in mid-morning the next day I was in bed in my digs (I had by then moved out of college). I was told later that I had made vigorous advances to the young lady I have mentioned, which were not at all repelled, and that I had eventually been brought home by her. On my mirror when I awoke I read a seductive message in lipstick. Three thoughts flashed through my mind: I had waylaid a woman and not a man (resolving that question once and for all), it had been the right woman and, most oddly of all, I had not been rejected. More than a little shocked at myself, I was nevertheless undoubtedly pleased. I had for the first time seen my way to having a girlfriend.

I shall be forever grateful to this lady (now dead) for teaching me for the first time to respect and to be responsive, if only spasmodically, to female outlook and feelings. She was high spirited and fine looking (too good for me, I used to think) and I felt for her a genuine affection. Another such might have found in me in some of my moods too boorish a companion: I was still determined to be side-tracked by no one and nothing. All the same the two of us had some splendid times together – whether at Stratford or in the gods of the Old Vic, seeing Gielgud or Olivier or Burton or wandering through heavenly Cotswolds blossoms on an Easter weekend. For the rest of my life I have not been able to see the annual blossoms without thinking of her.

I had reached by now a kind of peak in my Oxford life, more balanced than before with politics, student journalism, the Union and friends of both sexes, but still heavily committed to academic endeavour. I would work often through the night at my digs, from which I would emerge into the street at two or three o'clock for fresh air. This once occasioned the following interchange with the law:

Constable: What are you doing out at two o'clock in the morning?
KK: Thinking.
C: Do you normally think at this hour?
KK: Yes.
C: What are you thinking about?
KK: Henry VI.
C: Do you always think of Henry VI?
KK: No. I sometimes think of Edward IV.

No arrest was made.

Having, rather late in the day, decided to take a full part in the Union, I found myself asked to catch a train to Cambridge with the then president, Uwe Kitzinger, to represent Oxford in a Cambridge Union debate in which two debaters from the United States were also taking part. Uwe caught the train; I missed it. Since no form of public transport would get me there on time, there was nothing for it but to hitch-hike and hope for the best. The lorry drivers were friendly, and since the nationalisation of road transport was the most controversial issue of the day there was room for lively conversation. I had to change a couple of times and finally tore into the Union building at Cambridge with the debate well under way. Drenched with sweat and dressed in mufti, since there was no time to change into black tie, I took my place on the front bench, to a rousing cheer, shortly before the end of the next-to-last speaker. I had just made it. After three minutes I was called.

Apologising to the House for that near-approach to genius, an infinite capacity for missing trains, I reported on my experience with the lorry drivers. I had taken a poll, I said, on whether they would favour nationalisation. The result had been 100 per cent in favour: loud and prolonged applause from the benches on the left. I had then asked a further question. Why did they say that? The answer – also unanimous – was that a nationalised boss would be much easier to cheat: equal amount of applause from the right. I was then on my way, coming to grips, lightly, with the motion, which concerned, insofar as I can remember, Soviet boasts of spectacular achievement in civilian nuclear science. 'The Russians,' I said, 'have announced that with atomic energy they will be able to move mountains, Communist ideology evidently not having proved sufficient for the purpose.' It was, I think, my best speech ever. It certainly gained in impact by the last-minute drama of my (entirely unplanned) appearance. Percy Cradock, who was destined to be a very distinguished diplomat, sinologist and adviser to two prime ministers, was the president on this occasion and Ronald Waterhouse, the future judge and a lifelong friend, was the secretary.

My more serious speeches at this time were mainly connected with foreign affairs. While I supported Ernest Bevin's initial stand against the Soviet Union and his quick response to the launch of the Marshall Plan, I was very critical of him over Israel, over his unnuanced harping on the themes of the Cold War, and later over his rejection of the chance to take the lead in uniting Europe.

While A.J.P. Taylor very properly avoided any explicit prediction of a First (and I was myself intensely superstitious about taking anything for granted) what he said when discussing my future seemed to rest on the assumption that I would get it. He encouraged the notion of an academic career and I was happy enough to think of history as my first profession. However, I was increasingly taken with the thought of politics as my ultimate destiny. After four years in the army I had put thoughts of the diplomatic corps or any form of government service behind me, but I could not escape from the thought that, my life having been spared during the war and my having received free the advanced education at that time denied to the vast majority of my contemporaries, I ought not to indulge my historical hobby for ever. I should take some share of the responsibility for making the post-war world.

It seemed then to be very important that as early as possible I should write a book of recognised scholarly worth. I had a subject: the eighteenth-century politician Shelburne. There was something odd about Shelburne, the Prime Minister who took the decision to recognise the independence of the United States, which called for exploration. On the great issues of the day (such as relations with the American colonies) he almost always took the most enlightened and realistic view, yet became the most unpopular man in politics, personally distrusted and nicknamed 'Malagrida' after a deceitful stage villain in a contemporary play. He lost office in 1783 and never returned. Instead he retired to his country estate, succeeded his father as Marquess of Lansdowne and became the supreme patron of the advanced radical thinkers of the age, including Jeremy Bentham.

Shelburne's papers are at Ann Arbor in the state of Michigan and it struck me that it would be very pleasant to get a grant to go over and work on them and a great challenge to make sense of his character. I had already read many of the secondary sources. But Alan Taylor was not encouraging. 'You are not a Namier pupil,' he said, explaining that the formidable Polish-born Sir Lewis Namier had colonised that end of the eighteenth century and would undoubtedly put obstacles in the way of any outsider. However, he came up with an alternative: why should I not explore the life and career of George Villiers, 4th Earl of Clarendon, not Charles II's Chancellor and James II's father-in-law but the last professional diplomat to become Foreign Secretary (which he was three times) before Douglas Hurd? Like Tony Crosland, he died in office, in his case in 1870, when the Franco-Prussian war was fast approaching. Hiding my disappointment and thinking that in any case Namier might not still be around when it came to writing my second book, I was willing to go along with the idea and Taylor undertook to recommend me to the Bodleian Library to catalogue, at a small salary, the Clarendon Papers, which it had just acquired. My tutor, who was not immune to the pleasures of historical gossip, confided that Clarendon, when Ambassador to Spain, had had an affair with the mother of the Empress Eugénie. 'It would be a real scoop if you found a letter to him from Napoleon III beginning "Cher beau-père".'

Everything seemed set fair. I began to think of myself as the spoilt child of fortune, yet 1950 was to be the year of decline and fall. The earliest setback was political – the February election of 1950. In a spirit of bravado the Liberals had decided to contest all seats (though they only managed in the event to run candidates in 475 out of 625) in order to show that they too were in the big league. The voters were to have the chance of sending Mr Clement Davies to 10 Downing Street. Mr Clement ... who? Most Oxford Liberals, I suspect, privately shared my impression of 'our Clem' as an embarrassing blow-hard and hoped that the true leader, Sir Archibald Sinclair, the wartime Air Minister who had lost his Caithness and Sutherland seat in 1945 by a whisker, would be restored to us.

From our point of view the election was a total disaster. As we listened to the radio (only a few toffs had television), news summary after news summary throughout the night showed not only that the previous Labour landslide was melting away but that the Liberals were vanishing from the scene. With unbearable poignancy this was symbolised by a regular drumbeat, 'The chairman of the Liberal Party, Mr Philip Fothergill, has lost his deposit.' In truth 318 other Liberal candidates also lost theirs, but the single repetitive verdict (for Fothergill's result had come out early) on the candidacy of this prominent figure, now officially rated a frivolous one, sounded like a death knell for the party. The small, lively and a trifle foppish figure of the party chairman had cut quite a dash at Oxford in the last few years with his dynamism, his oratory, his hush puppies and his absurd moustache. Now the calm neutral voice of the BBC was dragging him through the gutter, like a Latin American caudillo overthrown by a *coup d'état*. And this time Sinclair lost by more than two whiskers.

Oxford Liberals huddled together in small groups, one of them in Robin Day's flat, nursing each other's loss of illusions and wondering what could be saved. Compulsory co-partnership was clearly not going to be the flavour of the month or indeed of the century. Where were all our policy resolutions now? My instinct was swift: the public had clearly expressed a verdict in favour of a two-party system, from which we must conclude that continued dedication to the Liberal Party must be regarded as the equivalent of a decision not to go into grown-up politics. If one was to be serious about eventually taking part in decisions about post-war policy one would have to be a liberal inside either the Conservative or the Labour Party. In favour of the first it was often said that Conservatives did not really believe in anything, so one could as well be a liberal in their ranks as anything else. This line of thinking was being promoted by Winston Churchill as Tory Party leader, no doubt because, having served both in both Liberal and Conservative governments, he felt that his career would be neatly rounded off by his ending up as both. In favour of the Labour Party, this would place me more decisively on the left of the political centre where I instinctively resided but then I would have to accept being called a socialist. Perhaps, though, following Ian Mikardo, I might champion the welfare state, greater equality, dissolution of the Empire and the end of the class system while going into denial about Clause Four of the party's constitution which spoke of the common ownership of the means of production, distribution and exchange. But was this honest? And I had meant to be an honest politician.

In the course of feverish coffee sessions in Robin Day's digs, which had by now become a regular feature of my Oxford life, I suggested that, since Robin's instinctive reactions seemed to be more of a conservative character, he should go in that direction whereas I might possibly join Labour. This analysis seemed too coldly rational to Robin, who objected with some pathos that we should then be in opposite camps. This, he thought, was not right. And in any case one should not be so brutally unsentimental in such a moment of grief. I was conscious of the irony that, being normally accused by my friend of entertaining too idealistic a view of politics, I was now identifying myself with the more pragmatic course. Yet was it more moral to pretend to be devoting oneself to politics while in practice not doing so (because of the certainty as a Liberal of being defeated), or should one bite the bullet and choose between the only two options that democracy had decided to enthrone? Awareness of this dilemma sharpened the sinews of my academic analysis but did not for the present solve my political problem. I felt more than ever that it must be on academic achievement that I should for the foreseeable future try to build a reputation.

No sooner had I renewed this resolve than I was made aware that my apparently inexhaustible talent for historical work was rapidly and incomprehensibly fading. I suffered from no loss of interest in the subject but I became uncomfortably aware of a swiftly advancing physical degradation; to my alarm I found that I could hardly see what was on the printed page or, more precisely, could not, save for very short spells, comprehend what I was seeing. Even worse, my historical memory, on which I had much prided myself, began to fail me. I mobilised all my mental strength to try to overcome these obstacles. This served for short periods, but then I found myself so drained of energy that I had the utmost difficulty even in rising from my chair. I had suddenly at 24 become an old man.

It was now Trinity term: the time had come for the final academic drive towards the Examination Schools when even those whose exertions had hitherto been in a minor key make a Herculean effort at self-redemption. I could manage little more than half an hour's serious work a day. Aware that my intellectual powers were failing, I realised that a First was now quite beyond my grasp. At first I thought it might be simply a problem of eyesight, but an optician soon deprived me of any easy escape. My vision was completely unimpaired. This was a savage blow. As usual, I kept my problems to myself. Now it is clear that I was suffering from ME (myalgic encephalomyelitis) but, though in 2002 the British medical profession at last recognised ME as a medical condition 20 years behind their American equivalent, even today there is little known about it. In my time it was a sickness without a name. I began to sleep late and to doze during the afternoons.

There were times when I used wistfully to lament at being thus stripped of my few scraps of comparative advantage. But my predominant mood was of gentle listlessness, of calmly observing myself, as if from the outside, going steadily, peacefully downhill. I doubt whether if I had seen a doctor he could have done anything for me. I confided in no one. I was ashamed of being thought a hypochondriac and did not want to be thought of as a depressive, since I had none of the hideous extremes of experience to which genuine depressives were liable. I was never, for example, in the least suicidally inclined. I had become passive, resigned, a spectator of my own decline.

While this was happening I became involved, owing to the generosity of my friends, in a tiresome controversy. In Trinity term 1950 Robin Day was an outstanding Union president. He had just completed a successful debating tour of the United States in the company of Geoffrey Johnson Smith, a handsome, likeable man who was known as 'the best dressed socialist in Oxford', not that he had expensive tastes but that he possessed to a marked degree the ability to wear utility clothes like a model, and he later entered the Commons as a Tory member.

Robin was triumphantly elected president on his return and while there was no doubt that he enjoyed his prominence to the full he was ambitious also for his friends. He hoped that in turn I would become president. I told him that it was not possible because by the rules my two terms in 1943 counted in the total period within which I was eligible to be elected. I could only hope to become secretary, the most junior of the offices, before my eligibility ran out. Robin was so emphatic that the rule should be changed to achieve consistency with similar changes already made to take into account Service-related breaks in membership that I eventually agreed, provided only that there was unanimity in the Standing Committee. This there was and the plan went forward.

Presently voices of dissent were heard from among the general membership, there were allegations against Robin of cronyism and the Standing Committee appointed a subcommittee to investigate. I went before the subcommittee, supported the amendment in principle, and then stated, as someone who might be expected to benefit from it, that I would not in any event be a candidate for the presidency. While this statement was extremely unwelcome to Robin, whose pugnacity had been inflamed by the opposition, there can be no doubt that it helped him to complete his term on a high note. I did, however, allow my name to go forward as the official nominee for the post of secretary for the Michaelmas term and was duly elected. Now that I could expect little else at Oxford, I told myself, I could at least head for obscurity as an ex-officer of the Union.

It was in a strange mood of abstraction and resignation that I sleep-walked into the Examination Schools. My condition had got worse during the term, although being at my brightest at lunch time I do not think my friends noticed any change in me. I even gained a certain satisfaction from play-acting the part of my normal self. In truth I slept for much of the morning and when I tried to work in the afternoon I could read very little. I went to a few revision classes, at which I occasionally roused myself to make the kind of remark that caused others to suppose that I was nicely positioned for a First. I knew better. I even felt a pleasurable relaxation as my life's ambitions were abandoned and I felt myself being carried by a quickening flood towards a mighty waterfall.

The examinations were a surreal experience. Time and again I said to myself in relation to a question, 'I had some interesting thoughts about this once but not now, some other time, when I am less weary.' My answers must have been lacking in spark and were calculated mainly to avoid dates and precise statements in view of the abeyance of my historical memory. When the week of intense testing was over I felt nothing, neither celebration nor regret, just emptiness and gentle alienation. I drifted home to my parents' house at Hampstead Marshall, told my mother quietly but firmly that a First was out of the question and waited for the axe to fall. The news that I had got a Second came as a genuine surprise and a huge relief. I have since never asserted even to myself that, had I been well, I would certainly have been in the top class, but I felt a certain pride that after such an under-powered performance I had avoided the academic disgrace for which I was prepared. Perhaps, I wondered, I would now recover completely: it might be possible to be an historian after all.

The condition known now as ME ebbs and flows. There are periods in which the sufferer feels better and is filled with optimism about the future, but moments thereafter of despair. I was fortunate that my natural temperament is an even one and thus was able to avoid the more extreme expressions of such changes in mood. After a period at home my spirits began to rise.

One major external development in the summer of 1950 influenced me greatly despite anything ME could do. I had all along been alert to the danger that France was making the same kind of mistake in relation to Germany that had proved so counterproductive after the First World War. Then on 9 May Robert Schuman, the French Foreign Minister, had held a press conference which had launched the scheme for a European Coal and Steel Community that held out the promise of lifting the question of Germany's future place in Europe on to an entirely different plane. It was one of those rare moments in history when a political initiative can change the whole context of events. It was a thrilling moment to be alive and I felt absolutely certain that Britain had to rise above the resentments aroused by the discourtesy towards herself occasioned by the mechanics of the announcement and should willingly embrace this entirely new concept. Just as NATO had reversed Europe's devastating loss of American commitment in the 1920s and 1930s and just as the Attlee government had by its welfare legislation averted the massive sense of let-down of the ex-Servicemen after 1918, so it seemed to me that now there would be a thrilling chance of escaping from the dreadful cycle of action and reaction that had plunged us into a second world war.

I enthusiastically joined the Strasbourg Club, which was named after the border city intended to symbolise the reconciliation, as it had previously marked the feud, of France and Germany. As such it was the seat of the institutions of the Council of Europe. At the suggestion of Peter Blaker I had decided to go with him to Strasbourg in early August to attend the second session of the Consultative Assembly made up of a selection of legislative members from the states in the Council. This was being promoted as the seed from which a united Europe would grow, though cautious governments (and none was more cautious than the Labour government of Britain) had ensured that all powers of decision were vested in a Committee of Ministers, with the Assembly in some danger of becoming a façade, a copy perhaps, I feared, of the Frankfurt Parliament of a century before.

Feeling that changes of scene might help me to shake off my troubles, I accepted the invitation of the Mitchison family, whose daughter Val perceptively thought I looked strained and tired, to stay for a week in their remote Scottish retreat at Carradale, near Campbeltown. Quitting a dinner party with the Benn family, I set out at night by tube for the Mull of Kintyre, by way of High Barnet, which seemed the tube station nearest to my objective. From there I got an immediate lift as far as Glasgow from a driver whose remarkable command of the history of ancient Rome made it quite difficult to keep pace with him. The rule of the house was that the various members of the talented Mitchison tribe, headed by the novelist and cultural historian Naomi Mitchison (known as Nu) and her barrister-MP husband Dick, were at liberty to invite their own guests to the large, dark, rambling mansion, isolated from all except a few fishermen. This resulted in some startling juxtapositions. The strait-laced young secretary of Dick's constituency Labour Party could be confronted at dawn by the opening ploy of a Finnish poetess, 'How active is your sex life?'

From Carradale I moved on to Strasbourg, without Peter Blaker who had been taken ill, being driven part of the way by Dick Mitchison with James Callaghan also on board. Having decided to acquire press credentials, I stepped for the first time on to the international stage as the fully accredited representative of the *Oxford Guardian*, of which, as already recounted, I had been the editor. The whole apparatus of the press room, commonplace for established journalists, filled me with awe and excitement. I eagerly scanned and analysed every document in sight, buoyed up by the discovery that I seemed to have recovered the ability to do so, and gazed at the brief, hastily scrawled messages on small scraps of paper pinned to the notice board, alongside a neatly typed appeal which read, 'Mr Norman of *The Times* has mislaid his copy and would be grateful to any finder who would return it to him.'

I noticed that in the interplay between politicians and journalists it was a distinct advantage to display physical bulk. Thus Robert Boothby stood four-square in the passageway and declared to all and sundry in his deep gravelly voice, 'If there is no regulation of white fish in the North Sea, there will be no more white fish in the North Sea.' He made this sound immensely significant to the obvious discomfiture of those Labour members within range who reckoned that Boothby had, compared with themselves, hitherto taken little interest in the subject. The second heavyweight attention-seeker was a German, Professor Carlo Schmidt, who, having been born in Perpignan, expressed himself with superb eloquence in French. Several of us, hearing that at the age of 17 he had, during the First World War, participated in the last great cavalry charge on the Eastern Front, begged him to describe it to us and were rewarded with a flow of language that rivalled that of Winston Churchill on Omdurman.

The main political debate at Strasbourg was between the functionalists and the federalists, that is, between those who wished to achieve political union by gradual, technocratic steps and those who wished to achieve the same end by adoption of large constitutional principles. The object in both camps was the same, but in regard to the British a basic misunderstanding underlay much of the discourse, because the others supposed that, being pragmatic, the British could be classified as functionalists, whereas in fact most of them were in neither camp, not sharing the common objective. However, some parts of Churchill's rhetorical language in support of a European army appeared to fit the aims of all and all were anxious to have the greatest living European in their camp. Churchill's young political assistants Duncan Sandys and Julian Amery laboured to edge him more decisively than he really cared to go in the same direction.

To the greatest possible irritation of members of the Labour parliamentary delegation, who represented the governing party, the leader of the opposition was the star of Strasbourg. Possibly on that account Labour had been content to downgrade their own team by having it headed by Hugh Dalton, who had once been a big beast in the jungle but whose career had been broken by a Budget indiscretion when he was Chancellor of the Exchequer. All the media interest was in Winston Churchill. Snippets of information wafted down to the press room from time to time from the mansion where he was accommodated. He had, we were told, managed to climb into his bathtub but had had the utmost difficulty in climbing out.

Thinking that I might as well start my new career at the top, I applied for an interview with the Great Man. I had not realised how rarely, except for American journalists, was such a request ever granted. Later when I was doing research for a BBC book on Churchill I came across an article in the *East African Standard* of 1907 on the eve of his tour of Kenya as Colonial Under-Secretary. Headlined as a future prime minister, the young Churchill had occupied the whole first paragraph explaining why, despite a rule of never giving personal interviews, he had been induced to make this one exception only because the journalist was Bram Stoker, whose *Dracula* he had so much enjoyed as a child. Having no such recommendation behind me I was told to speak instead to a Brigadier Jaspar Blount.

The Brigadier demanded what I wanted to know and my question was very precise. There had been circulated a lengthy draft, bearing the signatures of all the known advocates of a European federation such as René Pleven and Paul Reynaud of France and Paul-Henri Spaak of Belgium, in favour of the formation of a European army subordinated to an elaborate political apparatus. The suspicion could scarcely be avoided that the apparatus was, in the opinion of the authors, more important than the army. There was also another draft, in Churchill's name, which called for a European army *tout court*. A little later came a third, joining Churchill to the others, incorporating what was essentially his text but adding, in a phrase from the other document, 'subject to proper unified European democratic control'. In addition Churchill later accepted an amendment which would also have placed the army 'under the authority of a European Minister of Defence'. I told Brigadier Jaspar Blount that my purpose in interviewing his chief was to ask whether I would be right in concluding that by accepting the continentals' wording he was endorsing their federalist intentions.

The Brigadier grabbed numerous items of desk furniture in both hands. 'The old man feels that the Russians are massing together here,' said the great strategist, plonking a heavy item at one end of his desk. 'And we only have little packets all over the show', scattering small items at the other end, 'and he wants to bring them all together.' I tried several times to bring him to the political implications but nothing would penetrate the veil of incomprehension. I did not get my interview. Half a century later my researches showed that the Brigadier was approximately right. Despite the prompting of his acolytes, Churchill had paid so little attention to political structure that he was thinking of asking an American general to command the European army. And, to boot, he said he was not proposing to commit British forces to any 'sludgy amalgam'.

It was to be four more years before I was to shake hands with Winston Churchill. But I was in no way put down by this first rebuff. On the contrary, I thoroughly enjoyed my first experience of foreign journalism, returning with an article which was published in my small-circulation journal. I felt ready to come up as a graduate student for the Michaelmas term in Oxford in the belief that my difficulties were safely behind me.

3. 'Iconic' photograph at the Oxford Union.

CHAPTER 7

With ME to the Beeb

Michaelmas 1950 saw me back at Oxford with spirits restored. Historical research was my aim; in the face of my Second, the college renewed my exhibition. I would, after all, be able to prove myself a genuine historian. My subsidiary interest in the Oxford Union could be wound up in the office of secretary. National politics seemed on hold, offering little for the time being to seduce me from the life of scholarship.

I was to be rapidly and brutally disillusioned. Scarcely had I got down to work before I was again in the clutches of the strange lassitude of a nameless illness. At the Bodleian I obtained access to the Clarendon Papers but half an hour later I found myself staring uncomprehendingly at the pages before me. I slept long hours and when awake I often felt as if drugged. I could pull myself together for short periods and somehow managed to perform the not very arduous duties of my Union office but it seemed, as with King George V in January 1936, that my life, in any real sense, was drawing peacefully to a close.

There is an iconic photograph from this period (see facing page) published originally in *Picture Post* but afterwards much republished elsewhere. It shows me in profile reclining at my ease in the secretary's chair, in white tie, one button of my dress-shirt carelessly undone, eyelids confidently lowered over Roman nose, features to all appearances conveying that air, allegedly redolent of Oxford, of effortless superiority. In truth I was at that moment feeling done in, finished, without a future, sliding towards the abyss.

The Union secretary was entitled to a prime position in a major political debate. The evening that I was due to speak found me prostrated on top of my bed unable to galvanise myself to rise. Fortunately I had invited my girlfriend, or rather I should say ex-girlfriend, so much had I allowed contact with her to lapse, to come to the dinner and the debate as my guest. She arrived at my flat, not being wholly aware of my condition. She willed me to change into my white tie and tails and called up a taxi to get me the short distance to the

Union; I felt very weak but determined to last out the evening. The *Oxford Mail* had a reporter called John Smith who used to specialise in covering Union debates. The next day he wrote:

> For Mr Keith Kyle, secretary this term, [last night's Union debate] was a personal triumph. The former President of the Liberal Club once again proved himself one of the best undergraduate speakers of recent years and he got an ovation when he resumed his seat which many a Cabinet Minister might have envied.[3]

What in truth passed through my mind as I regained the secretary's chair was the thought of the Earl of Chatham (the elder Pitt) falling dying into the arms of his supporters at the end of his final oration in the Lords. Maybe I was going out on a high note but I was only 25. To anticipate a later book title, that of Caitlin Thomas, when the applause died away, I would have a long 'left-over life to kill'.

Indeed, a single favourable notice could not conceal the reality of my situation. As a last resort, I went to a doctor, unfortunately a rugger blue. When I told him that my illness was having a devastating effect on my capacity to work, he said with a sneer that I ought not to entertain any illusions about the superior status of academic activity. There were plenty of other things to do. This stark absence of sympathy alienated me totally from the medical profession for at least a decade. I was mentally good for nothing now. Should I emigrate to Canada, become a lumberjack and disappear without trace?

My final term at Oxford – since I clearly could not now engage with Clarendon – dwindled away. My half-lit days were diverted to an extent by a tiresome feud which had broken out between Godfrey Smith, as Union president, and Jeremy Thorpe as librarian. Jeremy, who was clearly going to be a major contender for the next presidency, had in his hyperactive style started usurping Godfrey's function of organising the visiting speakers. Exasperated, the normally mild-mannered Godfrey had punished Jeremy by dropping him from the order paper of the opening debate. The dispute was referred to a small subcommittee of which I, not being a candidate for future office, was appointed chairman. It was clear to me that Godfrey was correct that it was within the president's prerogative to decide the visiting speakers and that it was a recent custom, not a rule, that presidential contenders should speak in the first debate (as well as in the special presidential debate later on). As to how far Godfrey was justified in complaining about Jeremy's behaviour there were conflicts of evidence and, as Robin Day pointed out in a decisive summing up, we were in no position to require the attendance of the distinguished outside witnesses who alone could resolve the matter. Thus Jeremy escaped censure and won the subsequent presidential contest. The affair perhaps throws some early light on the high-wire performance, if not the sad finale, of Jeremy's career. But also the experience confirmed my view that undergraduate bodies were mistaken in seeking to ape the solemnity of adult institutions.

As the term came towards its end, it occurred to me rather late in the day that, as I was not getting any fitter, I ought perhaps to see the Oxford Employment Service about a job in case the Canadian option turned out not to be one. Feeling that I was to all intents and purposes unemployable, I put myself down for schoolteaching, since this was what others without any particular motivation were doing. Actually, over a fairly limited range of subjects such as history and English, I think I would have made quite a good schoolteacher. But this was never put to the test. Over the next few months application forms trickled in from various schools advertising posts at £325 a year (scarcely a living wage even by 1950 standards) but I was never once called for an interview, doubtless on account of my uncompromising refusal to indicate the slightest interest in supervising sport. But before receiving the first teaching application form I had just managed to take one other job initiative.

On almost the last day of the Michaelmas term, while idly turning over the pages of *The Spectator* in the Union's reading room where I dozed away most of my days, my eye fell on an advertisement for a Talks Producer in the North American Service of the BBC, commanding what was then the quite considerable salary range for a first job of £800–1,000 a year. With a huge effort I filled in the form, found with difficulty an envelope and stamp and managed eventually to post the letter. Having thus totally exhausted my drive for employment, I took to my bed and fantasised about Canadian lumberjacking.

My parents had been extremely gratified at my obtaining a degree and, witnessing their fallen faces when I proposed to apply for it by post, I had relented so that they were able to witness the full ceremonial at the Sheldonian. I there received two degrees. The lesser, a BA, I had earned; the greater, an MA, was by purchase, according to the fine old Oxbridge custom that to become a Master one simply needed to pay for a certain number of terms of nominal 'residence'. In my case this was already deemed to have been done by virtue of my period of war service.

I do not remember when or how I told my parents that I would be leaving after only one more term, but they were good enough to fix a day on which they would drive up to Oxford to cart away my possessions. The day they came was the worst of days and I had done nothing to prepare for my departure. I was dressed when they arrived but was lying on my bed in a kind of trance. My

mother, who had hip problems, had a bad spasm on her arrival and had to lie
down on the sofa, so that the two of us watched as helpless spectators while my
father, who could well have been pardoned had he displayed his temper, was
so far from doing so that he set to work without a moment's complaint to pack
my books and clothes and transport them to the car. I was much moved by
his kindness and ashamed of being able to do nothing to help. I could scarcely
speak, since my general nervous collapse was also by then affecting my vocal
cords. Helped down to the car and sinking in silence into the front passenger
seat, I was in this fashion driven away from the Oxford to which I had so often
come with such lightness of heart.

Installed in our elegant Queen Anne house at Hampstead Marshall, I was
sent out each morning by my mother who believed in the healing power of
fresh air and long walks. As the agent's son I was entitled to wander through
Lady Craven's substantial park and woodland but, as often as not, overcome by
my physical weakness, I was obliged to lie down in the grass until I was strong
enough to carry on. The weeks slipped by, the only events being the regular
arrival of the school application forms and my futile responses. Then at last I
was sent for by the BBC.

By the time I had presented myself at Broadcasting House in Portland Place
I was feeling quite ill, with the lowest of expectations and a sick headache. I sat
down disconsolately amid a room full of candidates for this one post. (There
had been, I was afterwards told, 500 applications.) They were all talking about
their broadcasting experiences, their technical backgrounds or their freelance
work. As each candidate went in I grew increasingly morose. At last it was my
turn. The first question from the bank of examiners was on some current issue
and immediately engaged my interest. Forgetting why I was there I started
discussing the matter in an animated fashion. The other board members joined
in so that I felt quite disappointed when the conversation was brought to an
end. My first thought when I left the room was joyful – 'I believe I've got it'
– then, as I left Broadcasting House and went out into the London street, ME
came down over me like a cloud.

As I got out at our country halt at Kintbury I was approaching total exhaustion. My father, alerted by telephone from London, had driven the one mile to
meet me. I moved towards him very slowly, putting one foot carefully in front
of the other for fear that I should fall down. Because of my slowness my father
ranted and raged about the immensity of the sacrifice involved in his coming
to meet me, not to speak of the suffering of my poor mother left all alone in
the house. I was by now beyond caring and was driven, in disgrace and as if to
prison, back to my home where my mother, who was perfectly well apart from

her permanent disability, received me with great warmth.

I drifted on with no word from the BBC of either acceptance or rejection. Something at the back of my mind caused me to hope but, as the days and weeks passed, it became increasingly difficult to preserve that front. At last I became aware of a job at the English-Speaking Union at £400 a year and, although I had doubts as to whether I could manage in London on that, it was a chance of getting away from home. I applied and was accepted.

My new employer was called Frank Darvall. In the 1930s he had had a glittering start to his career – Oxford Union debating tour of the United States, parliamentary candidate, author and diplomat. For some reason he had stepped off the Foreign Office escalator at the stage of First Secretary and had undertaken the running of what was partly a hotel and partly a soft propaganda machine in favour of good relations between Britain, the Empire and the United States. He was a big man physically, with a sonorous, caressing voice, a man whom one could visualise making valiant stands against anti-American assaults from all directions. Yet his broad shoulders sagged, his brow became moist and his cheeks flushed at the consciousness of the immense honour being conferred on him and the ESU by the presence of some unremarkable establishment speaker. He had the curious habit of reciting the complete title of one's job at every juncture. Thus I was always and repeatedly referred to as the Joint Secretary of the Programmes, Publications and Public Relations Department of the English-Speaking Union of the British Commonwealth. All the staff seemed to have designations of comparable length. I was the joint secretary because there were two of us. John Grist and I met on that first day and, circling around each other as puppies do on first meeting, discovered eventually that we were both frustrated candidates for the same post in the North American Service of the BBC.

That position had in fact been vacated by Tony Benn, who had managed to get into the House of Commons at a by-election for a Bristol seat that had been intended by Transport House (then the national headquarters of the Labour Party) as the means of returning Arthur Creech Jones, the former Colonial Secretary, to frontline politics. I had heard how patronisingly that senior politician had counselled this young rival on the railway journey to Bristol about the necessity of putting in plenty of experience in applying for seats, with an offer of help about possible opportunities that might later arise. Creech Jones had thus been gobsmacked when the recipient of that advice swept all before him at the selection conference. I had spoken on the telephone to Tony's beautiful American wife Caroline when I had first come up to London. She had told me that the BBC job was still there, that the candidates had been narrowed to two but that she feared the other candidate might be ahead of me. It was now plain to me that the other candidate was John Grist.

Four months into my first civilian job the BBC chose to come clean. There had been a blockage in the Foreign Office funds which was now happily over. Even better, there were now two vacancies instead of one in the North American Service; John and I were offered the positions. We had to file into the office of the Director, of whom we had become rather fond, to disclose to him the bad news that we were both leaving. Frank Darvall was gracious though flushed at this surprising setback to his plans. In this odd fashion I came one day to a hole in the wall at 200 Oxford Street and, like the white rabbit in Alice, disappeared underground to work in the BBC wartime studios, where, under Ivone Kirkpatrick and Hugh Carleton Greene, many of the famous broadcasts to occupied Europe and to other foreign parts had originated. I discovered an extraordinary rabbit warren of passages and studios at more than one level. To communicate there was a tannoy system which, we were told, had given George Orwell the inspiration for his novel *Nineteen Eighty-Four*. In some of the studios the river Fleet could be heard rushing beneath the floorboards.

The BBC, which thus became my therapy for ME, commenced with sport, a subject about which I knew precisely nothing and cared even less. With no instruction whatsoever I was directed on the first day to produce Eamonn Andrews, then a sports commentator, later better known as the original presenter of *This Is Your Life*. Descending to an even lower level underneath Oxford Street and confessing at once to Eamonn my ignorance alike of broadcasting and sport, I threw myself at his mercy. 'Do you know how to work a stopwatch?' he demanded. I said I did. 'That's all you're required to know.' I was launched on the career of a Talks Producer.

For other programmes there was a bit more to it and I was eventually sent to the BBC School, run by the historian of witchcraft Pennethorne Hughes, whose article on the role of the 'Mem Sahib' in burying the British Empire, 'The Women Weren't Wonderful', has already been noted. The Chief Instructor was Richard Burton's adopted father Philip Burton, who, with great rolling of the eyes, spiced his embodiment of the stage ham with repeated allusions to his brilliant protégé. John Arlott, the celebrated cricket commentator and one-time Liberal candidate for Parliament, made up the team. We were invited to judge the qualities and defects of different types of broadcasts, whereupon I formed an opposition front bench of myself and two others who systematically subjected each aspect of the BBC's style of presentation to what we took to be withering criticism.

As therapy the BBC was beginning to work. I know now, decades later, that, alarming as my symptoms seemed to me, other people can be struck down by ME much more severely and take much longer to recover. At this stage I could just about manage to read one newspaper a day and with some sense of eyestrain take in the scripts that had been submitted. Books were still out and I had an uneasy sensation of being forced to live off intellectual capital. Each work day left me unnaturally tired, feeling like a very old man. For the only period in my life I spent large amounts of time slumped in the cinema. Once when crossing Horse Guard's Parade I felt my legs sagging, my body shuddering with fatigue and the sweat pouring down my face. Painfully slowly I managed to reach a taxi. As usual, I confided in no one and managed to rally myself sufficiently to carry out my duties without disgrace.

The North American Service could be listened to as a continuous programme but its main function was to supply items for re-broadcast by American and Canadian stations. This sometimes caused embarrassment, as when a speech by Aneurin Bevan was chopped up by the American re-broadcaster to illustrate such unflattering features as lack of logic, unfair argumentation or other forensic faults. The programmes of which I was personally in charge gave me an invaluable introduction to the worlds of politics and journalism. Five days a week a news commentary, four minutes and 15 seconds in length, had to be supplied for re-broadcast throughout Canada. Speaker and topic had to be selected and the speaker rehearsed, with any necessary editing for timing and for content. Many of the speakers, such as Harold Nicolson, were expert broadcasters, but I used deliberately to experiment with others who were not. I also invited my tutor, A.J.P. Taylor, who was living in London on a sabbatical, to take part, realising that this was a risk from several points of view. There was, for one thing, his notoriously pro-Russian bias and his tendency to *épater les bourgeois*. I had briefed him on the need for balance but alarm bells were ringing when he turned up the first time with only 15 minutes to spare and no script. Seating himself down in the studio with a blank sheet of paper, he wrote rapidly with small, neat, very legible handwriting, winding up his argument at precisely the correct length and with faultless balance; I only effected two small changes where the transition from one brilliant thought to another was too abrupt. He became one of the mainstays of the series. Donald McLachlan, the foreign editor of *The Economist*, was another. One week I mentioned to him that I was about to go to Oxford to record a programme about a world conference of Quakers. To my surprise he invited me to send in an article about it to his paper. Since all writing in *The Economist* is anonymous I saw no need to inform the BBC. The article appeared unamended and had completely unforeseen consequences for my career.

An American called Ward Wheelock came to Rooney Pelletier, my French Canadian boss, and his Australian senior producer Peggy Broadhead, with a proposition. He had got an impressive list of Americans to contribute to a series of short talks, initially for radio but subsequently for a book, under the heading of *This I Believe*, and he wanted a matching array of British *prominente*. This Peggy charged me with producing. It was a strange experience persuading great varieties of celebrities to bare their souls in what for most of them was an unfamiliar and perhaps un-British exercise. The secret, I found, was to bin the embarrassing promotional material that came from Wheelock and instead to present this as a personal challenge, with the unspoken implication that it would be cowardly to refuse. Some people, like Tyrone Guthrie, the managing director of the Old Vic, and A.J.P. Taylor, seemed to have no difficulty at all; others – the aircraft manufacturer Sir Geoffrey de Havilland comes to mind – went in for intense intellectual and spiritual wrestling with themselves, in Sir Geoffrey's case in my presence, before anything remotely coherent came out. In this confessional my former tutor proclaimed quite brazenly that he had one set of beliefs that he had learned as an historian and another set that had sustained him personally from the beginning. The two did not match but he could not help it. Tyrone Guthrie, whose declared belief was that God and the Devil were merely aspects of the same idea and that a spectacularly successful career was only achievable at the expense of home-life or health or peace of mind, was at the height of his renown as a theatrical director and he invited me to come as his guest to the première of Marlowe's *Tamburlaine the Great*. As a marriage of great spectacle and great poetry this production can seldom have been equalled. And it was all the more remarkable in that for once Guthrie had achieved a near impossibility in getting the celebrated actor-manager Donald Wolfit, who normally only acted in solipsistic productions with third-rate supporting casts, to work as a triumphant member of a high-grade team.

Two prominent women whom I met over this programme – Lady Astor, who was the first woman to take her seat (though not the first to be elected) in the House of Commons, and Lady Violet Bonham Carter, whom I had met in Oxford days – were kind enough to take me up socially. Lady Astor used to invite me to film previews in Wardour Street, which in those days appeared to be attended largely by members of the aristocracy. At one such viewing I remember being introduced to the Countess of Dalhousie, who was without a 'g' to her name. Listening to her rattling away, dropping 'g's' as she went, it struck me as odd that, while absence of 'h's' would signify membership of the working class, loss of the adjacent letter was a mark of breeding. I also noticed that Nancy Astor, being much teased by the men for her teetotalism, rode such ribaldry with style.

Lady Vi was an altogether different matter. She was in every sense a *grande dame* with a superb command of spoken English equal only to that of her great friend Winston Churchill. She was a passionate Liberal but was in the process of being actively courted politically by the old man, who knew that an early re-run of the virtual dead heat of the 1950 election was his last remaining chance of regaining office. The failure of the Liberals, already alluded to, to make the spectacular comeback for which they had risked their all seemed to Churchill to open the possibility that the mortified remnant might be in a mood to supply the Tories with an extra margin of support. Asquith's daughter, whom Churchill had known and cherished for more than 40 years, should, he calculated, be the instrument of reconciliation of the two political streams, Conservative and Liberal, which had at different times run through his own career. At Colne Valley, the marginal seat for which Lady Vi was adopted as a Liberal, Churchill persuaded his unwilling party not to nominate a Tory candidate so as to give her a clear run against the Labour incumbent. Many Liberals found this hard to take but finally allowed themselves to be persuaded that their supremely eloquent champion should not be repudiated.

Later, when he was Tory Chief Whip (and I was *The Economist*'s political correspondent), Ted Heath told me that Churchill was the only man he knew who had attempted to shape his cabinet in order to suit a peroration. He had planned to say that his administration was both Conservative and Liberal since one could hardly say that a government that included an Asquith, a Lloyd George and a Rosebery was not representative of the Liberal tradition. Lady Vi was to be Minister of Education, but she failed to win a seat (because of Tory abstentions at Colne Valley) and then her brother, Lord Justice Asquith, turned down a subsequent offer of the Woolsack. Gwilym Lloyd George, the First World War leader's son, was indeed made Home Secretary. As for Rosebery, who had briefly been Secretary for Scotland in the 1945 transitional government, Churchill was told by the whips that his return to that office would cost all Scottish Tories their seats. Scoring only one out of three, the peroration perished.

Nineteen Fifty-One was the year of the Festival of Britain, in which the hitherto sad and smitten South Bank of the Thames was dressed in upbeat and witty apparel to celebrate alike the centenary of Prince Albert's creation and the emergence of London from the grim associations of war. For weeks I was stationed on the South Bank to arrange interviews with all and sundry about the particularities of Britain's renewal of gaiety. It was, it must be said, a more affirmative atmosphere than that which was to prevail in the Millennium Dome half a century later. The presiding spirit was Sir Hugh Casson, who told me that he saw London as a collection of villages, an observation which works in some parts of the capital (notably in Primrose Hill, where I now live) but manifestly not in others. In his contribution to *This I Believe* Casson had confessed that the great problems of life – religion, politics, world affairs – did not weigh heavily on his mind; he contented himself, he said, with trying to guard the innocent eye with which he was born and learning to distinguish the scholar from the style snob. On the South Bank we interviewed the poet Laurie Lee who was the licensed subversive on the block, authorised to prevent anyone from taking things too seriously. Because the 1951 Festival worked, having been written off in advance as a failure, similar predictions of fiasco about the Millennium Dome were to be mistakenly discounted 49 years later.

A small amount of patronage being now in my hands, I was naturally inclined, given my familiarity with the Namierite politics of the eighteenth century, to use this to the benefit of my friends, particularly those briefless barristers in pupillage who had to exist in London on negative incomes. For a weekly programme summing up the contents of the British weeklies, extracts were read by actors while the linking passages were written by a succession of my friends until I ran out of supply. Then I took up John Grist's plea for a bright young LSE graduate friend of his called Bernard Levin. He was being called up for National Service every three months but was declining on rather complicated grounds. Each time this was to bring either a fine (increased each time) or a prison sentence. He needed to earn enough money to pay the next fine but could not commit himself to a regular job so long as the prison gates were in prospect. There seemed to be something wholly admirable in having one national institution supply the wherewithal to defy another. Thus Bernard launched what was to become a spectacular career in journalism. He escaped prison and, when after a while National Service decided it could manage without him, moved on to be the pseudonymous political correspondent of *The Spectator*, transfixing the cast of Westminster under the Disraelian *sobriquet* of 'Taper' with devastating asperity. I also put Robin Day on the air for the first time on the occasion of a programme about the Oxford Union, with that ever fluent wordsmith Godfrey Smith writing the script.

My health improved to the extent that I was never forced to confess that I was in any way ill and was to be found during the day in an upbeat, sometimes slightly over-the-top mood. But I knew myself that recovery was still fragile, as many of my evenings and, towards the beginning, some of my weekends were spent slumped semi-autistically. In my second year at the BBC I began by degrees to feel robust enough to manage a little more reading and to think seriously again about the possibility of having a career. In the long run this could not be on the staff of the BBC, since this was organised hierarchically and I was already at the highest level that I would wish to reach. Promotion would shift me away from the work that interested me and into management and scheduling, which did not.

Being on the BBC staff was, where politics was concerned, almost the equivalent to joining the Civil Service. Though this was not strictly necessary I severed all connections with the Liberal Party. At the 1951 general election its popular vote had gone down to 2½ per cent. It seemed to have disappeared altogether from the radar screen. Purdah with the BBC gave me a further period in which to make up my mind whether to join a Tory Party without principles or a Labour Party with principles, many of which, however attractive at first sight, relied on assumptions about human nature which were perverse. Alongside this analysis which, I suppose, could sound cynical to some, there ran a great sense of awe for Westminster democracy. I thought that morally I ought not to be content (provided my health could be restored) with being for ever a commentator and never a participant in the public's business, an unelected critic rather than an elected legislator.

I got my first direct impressions of Westminster through my friendship with the Benn family. The former head of the diplomatic service Lord Vansittart had emerged as a potential British equivalent of the American Senator Joseph McCarthy, applying his technique of guilt by association to smear liberal-minded people as the friends of Communists. I was invited to the public gallery of the House of Lords to hear Lord Stansgate, Tony and David Benn's father, belabouring Vansittart for his remarks, which he did with the utmost vigour. Unlike Tony, Stansgate was a short man who became doubled up in the fury of his reproaches, wielding in his right hand, as if it were a mace, one of the individual sound amplifiers then in use. Tony, who had been raising the issue in the Commons, could be seen bringing messages to his father.

Fascinated by the drama of the occasion, I contrived (probably again through the agency of Tony Benn) to be present in the gallery of the House of Commons in May 1953 when Winston Churchill, who had taken advantage of Anthony Eden's illness to acquire for himself on a temporary basis the one major portfolio, that of Foreign Affairs, that had escaped him in the course of his career, opened a foreign policy debate. He had as usual written the speech himself, though it was sent to the Foreign Office for comment by a junior official who raised 42 factual queries of varying significance. The delivery was superb; it was one of his last few speeches of which this could truly be said. It covered a wide range of topics but the passage that remained with me was that which concerned the ongoing negotiations with Egypt about the British forces on the Suez Canal. 'We did not, let me repeat, seek these negotiations. We complied with the Egyptian desire for them. They asked for them and they have now – to quote the violent outpourings of General Neguib reported in today's newspapers – washed their hands of them.' The name of the Egyptian President was pronounced 'Neg-wib' and the reference to his handwashing was accompanied by the small figure of Winston Churchill slowly revolving in a circle and confronting in succession each of the crowded benches, mimicking as he did so the act of washing his hands. Total silence prevailed, everyone mesmerised by the master at his now rarely attained peak. 'We may await the development of events,' the old imperialist concluded, 'with the composure which follows from the combination of patience with strength.' For a moment I was able to suspend totally my sense of the recessional about the oration.

In the ordinary way I should have stayed with the BBC for longer than two years. But being in the business of producing broadcasts for the North American market it seemed to me desirable that I should take the first opportunity of spending some time in North America. In 1953 for the first time broadcast staff were made eligible for the Commonwealth Fellowships that had been hitherto only open to print journalists. The Commonwealth Fellowships were, as described in the biography of Alistair Cooke, a pre-war Fellow, a *de luxe* way of introducing the United States to young journalists. One spent a year in America, attached for a while to a university and for a while to a newspaper, and was supplied with a car to drive anywhere one wished through the vast continental country and with a reasonable income. It sounded too good to be true and the BBC promised my job back at the end of the year if I were to get it. I was conscious that I was taking a gamble with my health but if I was not to make a supreme effort now to lift myself out of my handicap, when should I ever do it?

I appeared before a board mainly of senior journalists headed by the editor of the *Manchester Guardian*. One of the members was Geoffrey (later Lord) Crowther, the editor of *The Economist*. Insofar as the other examiners were concerned, the interview went swimmingly but it was a different experience altogether in respect of Crowther. Himself a former Commonwealth Fellow, he cross-examined me at length about my ambitions and subsequent intentions. I was flustered and did not in my opinion answer well. I was left feeling very doubtful about my prospects. Three days later, before the results had been announced, my secretary received a call from the editor of *The Economist*'s office inviting me to come and see him. This struck me as somewhat irregular since Crowther was one of the judges who had yet to pronounce a verdict. However, curiosity prevailed and I presented myself at the Ryder Street offices of *The Economist* at the appointed hour.

'You may have noticed that I was being rather hard on you at the interview,' Geoffrey Crowther began. He was a fairly small man, rather frog-like I thought, and he spoke, as he wrote, with supreme lucidity. That had, I said, occurred to me. 'That was deliberate, because I wanted you to fail.' As I shifted slightly in my seat, the editor went on, 'But I didn't succeed and you will be offered a Commonwealth Fellowship.' A surge of joy welled up within me. But Crowther had not finished. 'The reason why I wanted you to fail was that I was about to offer you the job of the Washington correspondent of *The Economist*.'

Therefore, Crowther said, he must put a blunt choice before me, whether to become a Commonwealth Fellow or the Washington correspondent of *The Economist*. Did I, he first asked, know of any reason, other than the Fellowship, which would stand in the way of my accepting his job? I replied, 'Only three. I am not an economist, I have not been a journalist and I have never been to America.' He smiled indulgently. 'We would not have approached you without finding out about your reputation at Oxford University and we know that you can write.' It was then that I remembered the article about Quakers in Oxford. 'About how long do you reckon that you will need to make up your mind?' 'About thirty seconds,' I answered. I had known that with the Commonwealth Fellowship I would have been gambling with my health. While Geoffrey had been going on talking I had made up my mind to double the odds.

I served my three months' notice with the BBC, which included making an edited version of the Coronation service for the overseas service, and did another three months' apprenticeship in the old *Economist* office in Ryder Street. The first day that I was there I was rung up by the BBC and invited to broadcast – which I had never been allowed to do while I was still on the staff. I also got a glimpse of the popular standing of my new profession. Leaving a wedding, I contrived to have myself introduced to a striking blonde. She caught that I was a journalist and, not discriminating as to titles, ran away screaming, 'I'm not going to appear all over the front page of the *Sketch*' (she would have said nowadays, the *Sun*). That ensured that I knew where I now stood.

CHAPTER 8

With *The Economist* in America

The fog swirled round the faintly discernible limbs of the Statue of Liberty as the *Queen Mary* moved slowly into her New York dock in September 1953. I had been dispatched across the Atlantic in huge excitement by my father, who had initially been unable to understand why I would want to abandon after only two years the prospect of a lifetime career with an institution he had well-nigh worshipped from its creation. But he had taken soundings among the wealthy shooting and fishing tenants for whose weekend sporting comforts on the Hampstead Marshall estate he was responsible. Since, among such, *The Economist* was highly rated, he had been gratified by their warm approval of my appointment.

Thus happily it had been with my father's blessing, accompanied by frequent repetition of his two favourite pieces of advice – 'Marry wealth' and 'Don't trust any man further than you can throw him' – that I had set forth to adventure abroad. It was not the only advice I had received. Harold Nicolson, on being told of my impending departure, observed pensively, 'I think you will have a good time in America. The only thing you will miss will be the adult mind.' My father was good enough to come to Southampton dock and, being equipped with recommendations from Cunard directors and others, rushed around the decks until the last possible moment, thrusting these credentials under the noses of anyone arguably official with triumphant shouts of 'Influence! Influence! Influence!'

At last I was able to relax behind the two stout volumes of Morrison and Commager's *The Growth of the American Republics*, which were my leaving present from my BBC colleagues, the satisfaction being all the greater in that I found myself able for the first time in years to keep up the reading for hour after hour. My cabin was shared with a Mormon missionary returning from a couple of years of endeavour to convert the savages of Lancashire to the teachings of Joseph Smith, Brigham Young and the Church of Jesus Christ of Latter Day Saints. Unlike me, he was throughout the crossing very, very sick. Once ashore, Cecil (pronounced Sees'l by Americans) Thornton, the BBC representative in New York, with whom I had been corresponding on business for the last two years, greeted me warmly on the 50th floor of the Rockefeller Building, from whose windows I looked way down with shock and awe at the tip of a cathedral spire far below me. I moved on to Washington, where Robin Day, who had pioneered the New World a few weeks ahead of me, had found a flat which the two of us could share until I got somewhere permanent.

Robin's decision to give up his practice at the Bar had been a great surprise to me when he had revealed it when on a riding holiday in the Lake District. ('I prefer', he had said, 'to take my exercise sitting down.') I had seen for him a glittering career at the Bar. His forensic style of address seemed particularly suited to the art of cross-examination and he had acquired a genuine feel for legal issues, which indeed stayed with him throughout his life. Many of his later friends were to be the leaders of the profession (including Lord Irvine of Lairg who was the Lord Chancellor at the time of Robin's death) and he discoursed with them on level terms. Of no honour was he to be more proud than that of being made in 1990 an Hon. Bencher of the Middle Temple. But, having in 1953 after a couple of years of pupillage and practice acquired doubts about the law as the right avenue for his ambitions, he had decided to make a clean break and applied for a vacancy as assistant to Charlie Campbell, the legendary head of the British Information Services in Washington.

The Washington to which I came in 1953 was not the resplendent world capital of the twenty-first century. Certainly there were many elements of elegance about it – the Capitol Building, facing the wrong way because of a miscalculation of the direction in which the city was to develop, the Washington Monument, the White House and the Lincoln and Jefferson Memorials. Best of all was the splendid way the street plan of the city was designed to exploit breathtaking perspectives of the Potomac river. But New York was the commercial and cultural capital of the country; Washington was simply and solely the seat of government. It was a company town with many thousands of people depending on the three branches of government – executive, legislative and judicial – and with the crowds of lobbyists, hangers-on, media stars and general kibitzers that surround these endeavours.

My first impression was of 'an African city with a European quarter'. Most of the white population lived either in the northwest segment of the capital or altogether outside its limits in the neighbouring states of Virginia and Maryland,

4. With *The Economist* in America.

the first of which was still racially segregated and the second, a border state, carried more than a whiff of Southern manners. Partly because the District of Columbia (as the Capital area was officially called) had a black majority it was run like a colony, and a rather primitive one at that, by a committee of Congress dominated by Southern members. Thus the residents of the capital of the world's greatest democracy had no vote for national or local government (unless they had another residential base in one of the states).[4]

In the days before the John F. Kennedy Center was conceived the city was culturally under-developed. Its few theatres were 'dark' for most of the time; only one of them, a small theatre in the round, was open for performances during the whole year. Shows which would never make the big time staggered into Washington on their last legs, or else others that had already made it in New York, Boston, Detroit and Chicago wound up a long run in America's capital. By the time the musical *The King and I* arrived, the boy who had begun the run as the smallest child in the royal nursery of Siam had grown up to be the crown prince. Robin Day, who told me proudly when I arrived that he was dating the niece of the Secretary of State John Foster Dulles, was soon deciding that he was financially obliged to drop her because she expected to be taken to shows in New York. It was said that people could be divided into those who loved Washington and enjoyed visiting New York and those who loved New York. No matter what were its drawbacks, I loved Washington. Eagerly I breathed the air of its politics and I inhaled.

I was at first apprenticed to John Duncan Miller of *The Times*, who advised me on topics to be covered and was supposed to scrutinise my copy before it was sent. But this was a loose rein and, as he shortly afterwards accepted a job with the World Bank and was kind enough to advise that I was capable of standing on my own feet, I soon found myself opening my own office in the Washington Press Building. *The Economist*'s American Survey in those days was edited and partly written in London by two high-powered ladies, Nancy Balfour and Margaret Cruikshank, out of large packets of research material dispatched daily from Washington. Nancy was a small, squat, animated spinster, a dual British/American national with a pronounced Kensington accent whose ancestor was one of the founders of San Francisco. Her knowledge of America, which she visited every year, staying with cousins strategically distributed throughout the country, was encyclopedic and, though a trifle tetchy, she was a highly intelligent boss. Margaret was a much quieter individual but no less talented; an American, she was married to Robin Cruikshank, the editor of *The News Chronicle*, and in her time had delivered on the same day a *Times* leader and a daughter.

As Washington correspondent I usually contributed the principal article in the American Survey as well as anything else that caught my fancy and was acceptable to Nancy. To deal with specialist topics and to enable me to visit and report from other parts of the country I was allowed to place other contributors on retainer. They covered economic policy (Edwin L. Dale Jr), the Supreme Court (Adam Yarmolinsky, who had been Justice Frankfurter's clerk) and the Pentagon (Adam Watson, Susan Crosland's father). When I was away Washington politics was covered by William V. Shannon, a highly gifted writer on the *New York Post* and a very dear friend who went on to be a leader writer on the *New York Times* and US Ambassador in Dublin. We already had stringers in many parts of the country but I added to them, most notably in the case of Paul Jacobs, who because of his background as a trade union organiser and civil rights activist was, to paraphrase a celebrated commercial, able to penetrate parts of the (American) body which others could not reach. I used to file by airmail, sometimes literally entrusting it to the hands of the pilot, except for a single weekly booking of half an hour on Tuesday mornings with Cable and Wireless. I exchanged short messages with my editors on an exceedingly primitive fax machine which spun like a crazy top and gave out strange sounds and odd puffs of smoke.

President Eisenhower was in office all the time I was living in Washington. Unlike some of his successors he conscientiously held regular weekly news conferences which I always attended when there. He was immensely popular in the country and nothing that a rather unsympathetic Washington press corps could do, writing, for instance, of every unexpected event that he had received news of on the golf course, made the slightest difference. 'Ike', as he was universally known, was the original Teflon President, the man, to cite another commercial, on whom nothing could ever stick. His convoluted sentences, defying the normal rules of syntax, were reasonably intelligible if one shut one's eyes and concentrated on their oral punctuation. They were delivered with authority and charm but, when cruelly reproduced absolutely *verbatim*, down to every 'er' and 'um', in the following day's *New York Times*, they seemed to lack a good deal in clarity and precision. The humorist Jules Feiffer protested that he could scarcely be expected to satirise material that was like this to start with.

I never subscribed to the widespread view of Eisenhower as merely an impressive constitutional monarch who almost completely neglected his other function as chief executive. Later on therefore, when historians were given access to his papers and discovered the unsuspected extent of his activity in the White House, I felt no need to go along with the newly fashionable portrayal of him as a dynamic hands-on president. This was not really true either, especially after the major heart attack before the end of his first term.

John Foster Dulles, the Secretary of State, also gave a weekly news conference, at which he appeared as pedagogue to the press, the nation and the world, and, in contrast to the President, seemed rather too anxious to make himself understood. A man of lugubrious appearance, he spoke fairly slowly though not, in my recollection, as slowly as Anthony Eden used to claim. He was an international lawyer and a Presbyterian church official and before taking office had written considerably about foreign affairs. He appeared over-anxious to locate his answers in the general context of his intellectual processes and hence would volunteer thoughts beyond what he had been asked. It was then that he was in greater danger of committing his celebrated *sottises*. The doyen of the Washington press corps, James 'Scotty' Reston, the Scottish-born bureau chief of the *New York Times*, wrote with cruel accuracy, 'He doesn't stumble into booby traps; he digs them to size, studies them carefully, and then jumps.'

My first trip away from Washington was to Wisconsin. Here was a state which the books described as progressive but which had returned as one of its two senators Joseph McCarthy, the notorious abuser of human rights in the name of anti-Communism. As chairman of the Government Operations Committee, which gave him a wide-ranging remit to poke and tamper with whatever parts of the system he pleased, McCarthy had either intimidated or discomposed large swathes of present or former members of the Washington bureaucracy. He even penetrated the executive branch with his cronies and imitators, so that Dulles found it necessary to sacrifice a close political ally whom he had installed in a key position in the State Department because McCarthy had placed his black spot on him. Herblock, the masterly cartoonist of the *Washington Post*, portrayed this unfortunate individual sprawled on the ground with a dagger sticking out of his back spluttering in his dying words to an attentive reporter with a notebook, 'I thought my friend Foster Dulles was behind me.'

I used to attend meetings of Senator McCarthy's committee and sit on the press bench just immediately beneath the senatorial dais. The other members – McClellan, Symington, Mundt – seemed cowed by the chairman's pyrotechnics uttered in his rasping, rumbling voice. The committee was ministered unto by its young, rather loutish staff, who could be taken at first as naughty schoolboys but whose pranks were no joke to those who were ruined by them. They were Roy Cohn, a hard, cruel individual who was later to be characterised by his biographer as authentically evil; David Schine, the soft, handsome son of a millionaire hotelier, who was laughably described as an expert on Communism by virtue of a pamphlet slim in length and content; and, rather oddly in this league, Bobby Kennedy, the second surviving of the Kennedy brothers who outgrew this unpromising beginning to become a political phenomenon.

When I first went to see Bobby he was sitting on a desktop picking his teeth in the bowels of one of the Senate Office Buildings alongside the subterranean railway which conveys senators from their offices to the Senate chamber. I wanted to find out why McCarthy had considered it necessary to harass Harold Stassen, the Foreign Aid chief, about his failure to cut off all economic aid to Britain as punishment for our trading with 'Red China'. I found Kennedy monosyllabic and unsympathetic. The most he would concede, speaking through his toothpick, was that he supposed this would seem unfair – to the British.

Not unnaturally, Joseph McCarthy aroused strong emotions. I was at a party in New York which was attended by a man who turned out to be one of the Senator's few intellectual supporters. At one point in the evening he bore down on me and *The Economist* as representing everything undesirable that the Senator was against. Rather taken aback by this unexpected assault I parried it as best I could without making too much of a scene. He renewed his attack with added venom, whereupon my hostess, who had hitherto played no part in the discussion and who was, I think, a little taken with liquor, launched out with one of the most movingly eloquent statements I have ever heard in support of what at its best America has stood for ever since the Declaration of Independence. A short time afterwards I was in a Boston bookshop, looking at a pro-McCarthyite volume by Buckley and Bozell when I received what I can only describe as an unusual lesson in American salesmanship. 'I will not allow you to buy that book,' the lady behind the counter said in a firm voice. Her name she gave as Saucy and she turned out to belong to one of the wealthiest of the old New England families.

Only three Britons were generally known to the Great American Public – Winston Churchill, Bertrand Russell and Arnold Toynbee – and of these, of course, the greatest was Winston Churchill. He arrived in Washington with Anthony Eden, the perpetual crown prince, in 1954, during a break in the long conference at Geneva about French Indochina, which has been described as the last occasion on which Britain successfully performed as a Great Power. It had been a personal triumph for Eden, although less happily at the expense of John Foster Dulles. Churchill was keen to eliminate any discord. The British press had been summoned to the British Embassy; we were in for a long wait before the visitors appeared. Seen close to, I thought how much Churchill resembled the toby jugs of him which I had hitherto supposed were only a

crude approximation. He held out his paw to each of us in turn and delivered a
most graceful apology for having kept us waiting. He said he had had good and
constructive talks with the President. 'And now I am going to have a little nap.
The Foreign Secretary will answer your questions.' With this he disappeared
and we gathered informally round Anthony Eden.

I am unsure how it came about but after a while I found myself in one-
to-one conversation with Eden, questioning him in detail about the Geneva
conference. I thus became conscious of the nature of his charm. He never for
one moment took his eyes off me, as important people often do when seeking better company, and he concentrated on supplying this hitherto unknown
young journalist with detailed and specific answers. He said, for example, that
the Indian Krishna Menon (who was generally held in disesteem) had proved
on a couple of occasions at Geneva to be a very useful intermediary. After he
had gone, one of his secretaries approached me and asked what I thought of the
Foreign Secretary. I truthfully replied that I was rather impressed by him, both
by his diplomatic achievements and by his courteous manner towards me. 'You
wouldn't think that if you had to work for him,' riposted the civil servant. This
rather shook me as I had entertained a certain picture of the civil servant as
being discreet and loyal. 'He has a frightful temper, which he will loose off if
you haven't provided him with the right paperclips,' the private secretary went
on. 'I recommend you to read *Tribulations of a Baronet* by his brother about their
father. It runs in the family.'

In the early 1950s the United States was still adjusting itself to its new
world status, as was physically evident in its capital city. Many of the temporary buildings rushed up to accommodate the wartime bureaucracies had still
not been knocked down and replaced by permanent structures. In the country generally the air was full of uncertainties. Coast-to-coast all seemed in
thrall to a paperback called *Why Johnny Cannot Read*. Part of the answer to this
was supplied to me by the top Washington lobbyist for the National Education Association who, on coming to lunch, opined before being fully separated
from his overcoat, 'What you have got to realise is that a man is far more likely
to lose his job because he cannot get on with other men than because he cannot
read or cannot spell.'

Together with another young foreign correspondent, Amos Elon, then
the America correspondent of the Israeli daily *Ha'aretz* and later over many
decades perhaps the ablest Israeli interpreter of events in the Middle East, I got
invited by the ABC television network to take part in a half-hour discussion
with ABC's leading anchorman Martin Agronsky on the experience of being a
young, unattached foreign reporter in the United States. It was my television

baptism. All I remember of it now is that, after expressing my enthusiasm for many aspects of American life (including the American can-do attitude and the maturity and classlessness of American girls), I listed a few impressions on the other side of the ledger – no postal deliveries before one left for the office, the dumbed-down character of most television outside the Sunday ghetto to which political programmes were relegated, the appallingly prejudicial nature of press comment on criminal cases before they came to trial (there was a particularly blatant case of this at the time) and the performance of too many public functions by private enterprise. Now, half a century later, Britain has in all respects copied these features of American life.

Unlike most members of the British press corps, who were mainly concerned with foreign policy or, if not, with the freakshow aspects of American life and who, because of the five-hour time difference, were tied to a lunchtime filing hour, I filed for a weekly and was mainly concerned with American domestic politics. This meant that I spent much time with Congress and often came to interview politicians who did not see many foreign correspondents. After I had done a certain amount of travelling outside Washington, I developed a stand-ard technique. On my first sitting down opposite a senator or representative, he would, regardless of the question asked, launch into a lecture on the constitution beginning, 'This is a government of laws and not of men.' Patiently waiting to the end – which, in the case of Southerners, meant waiting a long time – I would ask a precise question about a recent political development in the politician's home state. The conversation would then rapidly switch from broad generalisations to particular confidences.

Lyndon Johnson was a very large and remarkably tactile man. When seated, he would thrust his face, with its elephantine ears, into yours and grasp you firmly by the knee. 'You've got to remember if you're going to run the United States Senate,' he told me, 'that small minds are attracted by small issues.' He referred back to the McCarthy censure debate, prior to which the expectant crowds in the public gallery were kept endlessly waiting while a single sena-tor murmured a speech to a chamber that was empty except for the presiding officer. The speaker was Senator George 'Molly' Malone of Nevada, a state where there is much sand and gambling and divorce but precious few people, but a state nonetheless which still boasts two senators as do New York and California. Senators, Johnson reminded me, have rights of unlimited speech ungoverned by any rule of germaneness. Malone had told Johnson that he was proposing to speak for eight hours in support of a tariff so high that it would make possible some potential local industry. Johnson had cut a deal with him that if he would limit himself to a mere four hours the Malone Bill would be slipped through the Senate before the end of the session. It would, of course, be too late for the House to do anything about it, but to voters back home Malone would look as if he had achieved something. Thus, four hours late, the McCarthy debate could proceed. By such shifts, Johnson told me, the Majority Leader could register progress.

Those who knew Lyndon Johnson would not be surprised to learn that he took advantage of my presence to vent a grievance, in this case against the British press. A Reciprocal Trade Act was going through Congress.[5] This delegated to the President for a modest period the powers held by the Congress to negotiate trade agreements. Without such authority trade agreements simply would not happen. It was a measure whenever it came up which was fiercely contested and was of prime importance to Britain and other trading partners. Johnson's grievances against the British were twofold. In the first place, our press had referred to 'Eisenhower's Reciprocal Trade Act'. 'But Eisenhower doesn't pass bills. It will pass because of Mr Sam and the Senate Majority Leader.' Then the British papers had dared to criticise him because he had allowed a wrecking amendment to be incorporated at committee stage and had not contrived to knock it out on the floor. But this showed little understanding of how the Congress worked. L.B.J. and Mr Sam between them had decided that the awkward amendment was better lost in the House. Then there would be a conference committee of the two Houses and an agreed text would emerge minus the obnoxious clause, on which there would need to be a final vote.

Senator Johnson concluded his little lecture with a flourish, for he was a great man for flourishes. A minion was summoned with paper and envelope. 'This is what Ah'm going to do with you. Ah'm going to write down the exact result of the final vote on the Senate floor and Ah'm going to seal it up and you're not to open it until the vote has taken place.' I obeyed the rules and did as he said. He was one vote out. Next time I was in the lobby of the Senate, Johnson was earnestly closeted with a group of senators, engaging in what he used to call 'belly-to-belly' discussion. He caught sight of me and lunged over in my direction, put his enveloping arm round my shoulder and proclaimed, 'Ah owe this young man a profound apology. Ah wrote down beforehand what the vote on the trade act was going to be. And Ah was one vote wrong!'

The great issue of race which underlay, often in an unspoken way, the multiple manoeuvres governing the life of Washington was brought to the forefront in December 1955 by the courage of an Afro-American lady called Rosa Parks, who in Montgomery, Alabama (a state in the Deep South), sat down in the section of a bus reserved for the whites. This wilful defiance of the state's segregation laws was followed by a massive boycott by blacks of the Montgomery buses. A packed meeting of blacks formed the Montgomery Improvement Association and drafted an impressive 26-year-old cleric, the Rev. Martin Luther King Jr, to be its president. The black elite of Montgomery were put on trial in the state court for conspiracy and I headed south in the company of my new friend Patrick O'Donovan of the *Observer* to cover it. O'Donovan's predecessor had been taken ill and I had been recruited to fill the gap until Patrick arrived. He was an accomplished reporter who had made his name covering the Korean War, a brilliant phrase-maker and a wit. For no good reason he claimed to be scared at the prospect of covering America, though his work was to show that he had no need to be. He got the *Observer* to keep me on retainer so that I could continue to lend a hand. He was splendid company except when, as sometimes happened, he had had too much to drink.

'I think I'm going mad,' declared Patrick as we left the empty courthouse in Montgomery, all set for the trial on the morrow. We had just been received by an elderly white-haired janitor, with an eerie resemblance to the Secretary of State. 'First of all I go to see John Foster Dulles, then I go to the CIA and see his double (the Director, Allen Dulles, Foster's brother), then I'm invited to use a swimming pool and meet John Foster Dulles in drag (a sister, Eleanor Dulles, also of the State Department) and now I come down South to the Montgomery courthouse and find a janitor who looks exactly the same as John Foster Dulles.' We went together to see Martin Luther King. I must admit that as soon as I saw him I felt the magnetism of the man (Patrick told me afterwards that I had been uncharacteristically deferential). It was immediately apparent to me why men and women so much older than he had wanted him as their leader.

I also went to see the editor of the local paper, *The Montgomery Advertiser*. 'We understand our Nigra' – a version of 'nigger' used in the South – he said. 'We are all Southerners, white and black, and we'll come along together in our own good time. Down here, we take care of them, whereas in the Northern cities they exploit their labour and take no responsibility for them.' He then launched into a tirade against the *New York Times* and other Northern papers which had agreed not to mention the skin colour of offenders in their crime writing, so that the fact that most of the crime was caused by blacks was withheld from their readers. Choosing a moment when he had to give pause, I asked what he thought of the Rev. Martin Luther King. 'Ah,' he said, as if awestruck, 'that is an authentic intellectual.'

The next day the world's press converged on the courthouse. The first person I caught sight of was a young redneck (as 'poor whites' tended to be

called, though this one seemed to be red all over) named Joe Azbell, to whom
I had been briefly introduced at the *Advertiser*. I had been told that he had had
little education but was a brilliant natural talent. His column in that morning's paper unquestionably gained far more in force and drive than it lost in
grammar, spelling and syntax. It was evident that at the courthouse where the
press was concerned Joe was the master of ceremonies. We found ourselves
being briskly directed to our seats, black reporters in one direction and white
in the other. But there was more to skin colour than met the eye. One white-
seeming gentleman called Brown was representing the National Association
for the Advancement of Colored People, the senior black rights lobby. He
being a small percentage off-colour (so to speak) was directed to the black
benches. However, the jet-black representative of the Indian paper *Madras
Times* was lodged on the white benches because an Indian, being a foreigner,
was objectively white. These events most conveniently supplied a theme for
King's sermon which I attended on the following Sunday.

The benches of the accused were crowded indeed, since the conspiracy
charge involved the leading figures of the black community. For me the most
dramatic moment involved Joe Azbell. He was called to the witness stand
because he had been the only white person present when Martin Luther King
had emerged as the black community's spokesman and leader. The key question that was put to him was whether, in his observation, King was party to a
pre-arranged plan to provoke a boycott or whether the decision to draft him
was a spontaneous reaction to events. The silence in the courthouse was total.
The accused evidently entertained little hope that this cocky white journalist would do them much good. Joe Azbell answered clearly and plainly. The
action had been spontaneous. There was a loud exhalation of many breaths.
The red-neck journalist had been fair to them.

CHAPTER 9

First Encounter with Suez

'We too have been invaded and ravaged by war but unlike Europe we have never had a Marshall Plan,' the lady in Prince Edward County, Virginia, said quite gently, as she showed me her garden. I was unable to withhold some measure of sympathy from a group of Americans who, living the life they had expected always to live, now found themselves, all unwillingly, in the eye of a legal storm. They had done nothing wrong by the standards of their state or, for that matter, by the standards of the United States Supreme Court prior to 1954, which had condoned separate but equal education of white and black children. Now in Brown v. Board of Education a unanimous court had decreed that separate schools were inherently unequal and liberals everywhere applauded the spectacle of judges legislating on a major moral issue on which legislators were not willing or not able to act.

Now, 18 months later, I was checking on the rate of progress of school desegregation in the South. I found that a visitor to a 'black belt' county like Prince Edward was obliged to 'conclude that the white population, which pays most of the local taxes, is utterly unready to comply with a court decree that does such violence to its basic sense of morality'.[6] Some with a sense of shame confessed past failure, school taxes being local, to vote a fair share of funds for black schools; but then when, with the Brown case pending, they had voted for a superbly equipped new high school to be run up for blacks, they had reckoned that their guilt had been purged.

As individual cases arose, with their ragged assault on the nerves of neighbourhoods throughout the South, the absence of a federal strategy for implementing Brown, which the court had said should occur 'with all deliberate speed', became obvious. One day I was summoned by my editor, Geoffrey Crowther, to lunch in a private dining room of his Washington base, the Cosmos Club. There were two other guests, two men who were to be seen regularly walking at a fast pace each working day between Georgetown (one of the two villages on the otherwise unoccupied land chosen at the opening of the nineteenth century to be the national capital) and downtown Washington. One was tall, could be taken for a senior officer of the British Army and was terse in speech; the other was short and inclined to be voluble. They were the best-known pair of walkers in Washington, the former Secretary of State Dean Acheson and Supreme Court Justice Felix Frankfurter, who had written the court's opinion in Brown.

Conversation for most of the lunch was confined to the other three, but at one point my editor turned to me to ask whether there was anything I would like to ask. The opportunity was not to be missed. I had been reflecting on the famous case of Worcester v. Georgia in 1832 when, the Supreme Court having upheld the rights of the Cherokee nation, President Andrew Jackson had said of his celebrated Chief Justice, 'John Marshall has made his decision. Now let him enforce it.' So I asked Frankfurter whether, when he was writing his decision, he had supposed that President Eisenhower would have some plan to enforce it. Felix Frankfurter flushed. 'I think that this is quite an improper question to be asked,' he blustered, reducing me to embarrassed silence. But I was to have a formidable advocate. 'That's just not good enough, Felix', declared 'the Dean', his moustache bristling, 'I think this young man is entitled to have an answer.' Thus rebuked by his constant friend, Frankfurter most unwillingly admitted that, yes, he had thought that the executive arm of government would have followed through on the social revolution he had launched.

I arrived in Jackson, Mississippi, the poorest state of the Union with the largest black population. There had just been some hideous examples of Jim Crowism, of intimidation of Negroes by the Ku Klux Klan. Despite being told that very day by the *Manchester Guardian* that the leading black organisation in the state, the NAACP, was extremely difficult to trace, I solved the problem by looking up its entry in the telephone directory. Once I had managed to explain that I had not said that I represented 'the Communists' I was promised a warm welcome. Only at the third attempt did I find a taxi-driver willing to take me to the black side of town, where I discovered a most gracious lady in charge of a neatly arranged office. She told me in soft, unemotional tones of the realities of belonging to an underclass defined by skin colour and raised her voice only when she came to her own epic struggle to be addressed by the authorities as 'Mrs' (and as a result she became the only person in the United States whom I invariably knew as Mrs). When it was lunchtime I invited her to be my guest, which was rather thoughtless of me because I was a white man in Negrotown and so banned from any lunch counter. She left me in the office while she got a takeaway. Afterwards she brought me to meet men and women who had only recently suffered abuse.

Not all my travels were so grim. A sweep of the mountain states in the northwest saw me driving into the desert of Nevada, past Lake Tahoe and the locations of many a cowboy and Indian movie, to come to rest in Las Vegas, where I arrived in time for Noël Coward's opening performance at Caesar's Palace. *The Economist* seemed to be known in these parts; at any rate I was provided with a seat at a front table by a public relations man who doubled as a member of the State Legislature. No doubt thanks to his efforts, the word got out that Mr Coward, having ventured out at noon, was, whether in the character of a mad dog or in that of an Englishman, feeling a little unwell. Tension having thus been built up, the Master gave us an immaculate performance, mixing old favourites with new ditties. Having personally no gambling instinct whatsoever I benefited from the peculiar morality of the Sodom of the Nevada desert: if you can resist one sin (gambling) everything else comes very cheap.

Some Hollywood stars disported themselves in Washington. The Italian Embassy for instance laid on a reception for Cary Grant and Sophia Loren, who were filming nearby. When I caught up with them they were lamenting having been kept standing in water the whole day. I found myself more in danger of drowning in the enormous liquid pools of Sophia Loren's eyes instead of concentrating on her more advertised charms. I was impressed by her well-spoken English and her courteous manners, contrasting them in my mind with the hoydenish behaviour of the bosomy American film actress Jayne Mansfield, who had been horsing around the capital to the sound of coarse Texan compliments. But once I had left her I was pounced on by a bitchy marchesa for my opinion of her fellow countrywoman. On hearing my favourable reply she hissed, 'Do you speak Italian?' I confessed that I did not. 'If you did you would know that she talks like a fishwife, what you call Billingsgate; all her films for Italian audiences have to be dubbed.' This was indeed a fascinating variation on the theme of Eliza Doolittle.

One of the minor pleasures of life in Washington arose from being invited to join a marching-and-chowder (i.e. dining) club known by the rather pretentious title of 'The Philosopher Kings'. These consisted for the most part of young men in or around government, including Elliot Richardson, the future Secretary of Defence, Attorney General and Ambassador to London, and Roger Fisher, then an Assistant Attorney General, whose delightful father had the odd hobby of keeping a record of the first time a colloquial expression turned up in the columns of *The Economist*. Each philosopher king in turn had to present a paper after dinner. Roger Fisher, for example, when preparing an *amicus curiae* brief before the Supreme Court about the boundaries between obscenity and free speech, invited our opinions on where to draw the line. Borderline exhibits were passed round. Eventually it came to be my evening to lead off and I chose to talk on 'America: Curator of British Political Relics', wherein I maintained that in a number of important respects the United States was more careful to conserve historic institutions than Britain.

The idea came to me when I read in the press that a lawsuit in Maryland had been determined 'according to the rule in Shelley's case'. I recalled with a start that in Britain this principle of feudal land law had been abolished in the early 1920s by F.E. Smith, Earl of Birkenhead, while he was on the Woolsack. It had been what he had sworn to do when, as a young man, he had for once been caught out by a question on the subject in a viva. The next major instance was the grand jury. When at Oxford I had learned from the great historian F.W. Maitland about its origins and importance in the development of English law. I also knew that, after years of attenuated use, the grand jury had finally bitten the dust in a statute of 1933. Throughout the United States, however, it is a most flourishing institution which, meeting behind closed doors, not only can determine whether an individual should be charged but can be given by a judge wider authority to probe suspicious patterns of behaviour. (It was before a grand jury that Bill Clinton was to coin the classic response, 'It depends what the meaning of "is" is'.) The morning after I gave my paper I received a phone call from Supreme Court Justice Frankfurter, whose clerk had been present at its delivery. He was checking that the English grand jury was really extinct and, on being told by me that it was, proceeded to amend a footnote in a judgement he was writing.

Warming to my theme I passed on to the sheriff. County sheriffs are indeed still 'pricked' every year in England but their duties are vestigial, falling very far short of the role of the Sheriff of Nottingham in the tales of Robin Hood. In the United States the sheriff is an important elected official who is frequently not only the local law enforcement officer but the tax assessor and jailer into the bargain. Then, I had been fascinated to discover that in Illinois, Indiana and a few other states the elected justices of the peace were allowed to take a percentage commission from the fines they imposed, this being precisely the old 'fruits of justice' about which the early law books waxed witty. Sometimes the sheriff was a fee-paid job, one veteran pol. in a Mid-Western county explaining to me in 1954 that his nomination for that office was the reward for a lifetime of 'shaking hands and ringing doorbells'.

Moving over to Congress, I pointed to the importance of the conference committees which are designed to iron out the sometimes quite substantial differences in wording of bills passed on the same subject in the Senate and the House. This copies precisely the old procedures at Westminster but in Westminster they are part of the forgotten past, though one such might have come in handy during the ping-ponging over the Anti-Terrorism Bill of 2005. The structure of national and local parties and factions within parties put me in mind more of Sir Lewis Namier's analysis of English politics in the age of the American Revolution than of anything contemporarily British. When I was in Indiana, for example, I had a long conversation with a park keeper who, suffering evidently from some form of Parkinson's disease, was attempting with shaking hand and no success to fix a (presumably loaded) pistol around his waist. His whole career absolutely depended not just on his party winning the next local election but on a particular local politician winning that party's nomination. In Chicago the equivalent of Edmund Burke's economical reform movement of the late eighteenth century to abolish anomalies and rationalise the system was being launched by a Republican, Robert E. Merriam. Like an eighteenth-century economical reformer, Merriam challenged item after item in the city budget by a process of truly Burkean cross-examination. Why, for example, were there 28 chauffeurs for gas meter readers? Answer: heavy slabs had sometimes to be moved. Why then were the chauffeurs women? They were the meter readers' wives who read the meters while their husbands moved the slabs. How come then that the women were nearly all widows? They were in fact party workers who did not themselves drive but hired drivers at a much smaller fee than they were paid themselves. This, to my delight, was purest medieval sergeanty. Readers of Edwin O'Connor's novel *The Last Hurrah* about the declining days of a big city boss will remember that provision is even made for the maintenance in some unexacting office of a court jester – the equivalent, one must suppose, of that twelfth-century Rolland who was given a manor by the king in sergeanty for which, once a year at the king's feast, 'debuet facere … unum saltum et siffletum et unum bumbulum – he must make a jump, a whistle and a vulgar noise'. Vulgar noises characterised many of the reactions to Merriam's campaign calling for Civil Service standards and fair access. 'I've done this job for 14 years,' an indignant Chicago alderman expostulated to me, 'and are they now going to make me purchase a pair of spectacles so that I can take exams?'

My paper received further outings on the BBC's Third Programme and, some time later, in the pages of *American Heritage*. I also began occasional contributions to *Punch*. Nancy Balfour had asked if I would be prepared to contribute a humorous or satirical piece for *The Economist*'s Christmas issue. I had declined on the grounds of not being a humorous or satirical writer but in the next few weeks the worm must have been turning inside my brain, since, with the Christmas season well past, I submitted a piece to *Punch* on the prospects of hereditary politics in the United States – the Kennedy clan showing more potential in this direction than the Eisenhower clan – and saw it promptly accepted.

Geoffrey Crowther had told me I could accept any invitations to speak that would at least pay for expenses, since he was anxious for me to gain experience of America away from the Washington beltway. The invitation I enjoyed most was an annual one from the University of Colorado in Boulder to take part in its spring World Affairs Conference. Colorado is a very mountainous state and Boulder is surrounded by very dramatic scenery. The conference was a massive assault on the consciousness of its students in the hope of making them aware of a universe outside the USA. An extraordinarily diverse programme would be drawn up by a committee representing the Boulder community as well as academia and an amazing number of visiting speakers were drawn in, usually by telephone, from all over the world. There were plenary sessions and lectures but, for most of the time, ten panels were meeting simultaneously for three or four sessions a day. Scholarship was respected and wit encouraged. We worked hard and played hard. In the evenings there was much carousal and not a little dalliance. Socialising was often centred on a steam-heated outdoor swimming pool; I have one vivid memory of swimming out in the middle of a snowstorm with a full whisky glass being floated out to me on a duck-board by a delicious young lady. Luckily I managed on my first visit to hit the right note in a plenary session and received gratifying applause. I am not sure that I ever equalled that performance but it was sufficient to ensure me a regular invitation to what Adam Yarmolinsky used to term 'the spring rites' so long as I was in the States.

My work in America continued to be immensely stimulating. Something more, I always felt, must be provided to *The Economist* reader than could be gleaned from the daily broadsheets and to that end I worked long hours in consuming large quantities of Congressional and think-tank reports. I buried myself in local papers from across the country, believing strongly that most politics was local politics, attended Congressional hearings and tried, without always succeeding, to stick to the gold standard set for me by the famous columnist Joe Alsop of four interviews a day. But I was still not completely well. I would be prostrated for days on end with recurrences of ME, and tortured by onsets of absentmindedness which fortunately were becoming rarer but perhaps for that very reason were especially disconcerting when they came. There was always the need to conceal from London the fact that I had problems with my health. And in any case what problems? ME had then no name, let alone a definition. My life was so busy that I could also have done without 'half-zheimer's'.

Once I was to fly to Detroit to interview two union leaders. Having stopped my car at a drug-store (chemist's) to collect a small item, I emerged from it having completely forgotten that I had been driving and caught a taxi to the airport. It was only when I was in the plane returning from Detroit in a happy mood after completing a very successful visit that I suddenly remembered where I had left the car. After long delays and at considerable expense, I recovered it from the police pound and then stopped for a moment outside my house to pick up my mail before going on to some other destination. The car was left with the engine running as I dashed in. Once inside I completely forgot about the car and settled down to various tasks. By the time I went out the police had returned the car to the pound. It was fortunate that I am by nature an even-tempered person, not much given to brooding. But during my working life I could never wholly make up my mind whether to fight these maddening handicaps or be resigned to them.

Nineteen Fifty-Six was to be a presidential election year and all seemed to depend on Eisenhower's health. He had had a bad heart attack in the previous October and Sir Anthony Eden, by now Prime Minister, had to be warned, to his considerable annoyance, when he was on his way to Washington in late January, that his time with the President would for that reason be strictly rationed. It was widely felt that so long as Ike was on board, the White House would remain in Republican hands and that without him it most probably would not. In response to a cry from the media that nothing should be concealed from the Great American Public, a heart specialist with a flair for publicity called Dr Paul Dudley White became overnight medical adviser to the nation. The canals and curlicues of the President's interior became as well mapped out and canvassed in the press and on the screen as any of the former general's battle plans. For long it seemed implausible that a second term could be considered possible. But Ike's popularity was undimmed and the irrepressible Dr White gave it as his professional view that a second term as President would be the best possible prescription for his patient's well being. Against such a verdict it would seem bad form to weigh the well being of the nation.

Foreign policy was not my principal sphere of interest in Washington but insofar as it impinged on politics, in regard for example to foreign aid and reciprocal trade, I used occasionally to write about it. I did go to Foster Dulles's briefings and had one rather special source in his brother, the Director of the CIA, Allen Dulles. This had a rather tragic origin. The young Allen

Dulles, the Director's son, had been to Oxford when I was up. A Balliol man, he struck me as the most right-wing character that I had ever met. I did not know him very well but I was fascinated how anyone so intelligent could be in possession of such extreme views. He was quite different from the aristocratic possessors of risible prejudices of whom there were still quite a number around. What impressed me about Allen was his rigid insistence on carrying his views to their logical consequences utterly regardless of what company that might entail. He was, for instance, much against Woodrow Wilson's attributing a moral quality to his recognition of foreign governments. In particular he attacked Wilson's failure to recognise the faction in Mexico that had seized possession of power in 1914. Because of this view Allen, the ultimate rightwinger, was in favour of the recognition of the People's Republic of China.

The young Dulles had served in Korea and had had half his brain shot away. Now he was living at home with a former Marine employed to take care of him. In appearance he looked normal but he lacked all sense of direction, remembered little and reconstructed endlessly the incident in which he had been wounded. His mother thought that the company of one of his old preKorean friends would jolt him into a more normal mood. I used to rack my brains to recall every topic we had discussed in our Oxford days because this had the electrifying effect of sparking off Allen to respond exactly as he used to do, giving his mother the thrill of hearing her son once more as she had known him. When the father felt I had done enough he used to signal me to accompany him to his study.

I would not say that Allen Dulles ever conveyed to me any real secrets but his judgements on men and matters at the highest level were well worth hearing and often were a good deal sounder than those emanating from other parts of the argus-faced American machine. 'What are they telling you in the State Department about Mendès-France?' he challenged me on one occasion, when that maverick politician seemed on the verge of office. 'They think he's a neutralist and wants to lead France out of NATO.' 'He's not a neutralist and will not quit NATO but he will bury the European Defence Community,' came the accurate forecast. It was useful that I was able to alert my editors about such judgements. How Allen Dulles would react to the Suez crisis will become apparent hereafter.

The presidential election campaign was moving on towards election day on 6 November. The news that came on 29 October that Israelis had attacked Egypt did not at first blush compete for the attention of Americans with reports of the campaign itself and also with the astonishing reports from Hungary that raised the prospect of an immediate unravelling of the Soviet empire in

Central Europe. In the course of the previous election of 1952 John Foster Dulles had preached that, rather than being satisfied like their opponents with containing the Soviet empire, the Republicans would see it rolled back. The slogan was much ridiculed at the time by Democratic spokesmen, but now suddenly on the very eve of the next election here was an old election promise that looked like being fulfilled.

On the morning of the following day I was in the Washington Press Club, on the top floor of the Press Building, scanning the agency tapes for news from the election front and from Hungary, when to my astonishment and dismay the chattering keys of the machine spelled out the terms of the Anglo-French ultimatum, nominally dispatched to Israel as well as to Egypt. My immediate reaction was that this had to be fraudulent and Egypt had to be the sole target. In some agitation I moved to the press bar next door and began talking rapidly to my American friend Ed Dale. His astringent mind endowing him with a fine propensity for querying any thesis with which he was confronted, he endeavoured to calm me down. While he succeeded to the extent of lowering the tone and moderating the language of my dissent I was in no doubt what I must now do. I went down one floor to my office, drafted two telegrams and sent them spinning on my proto-fax machine whose usual discharge of smoke seemed on this occasion more like steam rising.

To explain what the cables contained I must for a moment revert to my wish for a political career of my own. Observing politics from a distance of 3,600 miles I had by 1956 almost persuaded myself after all that anybody who was not a socialist could find himself a home in the Conservative Party. The current leaders – Anthony Eden, Rab Butler, Iain Macleod – seemed to be of a liberal disposition. I was now 31 (I had given a 'Farewell to Youth' party on my 30th birthday), I had not been a member of the Liberal Party for five years and I could not afford to hesitate much longer. It was in that mood that I had learned that Tory Central Office had decided that there were not enough of its MPs with interest in and knowledge of foreign affairs and that therefore it was on the lookout for potential candidates living abroad who did not have to be already members of the Conservative Party. For a start Sir Donald Kaberry, the vice-chairman in charge of candidates, was to visit Washington and interviews could be set up in the Mayflower Hotel. I wrote in and applied; the interview was set for 31 October. That was the date that the Suez ultimatum was to expire.

The two faxed messages were virtually identical and were sent to Central Office and to Sir Donald Kaberry at the Mayflower. They said that 'in view of the British and French aggression against Egypt at Suez I can see no point in going through with the interview'. I did not know whom else Sir Donald was interviewing at the Mayflower and whether he had any better luck with others. I had seen, as if in a blinding flash, just why I could never be a Conservative and why it had been a mistake for me ever to suppose I could have been.

The next day Ed Dale read to me the shorthand notes that his bureau chief, 'Scotty' Reston, had taken of the remarkable off-the-record encounter between the top American journalists and John Foster Dulles on the previous evening. It was at an elite dining club whose meeting with the Secretary of State had long been prearranged for the night of 30 October. When they heard about the ultimatum, Reston and his colleagues had expected that the supper would be put off, but Dulles was interested that his own version should inform press comment. He expressed his exasperation with British diplomacy in the Middle East, saying that the Americans no less than the British wanted to dislodge President Nasser, but that the trouble with the British was that 'they must have it by Christmas'. He told in some detail the story of how the British had suddenly cut off the usual exchange of information in the field among allies while Israel had been clearly mobilising and that the cable traffic between London (and Paris) and Israel had been vastly increased above normal. He referred to the latest news from Hungary, where the Nagy government had withdrawn from the Warsaw Pact and proclaimed a permanent neutrality. He said that in that case, and particularly if other Eastern bloc states joined a neutral belt, the United States would not need to defer so much as it had done to the colonialism of its NATO partners. I made two copies and sent them to my editor and to Hugh Gaitskell, the leader of the opposition. It was a relief to find that my own reactions were in harmony with those of all but one (Brian Crozier) of my colleagues on *The Economist*.

Once Eisenhower and his Secretary of State had assimilated the unpalatable 12-hour ultimatum, which had hit them just as Ike was entering the final straight of his election campaign, they felt certain that the British and French must have troopships 'just over the horizon', so that they could strike with maximum effect the moment the ultimatum expired. I saw Allen Dulles two days later. He had told his colleagues, he said, that they were quite mistaken to count on Britain being able to carry off a military coup with dispatch. Britain's military record was quite other. His special source, said the Director of the CIA, was a book about the Gallipoli expedition by the Australian author Alan Moorehead. This was not a lone example, I told him, and cited, among others, Walcheren, Tanga and Dieppe. One thing which he told me which I was not altogether convinced of at the time was that the CIA had had no advance warning. But subsequent research has shown this to be so.

The Suez crisis, which represented the only complete breakdown in the special relationship between America and Britain since the start of the Cold War, found Britain without an ambassador in Washington. The previous incumbent, Sir Roger Makins, had gone home to take up the Joint Permanent Secretaryship of the Treasury. His successor, Sir Harold Caccia, was coming out slowly by sea. When he arrived in conditions of great frigidity he was received with courtesy by the President when he presented his credentials but found that apart from this no one would talk to him. He approached some of us journalists, especially those representing papers critical of our government, such as Max Freedman of the *Guardian*, Patrick O'Donovan of the *Observer* and myself, and asked for help in reporting American policy. In the unusual circumstances it seemed the least we could do. The White House and the State Department continued to brief us during the fraught days that followed and we briefed the Embassy. Right throughout the large British diplomatic and military community men and women found their social as well as official lives in suspense, American tennis players telling their British partners that it would be better for the time being that they should not meet and British hostesses being bereft of their favourite guests.

Not all Americans agreed with this bleak demonstration of the social Siberia resulting from Washington's displeasure. I went to New York to witness the last stages of the presidential election. The vote was to be on 6 November, the actual day of the principal Anglo-French invasion (there had been air drops the day before). The final round in the clash of American politicians had coincided with the painfully slow advance of the armada across the surface of the Mediterranean. Adlai Stevenson decided to scrap his planned campaign for an all-out assault on the President for having been caught napping in the Middle East. I witnessed one Democratic senator go further. In Lower Manhattan Senator John F. Kennedy was speaking in support of a wartime comrade who was contesting a seat in the House and I heard him flay the administration for letting down America's wartime allies, Britain and France, in their hour of need.

On 6 November Eisenhower's electoral stock soared – his margin over Stevenson was nearly double what it had been in 1952 – and his Republican Party's stock plunged downward as the Democrats won the elections to both House and Senate. I realised that it was time for me to claim the home leave to which I was by now entitled when, in my passionate rejection of Eden's policy, I actually caught myself saying to American friends, 'What should *we* do now to stop *them*?' It was time to take stock of the situation in London. In any case Donald Tyerman, who had just taken over the editorship from Crowther, was keen to have me on hand to decide editorial policy on the prospects for rebuilding the Anglo-American relationship. So at the end of November I once more stood on British soil.

CHAPTER 10

Also Reporting for
The News Chronicle

'What do they think of Eden in the United States?' The question came in a deep, booming voice issuing implausibly from a frail, bejewelled old lady who had just moved slowly into her dining room clad in two fur coats, one on top of the other. This was the first time I had met my father's last employer, Cornelia, Countess of Craven, and I had been invited with my parents to lunch mainly, I suspected, so that I should answer precisely this question. I had it in mind that Anthony Eden had married as his second wife the daughter of Lady Craven's beloved friend Goonie, the sister-in-law of Winston Churchill. 'I am afraid that they don't think very much of him at the moment,' I ventured in reply. Lady Craven brought the huge ruby ring on her finger crashing to the table as she roared, 'I always knew young Anthony was rash' – the last word uttered with phenomenal emphasis. She put me in mind of Dame Edith Evans in *The Importance of Being Earnest* and, on a separate occasion when the name of that actress was rather naughtily cited by my mother, Lady Craven, raising one arm pronounced, 'A trifle maniérée, don't you think?'

The Westminster village, of course, was talking of nothing but Suez and the consequences for the Prime Minister's career and for relations with America. The fact that Eden had vanished on sick leave with the crisis he had caused unresolved and with British troops still stuck along a narrow and vulnerable corridor, with the currency reserves running out and with America being of no help whatsoever, could only aggravate the atmosphere. It did not help that the place the Prime Minister had accepted for convalescence was Jamaica, at the time a byword for the sybaritic life, or that in Jamaica he was the guest of Anne Fleming, who was known to Tory gossips as the mistress of the opposition leader Hugh Gaitskell, himself regarded by many Suez warriors as little better than a traitor. Feelings had run very high on both sides of the argument; seldom since the time of Chanak in 1922 (which in some ways Suez resembled) or even since the Boer War had the nation been so divided over an external issue, and, partly for that very reason, many people deliberately shut down all discussion, lest it do irreparable harm to families and friends who found themselves on opposite sides of the fence.

The subject, I found, had not been banned in the Oxford and Cambridge Club, to which my Oxford friend Ivan Yates, the snuff-taking socialist, had invited me for dinner. As Britain was suffering from a fuel shortage on account of Suez the club was very cold except for one small coal fire around which a group of young men had gathered after the meal. Ivan and I joined them. Conversation was in full swing. Each of the young men in turn was recounting his horror story of how an individual or an institution had let him down during the crisis by failing to back Eden. 'Of course, I've cancelled my subscription to the *Observer*,' said one, amid murmurs of approval. 'It's such a shame about the list of Oxford dons signing that letter to *The Times*,' said another. 'It means that I shan't be able to go to my tutor's sherry parties ever again.' There was a general sigh of sympathy. 'And then,' said a third man, 'there's *The Economist*.' The party then noticed the two of us sitting silently by the fireplace. 'Do you read *The Economist*?' I was asked. 'No,' I answered with studied venom, 'I write it.' There was a stunned silence and then, slowly and sadly the young men rose and without a word left the club.

Because of the petrol rationing the West End was like a village. Only taxis and buses were to be seen and one could race around the place with extraordinary rapidity. I took myself at the first opportunity to Westminster, where from the press gallery I saw the Liberal Jo Grimond very effectively skewering Selwyn Lloyd, the Foreign Secretary, who in his embarrassment was performing his famous stuck machine-gun act. I sent in a card for Sir Edward Boyle, who had resigned as Economic Secretary to the Treasury in protest against the Suez policy. He came into the lobby looking more like Billy Bunter than ever and, sitting down on the bench beside me, decanted from both pockets his entire constituency correspondence. There and later at his mother's flat Edward told me the Suez story as he had seen it from the Treasury, while I offered in return a Washington perspective. I asked him whether he had had problems with his constituency party, which was the Handsworth division of Birmingham. He said he had been summoned to a meeting to explain his deviant behaviour. In the debate following his speech there were two factions, each headed by a former lord mayor of Birmingham. One of them thought his conduct unforgivable and wanted him to be deselected for the next election; the other former lord mayor said that at the retirement of their previous Member they had deliberately set out to pick a young high flyer who would soon get office; Sir Edward had more than fulfilled the expectations they had had of him; any man should be allowed to make one mistake and they should be prepared to overlook this one. The second opinion had prevailed by about two to one. Only one speaker, a lady, had appeared to endorse Boyle's actual arguments. He approached her afterwards and thanked her 'for being my only real supporter'. 'Yes,' she replied, 'I think all the troubles in the world are caused by the Jews.' Edward had left the meeting a sad and troubled man.

After supper Edward took me to Pratt's for a brandy. We found Harold Macmillan at the bar surrounded by a circle of acolytes. He was of course one of the two candidates – Rab Butler being the other – for the premiership if, as expected, Eden found he had no alternative but to give up. Edward sat me down, supplied me with a drink and asked to be excused for a brief while. He then went over and joined Macmillan's circle. He was soon back, full of renewed apology, saying that he had felt bad at abandoning the Chancellor at such a critical moment 'because he used to need me to explain the figures to him, which he did not really understand'. I have often since wondered whether there was any connection between that remark and the fact, which later came out, that Macmillan gave the harassed cabinet the wrong figures about the loss of sterling on the night of 5–6 November. Edward was, alas, dead when I came to describe these events in my book *Suez*.

I was eager to piece together, from any source I could tap, the London end of the story. In return I found great interest in the motives of American behaviour. There was considerable surprise at my saying that Eisenhower and Dulles had written off Nasser some months before the Suez crisis had begun. One day in the 'Honky-Tonk', which was the staff's name for *The Economist*'s editorial dining room (properly called the Bagehot Club) where senior civil servants, politicians and economists came in to be debriefed, Sir Frank Lee, then Permanent Secretary to the Board of Trade, was being entertained. 'Suez will go down in the history books,' he propounded, 'as providing the proof that the theory that civil servants run the government is wrong. Over Suez ministers acted alone without the Civil Service.' I could not refrain from observing that, on the contrary, Suez would be noted because it had established the total indispensability of the Civil Service since ministers had made such a mess of doing things themselves.

Arising from one dinner-table conversation I was given the chance of writing about the Middle East crisis at greater length than was possible in *The Economist*. Lord Altrincham (later Mr John Grigg), the hereditary owner and editor of *The National and English Review*, commissioned an article entitled 'The Background to the Eisenhower Doctrine', laying out the American position on and after Suez. Grigg was later to claim with some justice that this was the genesis of my later book on the Suez crisis. Although the *Observer* tempted me with a better-paid job covering the Middle East from a base in Rome, I decided that for the time being I wanted to go back to Washington. The decision was helped by an initiative of Geoffrey Crowther, who by now, having handed the editorship over to Donald Tyerman, was the general manager of *The Economist* and felt I should be paid more so long as it was someone else who paid. Crowther was also on the board of *The News Chronicle*, whose much admired Washington correspondent, Bob Waithman, had died suddenly at the age of 49 and, since Bruce Rothwell, their New York correspondent, did not wish to transfer, it was arranged that, on a part-time basis, I should cover for the *Chronicle* on top of my duties for *The Economist*. For the only time in my career I was to function as a daily journalist.

The *News Chronicle* was a Liberal paper owned by the Cadbury family, which attempted, with some success, to combine a lively popular style and presentation with a responsible attitude to the news. It was in a way a 'lighter' version of the *Manchester Guardian* but its circulation of 1.4 million copies compared with the 4 million of the *Daily Express* and the 2 million of the *Daily Mail*, while its political influence went on declining with that of the Liberal Party. A year before, it had absorbed the *Daily Dispatch*, but this had brought in mainly Tory readers whose loyalty could not be guaranteed. The paper's first editorial reactions to the outbreak of hostilities over Suez had been equivocal and there had been much internal argument about the correct line to take. But then Michael Curtis, the young editor, had seized the helm and swung it decisively against the government. His signed article, splashed across two pages, had declared in capital letters 'THIS IS FOLLY ON THE GRAND SCALE'. At the end of the indictment Curtis had concluded, 'Only a miracle can save the Prime Minister now.' This was great for the paper's reputation among those including myself who felt that way, but was not good for circulation.

Back in the United States I enjoyed trying my hand at writing in a more popular style for *The News Chronicle*. I had to file at lunchtime because of the difference in time zones, though since Bruce Rothwell was the senior North American correspondent and space was very limited I was not required to do so every day. Some topics – such as the possible line-up for the next presidential election – were similar to those I was also covering for *The Economist*. Others, such as the criminal libel suit in California against the owners of a Los Angeles publication called *Confidential*, which I characterised as 'a sleazy, bi-monthly magazine which battens on the vulnerable private lives of celebrities, mostly in the film world', were confined to my daily journalism. I remember reporting in the *Chronicle* a rather scary hearing in Congress, during which Wernher von Braun, Hitler's rocket specialist whom the Americans appropriated at the end of the war, expounded on the space wars of the future. In this new world, for which America was invited to equip herself, the outcome of Armageddon would be determined by battles directed entirely from platforms outside the atmosphere.

I had been invited by the Canadian Institute for International Affairs to do a lecture tour under their auspices. When I was about to go I received a long letter from a Canadian giant called 'Tiny' Palmer, who had been quite a personality in the Oxford Union. The important point to remember when you go to Canada, he advised, is that most Canadians live close to the United States border and the life of all Canadians is conditioned by their attitude to that border. They either cross it when they are young and try to make a success of life in the big world to the south and sometimes come back triumphant or they don't cross it and, while imagining all their lives that they would have done better if they had, they spend their time proclaiming the sacrifices they have made for the sake of being Canadian patriots.

My arrival happened to coincide with a Canadian general election. Lester Pearson, known as 'Mike', who had earned a Nobel Peace Prize for his work as External Affairs Minister in creating the first UN peacekeeping force at the time of Suez, was seeking to be Prime Minister. His Conservative opponent was an old-fashioned blowhard from the sticks called Diefenbaker, who had headed a minority administration and was now seeking a full term. I was in Toronto for election day and was asked to a private house to watch the results. My hostess, a keen supporter of the Institute that was sponsoring me, told me that her cultural life was centred on New York. She made long visits there every year not only to take in the theatres but also to take in the United Nations. New York rather than Ottawa was her effective capital city. Eloquently, too, she spoke of the thrill of watching Mike Pearson take the lead in resolving difficult issues. It seemed to me therefore an anomaly that she was enthusiastically backing Diefenbaker to win against Pearson in the current election. How come? I asked. 'The trouble with Pearson,' she answered, 'is that when you listen to him you think that Canada is a great second-class power. But that's wrong. We are a twenty-second-class power.' Diefenbaker won. In Toronto my path was made smoother by the Canadian Institute's secretary who turned out to be an Oxford friend, John (now Lord) Gilbert. Later he stayed with me for part of a summer in Washington.

In Montreal I met some of the bright young men of the financial community. Most of them were British and most of the ones I met had double-barrelled names. Most of them were, I suppose, what on Wall Street are called 'masters of the universe', but they sounded like members of a persecuted minority. The French had begun to take over Quebec in a really big way; it was already heading in a direction which I was required in later years to report. More and more the use of the English language was being discouraged; the English community did not expect to be flourishing much longer.

It was high time that I got to know John F. Kennedy, who had only really emerged in the limelight (as the defeated candidate for the vice-presidency) during the 1956 nominating convention. When I went for the first time to his office I had scarcely sat down before he set about interviewing me. He had lived in England before the war, as he had come over with his father, the Ambassador Joseph Kennedy, who had given his son a lifetime subscription to *The Economist*. Now Jack Kennedy had a grievance: *The Economist* had introduced line drawings as part of its campaign to persuade potential readers that they did not need a PhD in economics before they could follow its articles. To the young Senator this seemed a fatal step on the road to (though he did not use the actual phrase) the paper's dumbing-down. I tried to reassure him; the aim was not to change the content, just to remove inhibitions against reading it. The thought crossed my mind that this man had more of a conservative temperament than I would have supposed. He had another question for me: who is 'Taper'? As previously noted, this pseudonym, after one of the two political fixers in Disraeli's *Coningsby* (the other was Tadpole), had been adopted by the writer of the caustic and hilarious parliamentary sketches in *The Spectator*. It must be doubted whether any other member of the US Senate would have heard of him. Kennedy was obviously disappointed when I revealed that 'Taper' was my old scriptwriter from BBC days, Bernard Levin. He had expected that some major political figure was sheltered by the disguise.

On one occasion Kennedy invited me out for lunch in the country. He picked me up at the end of the morning's hearings in a modest Chevrolet, observing good-humouredly, 'There goes the committee's counsel [his brother Bobby] in a Cadillac.' He drove me out to Normandy Farm, looking straight at me the whole time as we talked, never once keeping his eye on the road. He steered presumably by peripheral vision. I had to admit to myself that by the time we arrived his expert questioning had extracted all the information I possessed on the state of the Labour Party and the relative positions of Aneurin Bevan and Hugh Gaitskell. I propounded the thesis, which stood me well enough for the next two decades though not beyond, that despite all the noise, 'in the end the

Left never wins'. It was only when we settled down for the meal that I was able to draw him out on American politics. Though he would not say so directly it was apparent to me that he planned to go for the presidency, and though some people at this stage were inclined to dismiss him as a lightweight, that was far from my impression.

Later I came to know a young lady who had been one of Kennedy's girl-friends, not, I gathered, a small class, though I did not then realise what a compulsive womaniser he was. He was not, I was told, an elegant lover but this woman said that she had not minded his tearing her dress the first time because she knew he was rich enough to replace it. While many in the media must have had some idea of Kennedy's propensity in this regard, none chose to disclose it. There were limits, however, and since his marriage to Jackie there were dangers of these limits being exceeded. One day my friend requested me not to call at her flat that evening; she said she would explain the next day. The following day she told me that Kennedy had called her up and asked if she would be free as he desperately wanted to talk to her. He arrived at eight and for hours unburdened himself of his dilemmas. His marriage, he said, was a terrible mistake. Jackie hated politics and politicians. They were discovering that they had nothing in common. He stood a good chance of the Democratic presidential nomination, but his wife was unwilling to do anything to help him. Yet he was a Catholic and divorce would ruin his chances. What was he to do? My friend said that she had been firm and consistent. He must ask himself, did he genuinely, sincerely want to be president? If yes, there could be no question of divorce; he must come to some accommodation with Jackie.

It was instructive to learn what people find it necessary to do to qualify for public office. My high-minded Republican friend and fellow philosopher-king Elliot Richardson sat up late with me one night to discuss our attitudes to God. He first established that my position was one of agnosticism – that is, that it was not within the compass of a human being to know whether there was a deity or universal purpose, divine or otherwise. I was not convinced that Christ, for all his true saintliness, had been sent into the world to reveal the secret of these unknowns. Elliot said that his attitude was much the same, but in his case there was one difficulty. He was anxious for elective office, above all to become Governor of Massachusetts, and he supposed that for this purpose he would need a religion. Being an upright, rather buttoned-up Bostonian, this clearly bothered his conscience. Did I think that he was entitled, given the analysis that we shared, to term himself a Unitarian? There was at the time in Washington a hugely fashionable Unitarian preacher called Powell who had clearly appealed to him. I think I probably gave the project my blessing. Poor

Elliot, he was an admirable citizen and a highly intelligent man but not really cut out for electoral politics. He did manage, a decade later, to be elected as Attorney-General of Massachusetts, but when I was his guest at a swearing-in I had to push him forward into the limelight, reminding him that he was entitled by his office to be in front of the cameras.

One Republican who was not that inhibited was Richard Nixon. Our group of British correspondents was invited one evening to supper with the Vice-President. Very probably he would be the next Republican candidate and he was anxious to whiten his image, which to put it mildly was rather splattered, with parts of the world press. He was frequently portrayed at home and abroad as being callow, schmaltzy and McCarthyite. It was an agreeable evening during which he personally served us with a variety of cold dishes and talked about anything we brought up in a fluent, easy style. I cannot say that I had the feeling of having been in the presence of greatness or of being impressed by the novelty or depth of anything he said. But he did convey impressions of moderation and competence, particularly in the detailed handling of foreign issues. I remember remarking to a colleague after we left that he would make a good Assistant Secretary of State. As we now know he was far from being at the head of a list of people Dwight Eisenhower thought qualified to be his successor, but then those who were at its head were hardly an electable bunch. Assessing in *The News Chronicle* the prospects of a premature Nixon presidency brought on by another bout of Eisenhower's ill health, I acknowledged the hopeful evidence of Nixon's internationalism but concluded, 'Still sore about his bare-knuckle fighting in the past, would [the Democrat majority in Congress] be prepared to give him an even break?'

The Commie-baiting in which Nixon had once indulged was not over yet, although McCarthy himself was finished (he died on 2 May 1957, with his liver quite gone). Francis Walter was an elderly, distinguished-looking Congressman from a district in Pennsylvania; he was the chairman of the House Un-American Activities Committee, which had for long been called after its notorious first chairman, Congressman Martin Dies, the Dies Committee. I spent one morning on its press bench listening to the examination of Arthur Miller, the famous playwright whom I had previously met at the World Affairs Conference at Boulder. Miller had come to the attention of the committee because the State Department had refused him a passport to attend the European première of his play *The Crucible*, which is about the Salem witch-hunts but plainly carried contemporary echoes of the conduct of investigations by Congressional committees. The members of the committee took relatively little part in the proceedings; the interrogation was mainly carried out by the committee's hired counsel by frequent reference to the text of what he invariably called 'The Crushable', treating lines of dialogue as witness statements. After much of this, a committee member interjected the question which was doubtless on many minds, 'Why do your characters always have to be so pessimistic about America? Couldn't you write a play about the good things?' Miller fended off this question by the classic defence of writer's privilege and was unembarrassed by his signature on various joint letters alleged to have been promoted by Communists. He was only once shaken, I thought, when a member produced evidence that at the end of the war he had signed a petition for the death penalty to be passed on the poet Ezra Pound, whose pro-fascist beliefs had caused him to spend the war in Italy.

But the full drama of the proceedings occurred when, just as the committee was heading for a mid-morning break, one of Miller's few friends on the committee asked him when he would next need to use an American passport. To this he replied: 'Next month, when I plan to go to Europe with Miss Marilyn Monroe, who will by then be my wife.' Sensation! The press, who had had no advance warning, raced out of the hearing to man the telephones. No one was disposed to label Marilyn's future husband an enemy of the nation. In May 1957, when Miller was to face a contempt of Congress charge in the brand new federal court building in Washington, the heart had gone out of the attempt to pursue America's leading playwright.

Soon after I had come back to Washington I had received a summons from Geoffrey Crowther to Wilmington, Delaware. Geoffrey was married to an American lady who was a member of a wealthy Quaker family with an estate there, which gave him a comfortable base on his trips across the Atlantic. We discussed my future in the swimming pool. Geoffrey was flattering about my work and said that if I would like to keep the job indefinitely it was mine for the asking and that he was willing to make arrangements that would increase my income over time and would, if I wanted it, enable me to take an occasional sabbatical year with a university. I replied that if I were going to stay in America I should not stay in journalism; if I were going to stay in journalism I should not want to stay in America. After a couple more circuits around each other Geoffrey asked me to promise that I would give *The Economist* plenty of notice of any intention to leave. I gave him 18 months' notice on the spot.

The Council on Foreign Relations is a sister organisation to the Royal Institute of International Affairs in London, known generally as Chatham House. The two had been born at the same dinner party in Paris at which British and American experts at the post-war peace conference had agreed that their political leaders were not paying sufficient attention to their own expert advice. The experts also fancied the idea of carrying over into the peace the style of interdisciplinary work in close harness that they had found such a bracing experience in their Paris hotels. Since ignorant public opinion was so blatantly misdirecting the politicians, they must in future turn their hand to creating an informed public opinion. In the euphoria of that Parisian evening the mood was to create a single Anglo-American institute. But, it must be presumed, sober legal and political thoughts in the following weeks must have caused the scheme to be changed to allow for two separate bodies, albeit with identical aims, on the two sides of 'the pond'. It was this American institute that I was invited one evening to address.

I presented myself at the elegant Council premises in a tuxedo (American for 'black tie'), since the Americans are more formal than the British on such occasions, and delivered my talk after an excellent dinner. I suppose I must have spoken about British foreign policy but I remember only one feature of the evening. For the first and last time in my life I smoked. Sitting down to applause with the speech now over, I absentmindedly picked out a cigar as they were handed round. I realised that I was now committed though I had a sinking feeling that I had once been told that the first smoke often makes one sick. Thanks to having remembered a joke from a Christmas cracker I took the band off. Then I put the cigar gingerly into my mouth and inhaled. To my relief, although I sweated badly, I was not sick. I have never been tempted to repeat the experience.

Since I had committed myself to be elsewhere in 18 months I began, as that deadline grew nearer, to think where that should be. I had sketched an outline of a book I might write about American state politics but had not as yet found a publisher and a research grant, so I thought I would probably stay with journalism for a while and go to another part of the globe. I was approached by the *Sunday Times*, which thought that having covered one superpower I might like to cover the other. I toyed with this idea, but the more I learned about the restrictions which Moscow imposed on foreign correspondents the less keen I became.

At this stage my editor Donald Tyerman, who was famous for giving good advice to young people in the profession, came up with a new suggestion. Pointing out that I had as yet no experience of journalism at home, he offered me a job as political and parliamentary correspondent and added, 'If you still wish to be on your travels after two years we will not try to hold you back.' It was while I was considering this that I was asked to take part in a radio show that was conducted by two popular stars, Tex and Jinx Falkenburg, from a (not very clean) tabletop in a New York restaurant. The subject was American foreign policy and there was a mix of round-table discussion and response to incoming phone calls. It carried on for most of the evening, punctuated of course by commercials. One of the listeners was Dolly Schiff, who owned Bill Shannon's paper, the *New York Post*. She rang up the editor, Jimmy Wechsler, and told him to find me and offer me a job. Jimmy was able to reply that he was already meeting me in the morning. This had been prearranged for me by Bill, so that Jimmy could see whether he wanted me to write a regular London column twice a week. 'You are either a columnist or you're not,' Jimmy told me. 'It can't be taught or learned.'

With the extra income that this would provide, I decided that two years in London would make sense. It was to prove one of my best decisions, though it meant saying farewell to my host of friends, to my little house, to my very old but utterly reliable Cadillac, and to a country and especially its capital which had been good to me for five very formative years. If, in the years to come, I was to find myself at times critical of the United States, it would always be criticism from a foundation of love.

CHAPTER 11

Reporting British Politics

'We had hoped for better from a Liberal,' a party member said to me sadly when there appeared in print my first article as *The Economist*'s political and parliamentary correspondent, about the Liberal Party's 1958 annual assembly. Not having been to a Liberal assembly since I had been president of the Oxford University Liberal Club, I was now acting as journalist not as student politician. To judge from my report, my impression was of a mixture of 'blithering old age' and 'half-hatched juvenility'. Microphones did not work; more than once there was total confusion over what delegates were being called on to vote about. The party had filled the platform with its veterans like Graham White, the last Liberal Assistant Postmaster-General, and the 76-year-old party president, Sir Arthur Comyns Carr, who having been an MP for one year in 1924 had, he said, used that brief political opportunity to warn the nation that the Road Fund was not safe from being raided by the Treasury. It had taken only a year for such raiding to commence. As to affairs overseas Sir Arthur started off with the Boer War but reassured us ponderously that he was not going to say anything that would 'exacerbate' the situation in the Formosa (Taiwan) Strait, where there was a tense stand-off between the Chinese Communists and the Americans. This was followed by a debate on youth, which consisted, I wrote, of 'a series of self-conscious speeches defending "our generation" against the charge of being "angry"'. (It was only two years since John Osborne had famously coined the phrase 'Look Back in Anger'.) This, my first essay in reporting British politics after five years of the American equivalent, was perhaps a little cruel, but it went down well with my colleagues and could have helped shock the Liberal Party into pulling up its socks.

From Torquay I made my way to Scarborough where I was not all that complimentary to Labour either. 'Everybody was ready to admit that Labour was making no impact in the country but could not make up their minds whether this was the penalty for lack of the right policies or lack of the right

127

propaganda.' The existing policies, I was told by one party worker, 'leave us like salesmen without samples'. Even the raffish party chairman, Tom Driberg, made little impact, being 'not at all his usual flowing self', and even the party leader Hugh Gaitskell was 'interesting mainly in showing just how many cheers he can throw away when all the cards are stacked in his favour'. For a person used to the rough and tumble of American national conventions the casual brutality with which a handful of union leaders smashed the most earnest of opinions by the casting of millions of votes still had a capacity to shock. All this was distinctly old Labour. And so on to Blackpool where there was terrible anxiety among Conservative organisers over whether the representatives (as they were called) would misbehave during the debate on crime and punishment. 'From all sides they were being urged to take a firm grip on their emotions, lest the television cameras should catch rows of middle-aged women screaming for the cat to be used on sexual offenders.'

But the real drama occurred when the conference had closed. In those days the party leader did not risk compromising himself by being present at any of the actual debates. It was only when the conference was over that the representatives stayed on for a further day to receive the great man's speech in what was repeatedly referred to as 'a private meeting', though of course it was a meeting to which the press and television were given access. The proceedings on that day took on something of a sacerdotal nature. But Harold Macmillan's triumphant appearance in the Empire Ballroom to the sound of an organ crescendo of 'There'll Always be an England' was followed not by the opening of his speech but by the unscheduled blowing of a hunting horn. He was subsequently interrupted by half a dozen strategically seated members from the League of Empire Loyalists who, as the name suggested, thought that Macmillan was anything but loyal and took pleasure in shouting 'This is treason', rightly foreshadowing the Prime Minister's virtual abandonment of the idea of Empire. To most representatives this was like a noisy demonstration in church. They fell on the hecklers, wrestled them to the ground, beat them up and carried (or frog-marched) them from the hall.

I was doubling at the time as an adviser to Independent Television News and became involved in intense debate with its editor Geoffrey Cox and his colleagues. The question was whether clips from this scene, so distressingly counter to the traditional atmosphere of the encounter between the leader and the led, should figure in the evening's news bulletin. Commercial television, it should be remembered, was still struggling to assert its respectability in the handling of news. I passionately put the case for including the event – for what it said about the tensions inside the Conservative Party and for the very uniqueness of the episode. It was argued that we would be distracting attention away from the considered views of the Prime Minister. 'The age of deference is passing,' I said. The scene appeared, briefly but memorably, on the evening's screens. Six journalists who were there subsequently subscribed to a letter to *The Times* agreeing that 'excessive violence, amounting to brutality, was used to expel the interrupters'. The fate of Mr Walter Wolfgang, who dared to heckle Jack Straw at the Labour Party conference in 2005, was not without precedent.

Referring in *The Economist* to the three conferences together, I concluded that it was not the fault of party activists that the parties failed to offer voters clear-cut choices. If the activists could have had their way 'the voters could be presented at the following election with a choice between a party of unilateral free trade; a party of unilateral disarmament and abolition of public schools; and a party of hanging and flogging'. However, 'The business of the organisers of party conferences is to avert any such calamitous (and quite misleading) clarity.' In the case of the Labour Party this was done by marshalling the block votes of the trade unions against embarrassing policies; in the case of the Conservative Party, the actual motions on which votes were to be taken were so drafted that only by the most extreme intellectual contortions (which a few representatives were yet able to undertake) was it possible to be against them.

I had found myself thrust headfirst into the midst of the British political scene and frankly I loved it. Organisations such as the Bow Group on the right of centre and the *Universities and Left Review* on the opposite flank were both eager for me to attend their meetings as an honorary member. The first, being related to the party in power, was the more useful, the second the more exciting. Its crowded sessions were held in an extremely stuffy basement, a left-wing Fellow of All Souls College, Oxford, was in the chair, and everyone deliberately dressed down. A guest speaker was first given the floor and then thrown to the wolves, members vying with each other to show who could be rudest to him. At the first meeting I attended the guest was Dwight MacDonald, an American ex-Trotskyite who was introduced in lyrical terms by the chairman as being the dominant intellectual influence of his youth. As had appeared from his recent articles, MacDonald had, to say the least, modified his opinions over time. With supreme self-confidence he set out the way his thoughts had moved on. He was heard in silence, and then to his dismay his case and, what is more, his motives for advancing it were rent into tiny pieces. I looked forward with some anticipation to the next session when the victim was to be Anthony Crosland, whose revisionist book *The Future of Socialism* had recently appeared. But he must have been well briefed. In any competition in rudeness he was in any case unlikely to be worsted nor indeed was he. Stripped down to his red shirt he got his retaliation in first. By the end of the evening the scorners were scattered.

A week at *The Economist* started with an editorial conference on Monday morning, which always began with a statement from the business manager of the amount of advertising obtained for the forthcoming issue; this established its total number of pages. These were then divided up between the various sections, whereupon members of the editorial staff volunteered ideas, especially for the front leaders. Generally speaking the person whose ideas for the latter were accepted wrote the first draft, which was afterwards worked over by the editor. I got my fair share of front leaders, but by and large obtained more satisfaction from writing the so-called 'B' leaders (which were placed after the first two) because they were usually not interfered with and were less self-consciously editorial. The paper, when I was writing for it, was much given to the sustained metaphor, a form that set my teeth on edge, so that when I would see the published version of a first leader I had drafted I would curse the moment when I had made use of a metaphor which I would then find running like a virus through succeeding paragraphs of my prose. I also found the *de haut en bas* tone embarrassing when, in an article headed 'The Undistributed Middle', a concept which I had thought apt was preceded in the final cut by a lordly remark to the effect that, 'The New Year message from the new chairman of the Fabian Society ... would not normally be a subject for much comment.'

But these were trivial grievances. I considered it a great honour to be writing the *ex cathedra* opinions of such an admired organ and since the articles were unsigned I had in good grace to concede that an editor was entitled, especially on matters of style, to get his own way. Besides, in addition to the leaders, there were notes of the week, short pieces of three or four paragraphs on particular issues, to be penned, usually with relish, as well as a choice of books to review from those spread out on the editorial table for our selection. As the political correspondent I was frequently present at luncheons in the Honky-Tonk, the previously mentioned editorial dining room. The guests were not always conventional politicians. The most memorable of them in my time was Paul Robeson, famous for 'Ol' Man River' and other songs of the South but who had rendered himself virtually unemployable in the United States by virtue of his open and persistent support of the Soviet Union. Robeson had just come back from a tour of Eastern Europe and talked to us a little of his impressions of life on the other side of the Curtain but primarily about the predicament of members of his race. He had an extraordinarily melodious speaking voice in which he moved effortlessly from speech into marvellous song. Regardless of our view of his political premises he held us spellbound.

The Economist's political standpoint had been defined by the former editor Geoffrey Crowther as being that of the 'extreme centre', by which he meant that because one was non-Tory and non-Labour this did not have to imply a wishy-washy amalgam of right and left, but could be a radical alternative to both. This was a cause which as a political journalist I was perfectly happy to embrace. At Westminster, where I spent the bulk of my time, often arriving there from my Kensington flat by river bus, I encountered the strange rules of the self-governing parliamentary lobby. *The Economist* was reckoned by most people as being one of the leading journals in the country and it was true that its political correspondent was entitled to use the chamber known as the Members' Lobby. But, because we were a weekly, we did not qualify for membership of the lobby in the full sense of that term, that shadowy body of parliamentary journalists whose attendance at regular off-the-record briefings promoted most unsourced political stories.

When Hugh Gaitskell, the leader of the Labour opposition, heard of this he offered me a weekly one-to-one interview, during which he sometimes came out with unguarded remarks such as, 'Of course you realise that Ian Mikardo [one of the brightest of his parliamentary colleagues] is a secret member of the Communist Party.' Edward Heath, the Tory Chief Whip, followed suit and arranged for me to see Rab Butler, the Leader of the House, once a month. I liked both Gaitskell and Heath and valued my regular dates with them, but, looking back over the cuttings, I think I succeeded in preserving my professional detachment from both. I had a number of regular contacts in both parties. Enoch Powell, a man with whom I might be thought to have little in common personally, was one of the most valuable of these. Arriving at one of my parties, he announced, 'You may take it as a compliment to yourself when I say that there are not many people whose invitation I would accept in the foreknowledge that few of those present would be likely to be congenial to me.' Harold Wilson was likewise a valuable source. I remember vaguely an evening I spent with him and some lobbyists in a boat on the Thames, when he confessed that his wife's dislike of politics was one of the reasons he was not considered sociable – 'like Hugh Gaitskell' being the unspoken thought.

One article that I particularly enjoyed writing was entitled 'Set the People Free'. It was meant as a contribution to what later became known as the permissive society. I started with an endorsement of the independent candidacy for the Harrow East by-election of Sir A.P. Herbert, who had sat in the House for a university seat until these had been abolished and had made a career of challenging old-fashioned fustiness in an entertaining way. To finance his campaign he had published and put on sale a personal manifesto, which example should, I suggested, be a spur to other nonconformists. 'Are we living in an adult society or are we not?' I asked. I offered seven items for my personal manifesto: abolition of Lord's Day Observance laws, abandonment of the elaborate restrictions on pub licensing, repeal of the Labouchère amendment criminalising homosexuality among consenting adults, licensing of betting shops in place of the outlawing of off-course bets by cash, abolition of the Lord Chamberlain's control over the theatre, drastic liberalisation of immigration laws and legalisation of abortion at the doctor's discretion. Almost all of these proposals, excepting the item about immigration, have now been accepted, indicating how repressed a society it was to which I had returned. This piece appearing in a 'respectable' paper was intended as a wake-up call to people who might have thought they were living in an ideally free society. We received quite a large correspondence, most writers agreeing with six of the seven points but some dissenting strongly over abortion. I am surprised in retrospect that I had not said anything about divorce.

When in 1959 Parliament went into summer recess *The Economist* decided that there was not enough work for its political correspondent to do in England. So I was sent to Ireland. This was my first visit, north and south, to an island with which I was to become very familiar. My first date was with William Craig, the North's Minister for Home Affairs, who displayed his colour-coded street map of Belfast distinguishing the Protestant areas from the Catholic, the Shankill Road from the Falls Road. This was a vital key to the granting or withholding of permission for the route of street marches which were and are still an annual feature in the Ulster calendar. There was then a low-intensity war being fought by Republican bands across the border, which explained the spiking of many country roads crossing over to Northern Ireland from the Republic, to the great inconvenience of local inhabitants on either side. I went into the press gallery of Stormont, the triumphalist seat of the Unionist-dominated Northern Ireland Parliament, and listened to Question Time. One question which stuck in my memory was from a Nationalist member who wanted to know why the one half-time employment officer at Newry, a largely Catholic town with massive unemployment, was being withdrawn. The Minister replied that the government considered that it was a mistake to give the false impression that there was any demand for employment in Newry.

After inspecting Londonderry's walls and having noted with pleasure that one of the listed Protestant apprentices who shut the city's gates to the officers of James II was named James Stewart, I drove out into the Fermanagh country-side to see the Nationalist MP Cahir Healy, a charming, whimsical man who had been interned by the British during the Second World War. His whole career since the partition of Ireland, and in particular since his first election to Stormont in 1925, had been a dilemma. Either he attended the Belfast Parliament and did his best for his constituents or he abstained and thus highlighted his rejection of the whole idea of partition. He was a man who was obviously wracked by this problem and in the event pursued the two courses alternately. His gentle voice outlined the predicament of the Roman Catholic minority (a minority which considered itself part of the majority in the only unit – the island of Ireland – that it considered legitimate).

Having worked through a long list of Northern contacts I went on to Dublin, a city spoken of by many Northern Unionists in similar terms to those which many Englishmen at the time used of Moscow or as in the twenty-first century George W. Bush would use of the 'axis of evil'. I had only two introductions, one to Conor Cruise O'Brien, the brilliant polymath who had just scored high critical acclaim, including a lead article in the TLS, for his book *Parnell and His Party*, and James Meenan, a leading economist of University College, Dublin, who was our Irish correspondent. The reception accorded in Britain to O'Brien's book, while thoroughly deserved, carried with it an implication rather patronising to Irish historiography that at long last Ireland had managed to produce one historian who was capable of objectivity. It was a surprise to me to find that he was not in academic life but a member of the Irish Foreign Service. Not only that but at the time that I first met him he was serving as Head of Information at the Department of External Affairs and was running an Irish news agency set up to make sure that Ireland's bundle of grievances against Britain was well publicised in the world. My memory of 1959 thus carries with it a measure of irony in that Conor's views have in the years since travelled exceptionally far towards and even beyond the Unionist camp. Yet it was as an anti-partition propagandist that this remarkable man first presented himself to me as my host at one of the best of Dublin restaurants, where he tactfully abstained from offloading any anti-partition propaganda. He introduced me to his Minister, Proinsias Mac Aogháin, otherwise known as Frank Aiken, a former Chief of Staff of the IRA. Since Mr Aiken preferred to conduct as much as possible of the Republic's foreign policy in the First National Language, namely Irish, which was spoken by few except in the west, my host stood high in his favour, being fluent in that language, as he was in French and later became in Russian.

My second contact, James Meenan, wrote regularly for us from Ireland though, given his professional background, mainly on economic topics. He was an admirable tutor and guide during my visit, putting me up in the exclusive St Stephen's Green Club and introducing me to a wide circle of friends. One day we had lunch together in the club. The other tables were filled with prosperous-looking businessmen and professionals doing justice to the ample fare. Meenan surveyed the scene. 'That chap over there killed three people in the Troubles,' he said calmly. His eyes swivelled round to lock on to a rather overweight individual in a corner. 'He was responsible for five deaths, and that fellow over there accounted for another two.' By the time he had finished he had taken in most of the company. I grasped in a very direct way what it meant to live with a cult of the gun.

I had another glimpse of Ireland being dominated by history when I was brought into the press gallery of Leinster House, the seat of the Dáil. The competing parties were the Fianna Fáil in government and the Fine Gael in opposition. In one of my Irish reports for *The Economist* I cited an eminent authority on Irish politics for the view that the only difference between them was that leaders of Fianna Fáil turned up at the funeral of Henry Harrison, the last surviving member of Parnell's entourage, and the leaders of Fine Gael did not, though I went on, 'As with most Irish funerals there was more to this than met the eye. Parnell, a Protestant, died under the ban of the Catholic Church, having been an adulterer. Only Fianna Fáil felt it could afford to put his services to Irish nationalism first.' But it was the exchanges across the floor of the Dáil that revealed how much the parties were divided by history: Fine Gael standing for Michael Collins's acceptance of the Anglo-Irish Treaty of 1921 and Fianna Fáil for its rejection. I devoted a column in the *New York Post* to my thesis that Irish politics could only effectively be reported in the pages of *Le Monde*, since this was the only paper that regularly carried footnotes. Otherwise what was the reader to make of the taunt by one politician to his opponent, 'What did your family do with the Russian crown jewels?' Nor was this in any way untypical of the surreal exchanges that I witnessed.

One of my *Economist* reports from Dublin began, 'Mr Seán Lemass, the Taoiseach (Prime Minister), is described as "a realist" so often that one might suppose he was the sole exemplar of an otherwise extinct species.' But by the end of the article I was asserting as my most important discovery that, 'The absence of any serious expectation that the border can be abolished is indeed one of the most remarkable features of the Republic's present mood.' There was even, I found, an occasional article, as in the August issue of *Hibernia*, suggesting that the Catholic minority in the North should take a full and loyal part in its public life.

Despite the many attractive features I found during this first visit to the Republic, I also found a preoccupation with failure which is worth recording because it provides a benchmark against which to measure the radically reverse mood nearly half a century later. 'The word "failure",' I wrote then, 'is ubiquitous; failure to stem emigration, failure in industry, failure in agriculture, failure in education, the failure of Mr Patrick Kavanagh, said to be the best conversationalist in Ireland and therefore in the world, to find anyone worth talking to, failure to make the Irish language universal.'

Since I had been back from America I had been appearing quite frequently on the *Tonight* programme. News of the great success of what had originally been conceived as a mere device for filling up the Kiddies' Truce, the one hour of silence by which the BBC had hitherto undertaken to help mothers tuck their children into bed but which they had been forced to abandon by commercial competition, had reached me in Washington. Against (nearly) all expectations this *soufflé* of a nightly programme devised by Donald Baverstock and Alasdair Milne had risen to the point that it was the most talked-about show on television. Up-to-the-minute satirical songs, often written by my old colleague Bernard Levin, would be followed by a succession of items, some serious, others not so serious, but all containing a certain thread of individual quirkiness. Cliff Michelmore, everybody's favourite uncle, introduced the show with an air of beautifully relaxed command and Alan Whicker toured the world with his odd adventures. *Tonight* covered foreign items as well as domestic. In those days before transatlantic links I was often employed in doing a studio piece on some turn of the American scene.

I also appeared on radio programmes such as the *Brains Trust* and on the (one) commercial television channel. Shortly before the date of the 1959 general election was announced, President Eisenhower came over to Britain and we were told that he and the British Prime Minister, Harold Macmillan, were to be televised live just having a friendly chat as two old world-war comrades in the drawing room of 10 Downing Street. This was to be transmitted simultaneously on both channels. No one who wished to remain a viewer at that hour was to be allowed to escape it. Sidney Bernstein, the head of Granada Television, who was responsible for transmission on the commercial channel, decided that he was going to showcase the two statesmen with a difference. The moment that they had finished speaking his channel should contain critical analysis of what had been said. An American broadcaster was to be chairman and Marquis Childs of the *Louisville Post-Despatch* and I were to be the discussants.

We lined up in the studio to watch the two great men go through their

friendship routines. At the very last moment one of Bernstein's minions
signalled to me furiously from the wings with a message: 'Mr Bernstein wishes
that you should not on any account say that this amounts to the opening of the
general election campaign.' That had been precisely what I had intended to say.
I smiled inwardly as I reflected that while Bernstein was a courageous inno-
vator there were limits to what even he was prepared to risk, but I promised
obedience. The two principals came to an end, whereupon the two Americans
who spoke first showed themselves to be immensely responsible and respectful of their President when overseas and of his host. I decided to be different
and spelled out one by one the roster of Macmillan's attempts to slip into the
conversation requests for actions by the United States, showing that, polite
and cordial as Ike had been, in not one of these instances had he given away a
thing. Maurice Richardson, the television critic of the *Observer*, after applauding ITV for introducing some commentary, went on, 'Unfortunately, nobody
had anything to say except Keith Kyle, the new younger pundit who seems
much at ease in a TV studio.' Peter Forster of *The Spectator* evidently thought
that I was too much at my ease there. 'Mr Kyle has been bobbing up all over the
place lately,' he wrote, '*Press Conference*, *Brains Trust*, post-Ike comment, etc;
a young journalist with quite Byronic arrogance in the curl of his lip and a sharp,
unfaltering, enviably self-assured line of attack. A little of Mr Kyle and he will
go a long way.'

Harold Macmillan duly called an election, which some people thought
would afford an opportunity for a popular verdict on the humiliation of Britain
over Suez and the more recent scandal of the mistreatment to the point of death
of Mau Mau detainees at Hola in Kenya which had been memorably denounced
in the Commons by Enoch Powell. I toured the constituencies making reports
of the local campaigns. Some of the seats visited were being contested by my
friends. Dick Taverne was the Labour candidate for Putney. 'Really Bright
Young People are Joining the Labour Party' was the slogan that I found outside
his headquarters. 'Since Mr Taverne looks younger than his thirty years and
has a First in Greats, he presumably fits the bill,' I wrote, 'although it is a little
disconcerting to find that the sole policy item that is then picked out for display
is the undertaking to do away with the nominal fee for prescriptions at the
chemists.' When making enquires about Suez and Hola, I found general agreement that the voter was not much interested in foreign or colonial affairs or in
anything that did not affect his pocket. Journalism prevailing over friendship I
predicted that this time Taverne would not make it, nor did he.

In Hereford Robin Day was the Liberal candidate. He had already made
a name for himself among those who watched the new commercial televi-

sion. Alone among the three original newscasters of Independent Television News – Chris Chataway and Ludovic Kennedy were the others – in not being already well known, he had forged an individual path for himself as a fearless and well-briefed interviewer. His interview with President Nasser shortly after Suez was particularly distinguished. Hereford was at one time a Liberal seat, held by a very young Frank Owen, by now editor of the *Daily Mail*, and had very nearly been won back by him in a recent by-election. Owen was not prepared to try again and, since Robin had said to me that he would never forgive himself if he had not had at least one shot at getting into the House and since, despite my urging, he had insisted that he would only do so as a Liberal, I asked Jo Grimond, then the party leader, whether his candidacy for Hereford would be welcome. Grimond leaped at the idea and arrangements were speedily made for Robin to be nominated. This deprived him of his job of newscaster but fortunately *The News Chronicle* was still alive (just) and his income was assured by his being taken on as a columnist.

When I first arrived in Hereford I joined a press group which made a tour of the outlying villages that were also part of the division. They were very remote, both geographically and in spirit. One village we came to appeared to be inhabited exclusively by village idiots until eventually we found someone who could respond. Asked about the closing of rural primary schools which was a pressing local issue, this cheerful cynic replied, 'We haven't had a birth in the village for 14 years, we seem to have lost the art.' In the evening with Robin at his hotel he talked frankly of his experiences with local Liberals over the three months of his prospective candidacy. They were mainly very old – his chairman was an octogenarian – and very right-wing and far from the type of progressive party that Grimond was trying to build. Since Frank Owen's habit of being surrounded by adoring young women when on campaign had been so flatly disapproved of by the puritan element, Robin, still a bachelor, warned girlfriends not to come. Promptly there had sprung up rumours that it was very odd – wasn't it? – that the candidate appeared to enjoy only male company.

Robin urged me to stay long enough to attend the Saturday night hustings where the candidates traditionally spoke in turn before a crowd of several hundred from the back of a lorry in front of an immaculately restored Jacobean house in High Town, Hereford's centre. The Tory incumbent, Gibson Watt, spoke first, followed by Labour. By the time a bouncy, duffle-coated Robin started to lash into everybody in authority, to the huge delight of the mob, the drinkers were pouring out of the pubs. The Liberal candidate was in good voice and candle-end politics were to the fore. It was true there was one glancing reference to the Prime Minister as 'an Edwardian mountebank', which produced repeated shouts of 'That's libel! That's libel!' Finally the ex-lawyer had had enough of this and riposted with, 'It's not libel, you fool. It's slander.' But the biggest cheer was for a sally that went much nearer home. The Tory agent was called Alcock and the pro-Tory editor of the *Hereford Times*, which had accused Liberals of wanting to interfere with farm subsidies, was called Peacock. Hence Robin Day's last word to the people of Hereford was the formula, 'Alcock plus Peacock equals Poppycock'. At 11.30 drunken steel erectors stormed the Liberal lorry, shouting, 'What about the trade unions?' and a Tory heckler broke the Liberal mike.

The next day I had intended to leave but received a husky plea from Robin – after the previous night's shenanigans he had lost his voice – would I fulfil his speaking commitments in the villages the next day? Friendship prevailed. Fortunately the rest of the press had decamped, so that my desertion of the journalist's flag was not remarked on. I trailed around these beautiful and beautifully remote villages, not repeating Robin's demotic language but retailing as much of the Liberal message as I could remember – and thereby, as I was subsequently told, speaking above the heads of the audience. I was driven by the party agent, whom I had expected to take care of the timetable, but whom I soon discovered to be exclaiming after each meeting, 'Time for a wet!'

I went on to North Devon, where Jeremy Thorpe, who had made an unsuccessful run against the Tory incumbent in 1955, was seeking to reverse that result. Accompanied by his formidable, monocled mother, he was reaping rewards from his efforts to build up a powerful American-style organisation. 'This Time Jeremy' buttons were in massive circulation, there was a blown-up photograph of the candidate outside the Barnstaple Liberal Club and on hoardings through the constituency, and there were huge posters captioned 'Jeremy A Thorpe for the Future'. One literal-minded constituent objected to me that 'A' was not the candidate's middle initial. The time spent during the last four years in the constituency had perfected the Devonian accent into which the candidate slid for his dialect stories, like the one about the sabbatarian squire who would not permit the sale of Sunday newspapers within the village that he owned. Impeccably turned out, with just a hint of the dandy, Jeremy made a habit of literally leaping over fences to press his assault on Conservative dominance.

On paper Jeremy totted up for me the various factors that would fill up the 5,226 gap that separated him from a different Tory last time. The total fell 200 votes short. He then noted, with a flourish, that the psephologist David Butler had reckoned that the most that a candidate's personality could contribute would be 500 votes. 'I give them to myself,' he concluded, 'and therefore I predict a majority of 300.' His majority turned out to be 362.

My final visit of friendship was to a neighbouring constituency in Devon, Torrington, for which Mark Bonham Carter had been returned in a by-election in 1958. Mark was Lady Violet's son and a man of considerable substance in his own right. His mother had particularly asked that I should speak for him and I had agreed to do so on the basis of being a non-party political journalist who was willing to appraise Mark's performance at Westminster. I was all the more keen to do this in that he had played a prominent part in expounding the case for Britain joining the European Economic Community. I recalled the scene in the House of Commons during a debate on Europe when speaker after speaker was called first from government, then from opposition benches, each vying with the other in producing arguments for Britain staying out of the Community. Mark, not being a privy councillor, was not called until late in the evening when at long last the positive case for joining was for the first time, and to good effect, expounded by him.

Lady Violet and I both spoke at a big meeting in Barnstaple. Once again I thrilled at her superb delivery and the force of oratory that had first been deployed in the interest of her father in the famous Paisley by-election of 1921 – although, looking at the audience, I was bound to wonder how much of what she said (not to mention her grand manner) was connecting with its interests and aspirations. The young David Owen, the future Foreign Secretary and SDP leader, was canvassing for the Labour candidate in the constituency and in later years I used to reflect as to whether his lifelong disregard for Liberals had not partially stemmed from the noble vowel sounds that this great lady had distributed over the Devonshire countryside. Mark had told me what his target vote was and that, if he achieved it, it was improbable that there was room for a reserve army of Tories who had not voted in the by-election. The Tory agent told me that he knew exactly who his previous abstainers were and was confident that he would be able to produce them. He did and could. Mark reached his target but the Tories reached theirs and won.

In the 1959 election television was for the first time a major factor. Labour in particular made good use of the expertise of Tony Benn and the on-screen experience of Christopher Mayhew and Woodrow Wyatt to produce professionally slick election programmes that appeared to score heavily over the stiffer performance of the Conservatives. On the night of the result I was among the political correspondents who were corralled in the BBC studios to add our thoughts to the running commentary which was being provided by Richard Dimbleby and David Butler. In charge of us was Grace Wyndham

Goldie, a colourful BBC character who was known as 'the woman of iron whim'. Once it was apparent that the Tories were going to win by a convincing majority I began speculating privately to some of my colleagues about what cabinet changes Macmillan would effect. 'Go into the studio! Say on screen what you just said!' cried an excited Grace. When I had done so, Grace was dancing with joy: one more taboo about discussing politics on screen had been broken. One other 'green room' recollection remains of the scene of Macmillan's triumph. It is of a Young Conservative, with tightly laced leggings, confiding to me in the early hours of the morning that he was ashamed that his party had had an endorsement that it did not deserve after Suez and Hola.

With some exceptions in the West Country, it was already apparent that the television screen had taken over from the mass meeting as the main setting for political action. I wrote about this when covering a by-election in the Yorkshire division of Brighouse a few months later. Remarking how the appearance of microphone and cameras turned normally dour Yorkshiremen into raging partisans I observed that,

> To judge from the stormy broadcast meeting in Brighouse, which was utterly unlike any other meeting during the campaign, we shall soon become a nation of apathetic watchers of television shows portraying constituency after constituency as seething with political conflict and interest.

I was invited to join the British participants in the series of annual exchanges with German equivalents at Königswinter, an elegant resort on the Rhine. Dame Lilo Milchshack (as she later became) was the inspired impresario of this very successful effort to acquaint leading and potentially leading politicians and opinion formers with each other. On this occasion I formed particular friendships with two men from Hamburg, Theo Sommer, future editor and strategic thinker, and Helmut Schmidt, who was to become Chancellor. Opportunities to converse with fellow British delegates were also valuable. Travelling out with Lady Violet I asked her why in his peacetime premiership Winston Churchill had not done more to bring Britain into Europe. 'Alas,' she replied, 'he no longer had the strength to draw his own sword.' On the way out, with many VIPs aboard, the plane was surrounded by a dense fog; we circuited several airports and fuel was running low. 'There will be chaos in the obituary departments,' was Lady Violet's calm comment.

After the end of the exchanges at Königswinter some of us, including John Midgley, *The Economist*'s foreign editor, and myself were flown on to Berlin. It was before the days of the Wall, and John, who had previously been the Bonn correspondent of *The Times*, had arranged for the two of us to be received by the East German authorities. Accordingly we crossed the line into Communist territory, where, to my astonishment, I saw German guards performing the goose step, which I had hitherto associated exclusively with the Hitler regime. We were received by several members of the East German 'cabinet'. John, who was a fluent German speaker, conducted most of the conversation in that language, the youthful head of the Western Europe desk keeping me abreast by whispering in my ear. But I had the opportunity to put a blunt question to the Communist leaders about the large numbers of East German workers who were migrating to the West. Did not this represent a vote of no-confidence in the Communist regime? Quick came a slick response: these movements were due to very short-sighted calculations. The West German boom would inevitably be succeeded by a bust and then we should see Germans pouring back the other way. I later thought of that reply when the building of the Wall amounted to a confession of total defeat for this thesis.

There was at that time some reason for alarm in the uncomfortable situation of mutual deterrence, even if, like me, you thought it highly improbable that the Soviet forces would attempt to overrun Western Europe as long as the Americans remained involved. I once produced a scandalised reaction from a NATO officer by defining the number of British, French and German troops required as being simply the minimum needed to ensure that the Americans stayed. This was only indirectly if at all related to the numbers deployed on the other side. London was a scene of heated meetings in the late 1950s to argue about the morality and practicality of a nuclear strategy and I was involved more often as a reporter but sometimes as a participant. I was on the stage of the Central Hall, Westminster, in October 1958, for example, as a member of a group of questioners including Ludovic Kennedy who were there to interrogate three scientists, including the American Nobel laureate Dr Linus Pauling, about the stark realities of nuclear war and how best to avoid them. Pauling had been a leading campaigner against nuclear tests and in favour of nuclear disarmament, all of which had caused him trouble on entry with the British immigration service. The main pressure in Britain, led by Bertrand Russell, was in favour of our taking the lead in renouncing the bomb, on the assumption that America and Russia would then be forced by public opinion to follow suit. When it came to my turn, I asked Pauling whether he thought that unilateral action by Britain would have any effect. Anxious though he undoubtedly was to help the organisers of the meeting, Pauling, being an honest man, said that it would not.

In the new Parliament elected in October 1959 the first new member that I got to know was Margaret Thatcher. This was not owing to some preternatural foresight but because I had decided to write a series of 'B leaders' in *The Economist* about the processes of Westminster, and Mrs Thatcher had had the great good fortune immediately on her election to draw a winning ticket in the sweep to decide who should have priority in sponsoring a private member's bill. Her bill was to give the press access to meetings of local government committees and it clearly had the general support of the government. I saw her frequently during the next few weeks when she answered my questions, briskly and, so far as I could tell, candidly, about the influences and pressures that were being brought to bear on her. I came to admire her clarity and resolution and said at the time that she was obviously of cabinet material. Foresight did not carry me further than that.

Many post-election leading articles concerned the Labour Party, defeated as it had been for the third time in succession. There was no immediate threat to Hugh Gaitskell as leader (though Harold Wilson did challenge him the following year) but he himself was now of a mood to challenge the party over its greatest ideological symbol, Clause Four of the party's constitution which committed it to the common ownership of the means of production, distribution and exchange. It was this commitment which many party members passionately felt stamped them as socialists, with a cause that placed them above the trifling party politics of who's in and who's out. The trouble was, Gaitskell thought correctly, this very fact denied them the support of the full potential anti-Conservative vote and might well condemn them to permanent opposition. He therefore attempted at the end of November 1959 to pull off what it took Tony Blair 36 years later to achieve: the repeal of Clause Four.

The term 'Frognal Set' had entered political parlance because of the congenial company which Hugh Gaitskell was in the habit of inviting round to his house in Frognal Gardens in Hampstead. Roy Jenkins, Tony Crosland and Douglas Jay were at the heart of that company, but it could also include what might be called 'country members', of which I was for a time one. Following the election defeat, there was much rather unstructured conversation about the consequences for the Labour Party in which I took a part, though by no means a leading one. I was not, however, totally silent as was Charles Forte, the food retailer and hotelier, whom I had to presume was present as a token capitalist whose presence was a reassurance to Gaitskell that he could reach out that far.

A Labour Party conference was called for the end of November 1959 in the Opera House in Blackpool. A couple of days beforehand Gaitskell showed me a draft of his speech, making a point of apologising (quite unnecessarily) for having 'stolen' some of my ideas. This draft did not include the explicit proposal to drop Clause Four, though, as I remember, it said many things that were scarcely compatible with keeping it. On this occasion I drove up to Blackpool with the Italian count who was our labour correspondent. As we approached the black country I noticed that the tell-tale indication of our progress was that the lightning conductors on the churches were beginning to stand out, like hearing aids, from the increasingly dark patina of the steeples.

'For Mr Gaitskell,' I wrote, 'last weekend's Labour conference started very badly indeed,' with a stirring left-wing speech by the party chairman, Barbara Castle, quite evidently cast so as to put the leader on the spot. Hugh, I thought, was being too bleakly analytic in his preliminary dissection of the election result. But it was a deliberate choice to eschew all crowd-pleasing effects before coming down to the basic reforms that he considered indispensable for the health of the party, most especially, in a paragraph Gaitskell had inserted in a later draft than the one I had seen, the sacrifice of Clause Four. One speaker alone – Dick Taverne – spoke up for his leader and spoke as well of the necessity of ending class warfare within the party, 'Otherwise, as Mr Gaitskell sat on the platform silently taking his medicine, an extraordinary parade of affronted fundamentalists passed through the rostrum to ladle it out.' But next day was different. It was, I judged, the infelicities of a professional dramatist that marked the dramatic turn of the tide. Mr Benn Levy, the bearded playwright who looked like the prophet Moses, had every right to assume from the frantic applause for Mr (Michael) Foot's Marat-like denunciations of Mr Gaitskell (pointed finger and all) that the delegates wanted the leader out of the party. So Mr Levy said so; and it immediately became apparent that most people thought this was going a bit too far. This was the party that, with my eyes firmly open, I was indeed about to join.

CHAPTER 12

New York and Africa

Inow had to make two major decisions. *The Economist* told me in the spring of 1960 that, while my job as political and parliamentary correspondent remained perfectly safe for as long as I wanted it, I should let them know now if I still wished at the end of two years to be 'on my travels'. Secondly, I needed to decide about membership of a political party if it was still my intention to try for a career in politics. In reality this decision was about joining or not joining the Labour Party. The two questions were linked because I was in my 35th year and if I was really proposing to spend another period out of the country I ought to commit myself politically before I left or forfeit the parliamentary option. The temptation to stay in Britain was considerable. My combined income from *The Economist*, the *New York Post* and television was by my rather modest standards comfortable enough. For the first time in my life I had been able to afford the occasional luxury while two successive girlfriends had provided enjoyable company. The work was challenging, varied and full of interest. But I told myself that I was running the risk of settling into a groove, that I was still a bachelor with no responsibilities, still relatively young, and still open to try my luck in some other part of the world. Increasingly I began to feel that that part should be Africa and that I should go there in time to witness the process of decolonisation.

As to politics I found myself repeatedly challenged by friends and fellow journalists as to why I should want to give up the relatively influential and respected position that I was alleged by them to enjoy for the sake of the compromises, frustrations, dishonesties and uncertainties of political life. The answer, pompous but true, arose from the nagging feeling that, as my life had been spared in the war, I ought to be prepared to help make that system work for which I had been ready to fight and, if required, to die. I thought I had some at least of the qualities needed, that I was mentally resilient and morally tough enough to cope with the inevitable difficulties and disappointments involved. Being perpetually a commentator on the sidelines, though agreeable in itself, did not strike me as being sufficient. The tough problem that confronted me here and now was that posed by the proclaimed ideology of the Labour Party. Yet I had now reached the point at which failure to decide the question of membership would, in my estimation, amount to a serious moral failing. That I was a man of the left (or centre-left as I would now say) I did not doubt. I therefore joined the Labour Party. I do not remember when I told Hugh Gaitskell of this decision. I learned later that he had boasted a little that he had brought it about. What I did not do, so long as I was working for *The Economist*, was make a parade of it.

I can see, looking back more than 40 years, that the front leader entitled 'The Undistributed Middle' with which I opened the issue of 16 January 1960 must have been written with especially deep feeling. The undistributed middle of British politics was therein defined as 'that minority of liberally minded, robustly idealistic and not strongly partisan voters' against whom some members of the Labour Party wanted to 'raise an electric wire fence and a "keep out" sign to debar all who would not assume socialist stigmata, apparently chosen deliberately for their merit in frightening spiritual Liberals and Bow Groupers away'. This, I concluded, 'is an extraordinary direction in which to point a political party that is seriously seeking to convert enough marginal voters to replace the present government only four years from now.' Reading that again during Tony Blair's premiership I cannot help recalling that, when the short-lived Social Democratic Party came to be formed with policies resembling those which Blair was subsequently to make his own, I was to say that 'I have been an SDP member all my life'.

As 1959 moved into 1960 my interest in Africa mounted. In January a conference assembled in London to resolve the contradictions surrounding the British Colony and Protectorate of Kenya. I was commissioned by ITN to interview Tom Mboya, the brilliant young man who was being treated as if he were (though in fact he was not) the leader of the Kenya Africans. This was really my first close encounter with problems which were soon to engage me completely. Shortly afterwards, again thanks to Geoffrey Cox, I made my first trip to Africa. He had started a news feature programme called *Roving Report* and he wanted me to make one such report from Tunis, where the All-Africa People's Conference was to hold its second assembly at the end of January. *The Economist* was glad enough for me to go in return for a couple of articles.

The predominant cultural influence in Tunis was unquestionably French. Formulations in speeches and resolutions betrayed the Cartesian mindset. Two propositions stood out: *le néo-colonialisme*, under which the imperial powers, having left by the front door, would sneak in again by the back, and *la balkani-*

sation whereby the same satanic forces would foster secessions and internal conflicts. After much of this, Africans from English-speaking colonies such as Chief Enahoro from Nigeria represented a startling contrast with their pragmatic analyses of the problems ahead. The Ghanaians, though they spoke in English, seemed more aligned with the French since Kwame Nkrumah had propounded his own (sub-Hegelian) ideology called Consciencism whose published bible was largely couched in the algebra of mathematical logic. The saddest aspect of the debates was to listen to the South African delegates, because they seemed the most politically mature and the most 'ready' for self-government of those Africans present when one knew they would be the last to get it.

On 27 January, right in the middle of the Tunis conference, sensational news arrived from Brussels, where a conference was being held on the future of the Belgian Congo. The Belgian government had just announced that this enormous colony, which lacked any preparation whatsoever for self-government, was to be independent in six months. It seemed to the assembled Africans as if a miracle had happened: if the Congo could in one leap be free, could the rest of Africa be far behind? There was a spirit of joy and elation at what seemed the absoluteness of the achievement and a mood therefore to reject any halfway house such as was being negotiated at Lancaster House over Kenya, when nothing was being said about ultimate independence or the freedom and future of Jomo Kenyatta. Because Tunisia was a frontline state in the ongoing war between the Algerians and France I was able to meet a number of the leading figures in the Algerian National Liberation Front, the FLN. I did not find them a particularly united band and was able to supply some detail about the internal intrigues in *The Economist*'s *Foreign Report*, an affiliated publication which was sent to special subscribers.

I was able to see a little of Tunisia while I was there, being taken by Cecil Hourani, of my Oxford college, to Sidi Bou Said, the Hampstead or Greenwich Village of the state where he and his Iraqi wife had a little jewel of a house adjacent to the Mediterranean Sea. Cecil, a Lebanese who was President Bourguiba's personal adviser, was shortly moving into a restored fort and tried hard to persuade me to rent or buy the house from him, eloquently arguing the case for basing a freelance career on Tunis as the bridge (or did he say gateway?) between Europe and Africa. I had been inoculated by A.J.P. Taylor against the fallacy of bridges and gateways and could in any case not afford such a commitment. But it was a beautiful house and, for the first time in my life, I found myself half wishing I were well enough off to undertake such an investment.

From then on I followed the developments on the African scene as closely as I could, poring over the daily bulletins of the BBC Monitoring Service's section on Africa. *The Economist* sent me to cover the press conference organised by Associated Rediffusion TV for the arrival in London of Dr Hastings Kamuzu Banda, the Nyasaland nationalist leader newly released from prison. Rediffusion was the first commercial company to receive a licence to transmit in the London area and Jeremy Thorpe who was working for it had got a scoop. Thanks to his friendship with Dingle Foot, the lawyer who had represented Dr Banda while he had been locked up in Nyasaland (as Malawi was then called), Jeremy had been promised the first interview with the newly released man and had been able to join at Rome the plane bringing him to London. Banda had in fact lived most of his adult life in Britain, where he had had a successful practice as a physician and had only returned to his native land at the urgent request of young nationalists who had wanted a mature hero to front their campaign. They had not as yet entirely grasped the nature of this particular hero. The White Paper explaining the disturbances that had brought this obscure colony into the headlines had at one point reproduced the correspondence between one of the young nationalists and the legendary but as yet unknown figure of the doctor. In respectful language it had been explained to him that African custom, in contrast with those European habits with which understandably he would be more in tune, required a supreme chief to be boosted to high heaven. Dr Banda would have to put behind him the English-type reserve that he would no doubt have acquired. Never did a letter turn out to be more ironic since 'the great Kamuzu', as the little doctor soon chose to be called, proved in the event to have the biggest ego in the whole continent. However, when he turned up with Jeremy as his companion he was on his best behaviour, with countless benisons rained on 'that great Christian gentleman', Iain Macleod, the new Colonial Secretary who had released him.

The trouble with Nyasaland was that its case was not anything like so simple as that of a small black colony wanting independence. With a great expenditure of effort, first a Labour government and then a Conservative one had solemnly gone about making life difficult for themselves by constructing a Central African Federation that tied Nyasaland in with the two settler-ruled Rhodesias (present-day Zambia and Zimbabwe). I had raged against this doomed concept in an English-Speaking Union debate in 1951, and Lord Stansgate, Tony Benn's father, had accurately foretold the luckless project's fate in the House of Lords. The condescending phrase that 'hindsight is a wonderful thing' is nowadays used far too glibly. A bit of foresight would sometimes not come amiss.

On this occasion the little doctor kept himself well under control. There were no hysterical screams of 'I will smash their stupid Federation!' that closer acquaintance was to make only too familiar. Now he was the hard-done-by moderate, with, however, an inflexible resolve to sever the constitutional links with the Rhodesias. In retrospect the occasion has acquired for me a quite special resonance. Rediffusion, having at first grasped their exclusive interviewee to their bosom, had begun to have qualms about denying him to the rest of Fleet Street. So the press were invited to the studio, Jeremy Thorpe was awarded the first ten minutes and then the questioning was handed over to the rest of us. At the last minute the producers panicked because enough of the press had not turned up and production staff were shovelled in to fill up the gaps. One rather special young lady positioned herself behind me. We did not speak but when I rose to put my question she duly appeared in the frame. Her name was Susan Harpur. Two years later a sharp-eyed colleague of hers sent us a still in honour of our engagement.

Domestic politics and fresh African interests had not eliminated my interest in American affairs. While I was in London I used frequently to handle American items on the BBC *Tonight* programme, and *The Economist* from time to time called on me to help with the American Survey. I resolved that, although my next long-term destination was to be Africa, I should first make a return visit to the United States. I had the offer of a lecture tour, the BBC *Tonight* programme wanted me to cover the Democratic nominating convention and I had a fancy to become an accredited UN correspondent in New York. With all these purposes in mind I wound up my two years as political correspondent with *The Economist* and set forth in a new capacity as a freelance. Remembering, however, how important it was to have some form of accreditation I signed up with a small weekly called *Time & Tide* and thus for the next few months – and probably for the only time in its life – this organ boasted an official correspondent at the UN.

I had never previously attended sessions of the UN Security Council and listened through earphones to the downbeat accents of the interpreters, which have on the listener a perversely hypnotic effect. Journalists were allowed to mingle with delegates in one of the main lounges of this great slab of a building whose shape has so imposed itself as a symbolic presence through decades of international crises; and I would find myself sinking into comfortable armchairs to exchange gossip with a fascinating variety of individuals. I remember an occasion when I encountered the Ambassador of the newly admitted Maldive Islands. (He was a student already in the United States so that his newly independent government did not have to find his airfare.) He described to me in humorous detail how delegations and groups had made tracks in his direction to sign up this new Assembly vote to various causes. In this race the Russians were first off the mark. The most interesting encounter was with Patrice Lumumba, the Prime Minister of the Congo. Though I was to go to his country many times he was already dead by the time that I first arrived there. He struck me as over-excitable and full of resentments but I wished him well.

In the Coliseum in Los Angeles the Democratic candidate for the American presidency was to be chosen. Senator John F. Kennedy was up against Adlai Stevenson, who still commanded strong emotional loyalties, and Lyndon Johnson, the Senate Majority Leader, who patted the grey hairs behind his ears to indicate before the Massachusetts and Texas caucuses that a boy could not be sent to do a man's job. But, as before in 1956, the calculations and combinations which gave him mastery of the Senate failed to work with the totally different arithmetic of a national nominating convention. I was filming the whole chaotic scene. With typical American generosity I had been lent a house belonging to a friend of a friend which was in easy reach of the convention. A bus route stopped dead opposite both the house and the Coliseum. I caught it after the hoopla of Kennedy's achieving the nomination in the face of the conventional wisdom that since the Democrat Al Smith bit the dust in the 1928 election it would be suicidal for the party to risk offering a Roman Catholic candidate for the White House. As the only white passenger in a busload of African-Americans, I was beckoned over to a seat next to the driver. 'The Democrats have just made the most terrible mistake,' he said. 'Oh,' I said, 'why so?' 'By going for Kennedy they've made it impossible for me to vote Democrat. I can't have the Pope deciding where I'm to send my kids to school.' It did occur to me to try a brief sketch of the American constitution but I thought better of it. 'What are your politics?' I asked instead. 'I'm a socialist,' he answered promptly. Rather naughtily in view of the extreme prejudice with which the socialist label was judged in the States, I begged him earnestly to launch a 'Socialists for Nixon' campaign.

Vice-President Nixon was, without much difficulty, selected as the Republican candidate. In the early phases of the campaign the feeling was often expressed that neither he nor his Democratic opponent was mature enough for the job. Combined with the elitist view that Eisenhower, though great at playing the role of president, was not really doing the work, this explains the applause in the nightclubs for Mort Sahl's pronouncement, 'Confronted with a choice of Kennedy or Nixon I shall vote "No" and keep the White House empty for another four years.' Even in England, to my own mild embarrassment, my report in *Time & Tide* from the Los Angeles convention was accompanied by a cartoon of Uncle Sam holding up by the wrists way above the ground the small figures of Nixon and Kennedy, with the caption 'And now we have the junior featherweight championship'. But it was true that by the time internal balances within each party had been worked out policy differences between the two parties were not that significant.[7]

In the middle of these proceedings Castro turned up in person in New York, and not only Castro but also Khrushchev together with half a dozen of satellite heads of state and government. They had decided, exceptionally for those days, to head their countries' delegations to the annual UN General Assembly. As I put it in *Time & Tide*:

> In nearly every respect New York is one of the least suitable cities in the world
> for the headquarters of the UN and nothing but the compelling need to prevent
> the United States repeating history and taking itself off into the isolationist
> void could have induced the victorious Allies to have agreed to it after the
> Second World War. It is a large polyglot city, notoriously capable of producing
> volatile mobs from almost every country represented; it is on the soil of one of
> the Great Powers; and, to make matters worse, the Annual General Assembly
> must coincide every fourth year with the American Presidential Election.[8]

But the deed was done, New York had become the UN's permanent host, and the United States was obliged to accommodate itself to the presence of whomsoever were the chosen representatives of the member states. With clenched teeth, Khrushchev and Castro were given visas for the island of Manhattan and nowhere else. Castro moved into a hotel in Harlem and was lionised by the black community. Khrushchev, who came by sea, accompanied by the Communist leaders of Hungary, Romania and Bulgaria, was located in a medium-sized hotel from whose convenient balcony he bandied words with the world's press beneath, with the aid of his gifted interpreter, Oleg Troyanowski, later Ambassador to Tokyo, who caught the tone of the exchanges so perfectly that we who were standing below had the illusion of conducting direct exchanges with the Soviet ruler with no barrier of language. In the course of these exchanges Khrushchev declared on being asked when capitalism would come to Russia that it would occur 'when pigs learn to whistle'. The USSR, he said, was going shortly to overtake the USA. 'We will bury you.'

The Soviet leader was not one to observe the polite conventions of the General Assembly. When Harold Macmillan was beginning a carefully prepared exposition of the West's requirements of fierce safeguards and intrusive inspections to accompany any agreement on disarmament, Khrushchev interrupted to say he would accept all these controls even if drafted by 'the worst enemy of socialism' if the West would accept total and complete disarmament. There being no translation facilities available for such an unprecedented departure from the stately procession of speeches, Macmillan got away with disposing of the heckling with a cool parliamentary gesture such as Americans found charming and terribly English. Since I still retained a little Russian from my army days I more or less followed the drift of Khrushchev's remarks and was able quickly to check my impression with a more reliable linguist. I argued in *Time & Tide* and in a much longer piece for the American journal *The New Republic* how Khrushchev's daring gesture could be taken advantage of, though the idea, much canvassed in left-wing circles, of Britain disarming ahead of others seemed to me an undesirable weakening of the vital link of America with Europe.[9] I witnessed Khrushchev continue to perform, including the occasion when he underlined his point by banging his shoe on the podium. He ridiculed Eisenhower for only giving up one day to come to the UN building and announced that he was staying for a month. Rather farsightedly, as it turned out, I remarked that Khrushchev looked as if he were being reckless at boasting of his secure position at home despite being away so long. In 1964 it was to be the amount of time he spent on foreign ventures and some of the reckless commitments he had been willing, without any authority, to make during them that formed a major part of the bill of indictment brought against him by his Central Committee comrades.

Although television was really coming into its own in the 1960 election there was as yet no transmission by satellite across the Atlantic. As the ITN commentator on the election results I was positioned in a small New York studio with the television channels in front of me and the ability to make voice-only injections into the live programme at home. The master of ceremonies in London was Brian Connell, who having started his career as a professional historian (specialising in editing documents of the Palmerston family) had passed from that to being a foreign correspondent for *The News Chronicle* before committing himself to television. He now had lines open to Moscow as well as to New York. I would press a buzzer when I had something to say and hear Connell, in his ripest 'lord of the universe' manner, declaim, 'Do we have Moscow? No, it's New York.' I had the ITN boss, Geoffrey Cox, with me in my studio. On the basis of the early returns – and my own 'gut feeling' already committed to paper – I was predicting a Kennedy victory. Cox got more nervous as the evening proceeded – and rightly so as later returns began to paint a different picture and I really had had no right to have made such a confident prediction that early on. 'Don't you think you had better withdraw your prediction?' Geoffrey asked. Stubbornly I decided not to – some states that I had reckoned to be key had, after all, gone Democratic – but, in deference to my employer (and in recognition of reality) I did say that Kennedy's lead was now smaller and less assured than had appeared earlier on. To my relief I was not obliged to retreat any further. My audience, I was told subsequently, gave me credit for being right without noticing how close I had been to being wrong.

Afterwards I wrote in some detail in *Time & Tide* about the nuts and bolts of Kennedy's so slender victory and about the process of putting together a new administration. I was greatly helped in preparing the second of these pieces, which was titled 'The sweet smell of market research', by my friendship with Adam Yarmolinsky, *The Economist*'s Supreme Court correspondent who was one of the small group entrusted by Kennedy with the task of winnowing out the possibilities for office. I had, for instance, been informed of the likelihood of the new president of Ford Motors, Robert McNamara, becoming the Secretary of Defense before either McNamara or Kennedy had focused on the matter. This serves to highlight one of the most striking differences between the British and American forms of democracy. In Britain members of a new government will have been working together in the Westminster village for decades and even those not personally familiar to a new Prime Minister will have been under the sights and with their most intimate characteristics recorded in the notebooks of the whips for the whole of their political careers. In the United States, where the executive is not part of the legislature, it seems a matter of chance whom the new chief executive knows or otherwise a function of his talent scouts as to who gets called to his attention. Also in Washington far more layers of government than in Whitehall have to be renewed. Kennedy, not a very assiduous senator, seems to have known remarkably few candidates for appointment, but nevertheless the distinctive spirit of the new regime became immediately apparent: 'A certain breezy irreverence,' I identified as 'the dominant tone on the New Frontier, to adopt the now fashionable vocabulary, which few who have been to Las Vegas must be able to take too seriously. (The *New Frontier* has for long been the name of a gambling joint on the Strip there.).' I warned nevertheless that 'A bracing and on occasions devastating astringency will underlie the apparent casualness of the new White House. ... Many of those who have been moaning for years about the absence of American leadership will be moaning about its upsetting versatility before long.'

One startling facet of this distinction between British and American institutions provided material for a long piece in one of my 'strings', *The London American*, which was being edited by Derek Jameson, the cockney chappie who was later to edit the *Daily Express*. On returning to America I had been particularly incensed by a radio talk given by a visiting Englishman, a former Deputy Speaker of the House of Commons, who had been spelling out very slowly and deliberately that the British way of doing things rested on the separation of powers. Since this is true of America but not of Britain this seemed a peculiarly perverse observation. Of no office was this more the case than that of Lord Chancellor, who was head of the judiciary, speaker of the House of Lords and a senior member of the cabinet. Forty-three years before it was proposed to end this anomaly, I described, with lip-smacking relish, the history of this historic post, with particular regard to the early eighteenth century, which had seen America's trend-line splitting off from that of Britain. A shorter version appeared in the *New York Post*, which to my relief continued to print my column even while I was in the States.[10]

Although spending most of this visit in New York I had been given the free use of a basement in Washington by a remarkable man called Roger Hilsman, who had had a spectacular war as a commanding officer with Merrill's Marauders, the American equivalent of the Chindits during the Burma campaign, and who was to have senior office in Kennedy's State Department. He was a member of a group of strategic thinkers planning for the next administration and invited me to come along to one of the sessions. Some ideas discussed made a lot of sense but I listened with mounting disbelief to what was proposed for Vietnam. In brief it was to be Merrill's Marauders many times multiplied. Much as I was inclined to applaud the American can-do spirit, this particular application of it left me feeling distinctly queasy. My opinion was not invited and in view of my host's hands-on experience I did not feel qualified to volunteer it but I thought that I detected trouble ahead.

In January I was in the press gallery of the Senate in time to hear Vice-President Nixon, as presiding officer of the Senate, solemnly proclaim the result of the ballot of state electors which always in practice enshrined the verdict of the previous November. It was the first time a vice-president had been obliged to announce his own defeat since John C. Breckinridge had confirmed the election of Abraham Lincoln a hundred years before.[11] After a couple of articles on Kennedy's cabinet and his likely relations with the new Congress ('there is in reality complete deadlock between the President's supporters and his opponents'[12]) I was back in London, equipped with commissions from the *Christian Science Monitor* and the *Atlantic Monthly*, to help finance my coming African adventure.

In Africa I was now very much on my own; my job for the BBC would be what I cared to make of it. Never before had a television programme outside the News Department had a resident correspondent abroad, but this was just typical of the spirit of innovation that *Tonight*, now under Alasdair Milne's leadership, was famous for. I had to swim or sink. I was not on the corporation's staff and except for the *Tonight* office in London I had no backup of any kind, no camera crew, no office, none of the devices like the satellite telephone that keep the present-day broadcaster immediately in touch, and no experience of television production. Any filmed report would have to be physically dispatched from an airfield.

Most Europeans (and Kenya was a place in which an Englishman had no objection to being called a European) still behaved as if they were yesterday's men and clove socially to a whites-only world, while a quite small minority, mostly academics, a few of the journalists and missionaries (including my Oxford friend Stanley Booth-Clibborn), by contrast treated Kenya as a black African state in waiting and lived their lives accordingly. Twice in the course of the next two years I was told by European colleagues that I was in danger of earning a bad reputation among 'our own people'. These were warnings that I ignored and was at no point sorry that I had done so. Unless I had clearly supported *uhuru* (liberation) I would not have been received so openly by people I aimed to understand.

Absorbed as I was by the gathering pace of Kenya politics I soon found myself switched to the rapidly deteriorating scene in the Congolese province of Katanga. I joined the press corps, based on the E'ville hotel, the Leo II, which seemed sometimes to consider itself as being 'embedded' (to use the twenty-first-century term) with the Tshombe regime. Personally, though I was often in the Leo II, I chose not to stay there but in a small studio flat which I rented nearby.

There were no reports coming out of the UN. In these circumstances it seemed to me imperative that I should go and see them. When I made some enquiries, some of my journalistic colleagues took a dim view of my interest. 'This is a war situation,' I was gravely told. 'And if you find yourself on one side you don't try to report the war from the other.' This was an analysis I was unable to accept. With a very able BBC sound correspondent, Donald Milner, taking the same view, we decided to seek some assistance from the Americans. It turned out that they went to see the UN every day, following an obscure route that wove a way through the African townships. We followed the American vehicle but at one point lost it and found ourselves confronted across a stretch of grass by a squad of gendarmes with rifles cocked. We halted and Donald, whose French was more fluent than mine, got out of our car and walked slowly but firmly towards the guns levelled at him. Halfway there, he coolly took out and lit a cigarette. Fortunately he had in his possession a pass signed by the Katangese Interior Minister, a sinister character called Munongo. After what seemed an age the guns were lowered and Donald returned in the same unhurried manner in which he had gone out.

We finally reached the UN headquarters which was established in a large villa called 'Le Clair Manoir' which may have at one time possessed considerable elegance but was now looking distinctly the worse for wear on account of the number of hits and near-misses it had received from mortar shells. The roof in particular was puckered so that it let in the rain, which arrived in that season in short, sharp showers. The place was described to me as a former bordello, but whether in jest or not I did not discover. Inside one of those rooms which did not let in the rain sat two senior UN figures: George Ivan Smith and Brian Urquhart who, except for a badly dislocated nose, appeared to be undamaged after being beaten up by the Katangese gendarmerie the day before. They were reading to each other passages from the seventeenth-century Welsh metaphysical poet Henry Vaughan. It seemed to me to resemble a British Council set in an Ealing Studio comedy. On second thoughts, I concluded that Vaughan was a healthy distraction from the only source of information regularly reaching them from the outside, namely their appalling press notices derived from my pro-Tshombe colleagues. We, I think, cheered them up, since we were the first journalists to reach them and moreover were in principle supportive of the UN's aims.

With the UN interviews in the bag we threaded our way back through the townships and made for the 'presidential palace' where a press conference had been called. It was held in the open air in front of the palace and Tshombe, wearing that puzzled, suffering look that his official portraits had made so familiar, was in full flow when the UN bombers began to fly overhead. His French press officer rather sharply ordered him indoors and he rather humbly obeyed, but the UN was not gunning for the 'president' but, as I had previously been briefed, was out to strafe the offices of the Union Minière, the Belgian copper giant, which was allegedly harbouring the arms stores of the gendarmerie. I realised, having been told of UN plans to cut off the city, that I had left things rather late for getting out with my film across the border to Kitwe, Northern Rhodesia, to catch the London plane. I decided not to risk the direct route but to go by a roundabout alternative, much longer and by much rougher roads. My press colleagues at the Leo II begged me to take duplicates of their reports, having entrusted the top copy to the Swiss economist whom Tshombe had made his Minister of Finance and who had left by the direct route, declaring himself fed up by the whole business and bearing a boot-box crammed with currency. The ITN crew asked to be included in the same service. I was not sure of the correct protocol here but I took their film anyway.

With my two-man crew I set out through the townships by muddy, unmetalled track. About halfway along we came across a row of trucks, containing illegal supplies from Rhodesia to Rhodesia's friend Tshombe, all wrecked, each one toppled over, alternately on the left and the right shoulder of the track. The African drivers, while not overtly hostile, were distinctly unforthcoming and, as they were not Swahili-speakers, we could find no language in common. We made it to Kitwe at five in the morning. There was no plane till the afternoon, so I could have had some sleep. But the post office opened at seven and I forced myself to stay awake to see my colleagues' dispatches transmitted by telex. For the first time I examined them and read the dramatic accounts of how the UN had made a last desperate attempt to kill Tshombe by assaulting his palace. Then at seven I handed them in (unamended, of course).

I was soon to discover that these were the only copies that would arrive. The car containing the elegant and polished M. Favre and two journalists, one of them the correspondent of BBC News, failed to stop at a road-block that the Swedes were just beginning to erect as part of the UN blockade. The Swedes let go with a bazooka, the Swiss was killed and the two journalists severely wounded. It had been the right decision to take the long way round. A phone call told me too that I had been wise to leave by any route since a mortar bomb had landed on and had demolished my studio flat.

'The greasepaint is never far from the bloodsmear,' I wrote. 'Amid all this clowning old ladies and young children died. And the mortaring in the streets of E'ville is only an off-stage incident, news of which is brought in, as in a Greek tragedy, by messenger to the scene of the real battles, those which go on in the Brussels board rooms of the Société Générale and the Union Minière and which will decide whether Katanga is to be independent or part of the Congo.' It seemed sometimes as if my life has been spent in the working out of the themes of the great political philosophers, above all of Hobbes. Only when I was in the Congo did I step over the edge of civilisation and feel what constituted the state of nature. E'ville was a kind of halfway house, the rest of the Congo being much worse. But one saw comfortably well-off Belgian *colons* faced suddenly with the prospect of the disappearance simultaneously of almost all their previous assumptions. 'Before independence I never had to lock my door,' wailed a Belgian housewife. Both in Katanga and even more so in other parts of the Congo which I came to know later, there was a sense of the fragile bonds of society suddenly being snapped or falling slowly into decay, although also one came across instances of ceremonies and practices from more regular times surviving the collapse of institutions that had once

given them meaning. It must have been rather like this in England – and elsewhere – after the collapse of Roman rule. In the Congo nothing was certain,
all was contingent. And in Katanga there was the special moral complexity
that arose from the fact that from the white minority's point of view the last
props of civilisation were, as they saw it, being knocked down by the organisation created to uphold civilised standards. I began to get the feeling, which
often recurred later, that I would only really be qualified to write undergraduate essays when I was very old.

Paradoxically, the time I was actually closest to death was not in the Congo at
all but in the comparative safety of Kenya. The colonial government, wrestling
with very serious flooding mainly in the Maasai area, offered journalists facilities to fly down to the Southern Province to see what the administration was
doing to rescue the tribe. We landed in our small Cessna aircraft at the district
commissioner's headquarters after overflying these sad sights. Kenyan officials,
British and African, had indeed achieved miracles of improvisation to save the
Maasai and a few of their cattle, but the scene was desperate. My cameraman,
Pius Menezes, a Goan resident in Nairobi, who felt so emotionally involved
in the Maasai tragedy that he actually volunteered to do the work at his own
expense (although I would not permit this), slaved away at getting the most telling images. The South African pilot, who seemed to me very nervous (having, as
he subsequently informed me, only just qualified) was constantly urging me to
speed Menezes on. As soon as I decently could I ordered us into the air, I sitting
in the co-pilot's seat with Menezes in the rear. We took off and in a short while
it struck me that we were not going to make it above the line of thick jungle that
was approaching. Should I tell the pilot? I reflected that he must know better
than I what the score was and, since his manner was anyway nervous, it seemed
a mistake to wind him up. So I kept my peace but took the precaution of moving
my knees so that they were no longer directly under the dashboard. I also made
certain that I remembered the sequence of events in case I survived and was
required to give evidence in a court of inquiry. My main thought on impact was
how astonishingly like air crashes in the cinema it was, when I had always found
them singularly unconvincing. (I had exactly the same sensation on 9/11 when
many years later I watched on television the twin towers of the World Trade
Center in Manhattan crumble to the ground.) The jungle at the point of impact
was very thick and brought the Cessna to an early halt. I jumped out, a trifle
shaken but completely unharmed. It had all happened within sight of the district
commissioner and the rest of the press. The pilot was also unharmed except in
pride (he decided never to fly again) but Pius Menezes, the hero of the trip, had
serious (but not life-threatening) injuries.

In response to the pilot's qualms I had taken off without doing the into-camera commentary. Still feeling a bit stressed I wrote it on the plane which was found to take me back to Nairobi, while another one was rushing Pius to hospital. The press department, whose expedition this had been, produced another camera for me at the airport and, looking, I trusted, as calm as if nothing untoward had happened, I voiced my impressions of the Maasais' fate. I airmailed the film and telexed *Tonight*, and only then allowed myself to realise what a narrow escape I had had.

There is a postscript to this story which was luckily unknown to me at this time. Richard Lindley, in his distinguished history of *Panorama* (Politico's, 2002), the long-running BBC weekly current-affairs flagship, uncovered a memo from my boss Alasdair Milne to his superior complaining that 'Kyle dispatched his story to us late last week and it was cut and ready for transmission tonight, Monday. … I discover from the Ed, *Panorama*, that on Friday morning he dispatched Robin Day to Kenya to cover the same story. … I have agreed to withhold the story on which there is no doubt we had prior claim.' [13] So it was never transmitted. This is the luck of journalism. I did at least get an article called 'Noah of the Famine Lands' in *Reynolds News*.[14]

In the spring of 1962 I suddenly reached the decision, almost on a whim, to fly back to London. I had not in my mind finished with Africa but I had a feeling that it was high time to touch home base. It was a decision I was never to regret.

CHAPTER 13

Europe and Matrimony

I arrived in London with no clear idea of what to do next but with a cheerful assumption that something would turn up. Two things did: Alasdair Milne, who seemed to be not at all put out by my abrupt decision to quit Africa for the time being, commissioned a script for a documentary about the situation in the Congo. And the *Sunday Times* invited me to become their columnist on European Economic Community affairs, the Macmillan government having at last decided to give up inventing alternatives to the EEC but instead to seek to join it. This had been what I had wanted since the very inception of the Schuman Plan, so that I felt it to be great good luck to be directly involved. Indeed I was so pleased that I overlooked one drawback about the proposition that had been put to me. The foreign editor, Frank Giles, had said that since he had a special affinity with the French my presence in Paris would be unnecessary but that once the negotiations got really under way I should base myself for most of the week in Brussels. I was later to discover that I had acquiesced too readily in this division of functions; my lack of contacts in Gaullist circles was to make me too optimistic about Britain's chances of passing muster with the General as a genuinely European state.

I did not lose my interest in either the United States or Africa. I wrote a long review article in *Time & Tide* on the 1960 American election, welcoming Theodore White's pioneering survey while listing seven factors that he had omitted, including Kennedy's demand for a more aggressive policy towards Cuba as against Nixon's defence of American propriety in regard to the UN. The BBC World Service and, more occasionally, the Home Service used me for comments on African developments, while a social encounter with the Colonial Secretary, Reginald Maudling, led to a memorable interview in Whitehall.

Maudling was a remarkable but now largely forgotten figure in the Conservative Party. He was a large, shambling man with the type of brilliance that caused him to be admired by top civil servants. Along with his slow

161

movements went an exceptionally quick mind. I knew him, though not well, as a result of having been a political correspondent, and when Iain Macleod left the Colonial Office I was not sorry to learn the name of his successor. Maudling had come out to Nairobi shortly thereafter to try to sort out the muddle into which Kenya's constitutional talks had fallen, on account mainly of the political parties' different approaches as to how an independent Kenya should be governed. The Governor, Sir Patrick Renison, whose florid countenance and cloth ears were insufficiently compensated for by his undoubted honesty and patent goodwill, was proving to be a blundering chairman with an insufficient sense of urgency. Maudling had seemed to transform the hitherto heavy atmosphere so that in a couple of days apparently intractable issues appeared manageable after all. Superior intellect linked to an approachable manner corresponded to what African politicians thought they were entitled to expect from a British statesman. Once he had vanished they waited expectantly to see whether delivery would be prompt.

When Reginald Maudling caught my eye at a cocktail party he shambled over to greet me like an actor looking for first-night reviews in the early editions. 'Hello, Keith. What do they think in Nairobi about how I did?' I replied that the Africans felt that he had done pretty well. 'Call my secretary in the morning and arrange to come over for a talk.' On keeping the appointment I was interested to find the Minister behind a large desk entirely devoid of papers. Nor was there anyone else present. The trouble with Maudling, I had been told, was that along with being very bright he was also very lazy. It was not so much that he neglected his homework as that at an early age, perhaps at university, he had discovered that he had a great capacity for absorbing material at the very last minute and had acquired the habit of relying on that gift too readily.

He began by repeating his question of the night before. I replied that my impression was that the Africans thought well of his untangling of key problems while he was in Nairobi but that they were reserving their final judgement until they could see whether his promise to appoint two commissions would be swiftly carried out. Maudling affected to be incredulous. 'You don't mean to say that they are really worrying about the commissions?' 'Yes, I do. They regard their rapid appointment as the measure of your sincerity.' 'Well,' said the Minister, 'I thought [name forgotten] might very well chair both of them. But he was yachting in the West Indies. Then I thought of [someone else] but I was told he was in New Zealand. So I thought I would leave it until after the summer.' I told him that that would not do. Maudling, who had parked his long legs on his desk, seemed mildly surprised but not offended by this opinion. He went on to question me about the personalities involved.

Time passed and twice I made as if to go. I had a further piece of advice to give but felt that this should take the form of a parting shot. However, the Colonial Secretary was in no hurry and obviously wanted to continue the Nairobi gossip. There was no outside interruption to the relaxed, placid scene. When finally I rose I said there was just one matter that I felt it necessary to mention. That was that his clumsiness as a constitutional arbitrator made it imperative that Governor Renison should be replaced. I suggested that his successor should be Malcolm MacDonald, who had the appropriate temperament and sensitivity for the task. MacDonald, the son of the former Labour leader Ramsay MacDonald, was himself a former Colonial Secretary and then had been Minister of Health during the Battle of Britain. Churchill had sent him to be High Commissioner in Canada, the first of a succession of often tricky Commonwealth and postcolonial jobs which he had carried out with notable success. I had been right to leave this question till the last, as Maudling's mood changed, though more, it seemed to me, as a matter of form than because he was genuinely discountenanced. This was a subject, he said, on which he could not possibly comment. I replied that I had not expected him to, but, as he had requested my frank opinion on the Kenya question, I had felt it was my duty to give it to him on a really critical matter – and then I left.

There is a postscript to this incident. Some years later, after Kenya had become independent, I was discussing it with a senior civil servant at the Colonial Office, who said that it was a good illustration of the different characters of Reginald Maudling and his successor in the post, Duncan Sandys. At one point Maudling had reached the same conclusion about Renison as I had myself and had consulted his Permanent Secretary about the method for removing an incumbent governor. The Permanent Secretary had reasoned with his Minister, pointing out that Sir Patrick had worked very hard, that he had not had a proper break for several years and that, rather than have a hitherto successful career ending in failure, he should be sent on a long leave during which the constitution could be worked out under the aegis of his deputy. This had seemed to Maudling an adequate solution of the problem. The only drawback was that, contrary to the expectations of the local politicians and press, Sir Patrick Renison turned up again at the end of his leave. He was seen in action by Duncan Sandys, Maudling's far from emollient successor, who immediately sacked him with such scant ceremony that he won genuine sympathy even from those African politicians who had hitherto displayed little regard for him. Malcolm MacDonald was appointed as his successor and saw Kenya through to independence and beyond.

My main interest and enthusiasm was now devoted to Europe. Since my
visit to Strasbourg in August 1950 – and a second one in 1952 – I had been
familiar with the grammar of Community politics and more profoundly and
over a longer period I had wanted the conventional pattern of sovereign states
to be drastically modified so that 1914 and 1939 could never recur. Yet at the
same time my period as a political correspondent, though relatively short, had
been quite sufficient to convey the lesson that enthusiasm for such a change
would in my own country run against many dearly held instincts, not to
mention problems created by the Commonwealth.

Britain, I wrote, had gained caste among Europeans by talking about the
essentially political character of the Treaty of Rome, but, I warned, 'if Ministers try to sell membership of the Common Market to the British public in
primarily political terms they face the danger of having to answer awkward
questions about the possibilities and implications of political federation'.[15] The
excitement, as I saw it, of the Community method lay in its disregard of familiar categories. It partook both of political process and continuous diplomatic
negotiation and the relationship between these two features was a dynamically
changing one. There would be an unending dialectic between the European
idea and the interests of the nation states. The European Commission was
there to see that Community decisions were actually carried out, a fatal weakness, as A.J.P. Taylor had taught me, of many a conventional diplomatic treaty
or military alliance lacking provision for staff talks. Its undemocratic features
were there precisely because public opinion was not yet ready, might indeed
never be ready, for the direct election of a European government. One had to
start somewhere and the balance between Council of Ministers and Commission seemed (and still seems, 40 years later) the most ingenious way to begin,
while avoiding the ideological complexities of a political federation. As I put
it in 1962 the European movement 'offers Britain, which knows something
about the style of a Great Power, a share – and a potentially large share – in a
great new experiment on the Great Power scale'.

In Brussels I felt absolutely in my element, though there were surprises. On
my first day the newsvendors for *Le Soir* carried a banner to the effect that Paul-
Henri Spaak, the best-known Belgian politician, whom I had first encountered at Strasbourg as president of the European Consultative Assembly, had
come out in favour of federation. Excited at the thought of a major move in
European politics I devoured the lead article only to discover that the great
man was committing himself not to integrating a continent but to splitting
up 'gallant little Belgium' into still tinier pieces. I had clearly much to learn
about continental politics. Along with my colleagues I shuttled between press

briefings by the various delegations and got to know the two Ted Heaths. Ted
Mark I held himself very stiffly so that his neck bulged and his cheeks flushed
as he pronounced dalek-fashion the chunks of prose that had been prepared for
him. This part of the briefing would be filmed and was for the benefit of news
agencies and the daily press, whose representatives scuttled off to relay the
bromides by telephone. Then Ted Mark II, for those interested in background,
would swing into action. He would lean confidentially on a table or perhaps
sit on it. His highly mobile shoulders would shake and vibrate as he graphically
described the choreography of the latest negotiating session, the attitude and
gestures of individuals among his opposite numbers, the hints of progress or
retreat. We British correspondents had the advantage of an agent within the
Six, as the existing members of the club that we wished to join were called. He
was Dr Joseph Luns, the long-time Dutch Foreign Minister, whose partisan-
ship for British membership was unconcealed. Perhaps for that reason Luns did
not, however, manage to convey the depth of Gaullist hostility. Indeed even
the French negotiators may not have realised it.

I must admit that for most of the time in Brussels I was 'on a high'. I even,
contrary to my habits elsewhere, became a frequent attender of night clubs.
But I am glad to say that on rereading my reports I do not find them excessively
optimistic. They will have suggested to readers of the *Sunday Times* that Britain
was not going to get her way in the accession talks on anything substantial,
though the odd gesture would perhaps be made in favour of the interests of the
Commonwealth. 'There are two documents as a basis for negotiating [about
imports of foodstuffs from temperate zones] – that of Britain and that of the
Six,' I observed bluntly at the commencement of an article on agricultural
policy on 22 July. 'But for all practical purposes one can forget the British
document – it is a dead duck.' [16] Then occurred one desperate Saturday night
at Brussels on which we all sat around waiting to see if the Six would agree to
give the British the outline of an agreement that could be put to the coming
conference of Commonwealth prime ministers. The French were determined
to nail down first among the Six fresh details of the Common Agricultural
Policy, which they knew would be unpopular in Britain, so that these, having
thus become a part of the *acquis communautaire*, would have to be swallowed
whole by a new member. And in any case the French did not rate very highly
the need to oblige Commonwealth prime ministers. As the night wore on brief
messages would come out from time to time. They were still at it when my
ultimate deadline for a Sunday paper approached. Someone from the British
delegation came out and said that things had started to go rather better. An
agreement might be arrived at after all. I hastily conveyed this thought over the

phone to London. It made the *Sunday Times*'s front page headlines the next day. Unfortunately by the time that they were read the negotiations had collapsed. It had not been my most distinguished contribution to journalism.

It was not until the following January that De Gaulle vetoed Britain's accession and I notice that most accounts of these negotiations imply that there was thought until then to be a real chance of their success. I am bound to say that that was not my impression. Everyone supportive of British membership was immensely depressed by the August failure, and being given the chance to stay on by the *Sunday Times* I had little difficulty in opting instead to accept the BBC's offer to return to Africa. There was, however, a rather important item of unfinished business to complete before I departed.

My routine in covering the European negotiations had been to spend about four days a week in Brussels and the remaining three in London, where I stayed at the Reform Club, or in visiting my parents. I was rung up one day by a producer from Rediffusion, the television company which had the franchise to transmit to the London region on weekdays on the (one) commercial channel. I was asked if I would care to be an interviewer on a series called *Questions in the House*. This programme had been devised by the retired naval captain on Rediffusion's board as a means of rallying political support for the company with a view to the extension of its franchise. Ordinary backbenchers at Westminster had become very jealous of what they considered to be a small group of oddballs (like Michael Foot and W.J. Brown) who appeared to have a monopoly of screen time when it came to discussion of current affairs because producers could be confident that they would utter something controversial and entertaining. A.J.P. Taylor, though not a parliamentarian, would usually be included, the populist aspect of his personality guaranteeing that fireworks would ensue. Captain Brownrigg, bestriding his office like a quarterdeck, was going to see that there was a programme on which typical backbenchers could have their say. Every week he ran through the parliamentary orders and picked out three questions that were to be asked about local matters. Camera crews went to each constituency selected, the background to the question was examined and at the end the conscientious MP was displayed in action championing his electors. I was asked to be the interviewer for one of these segments, examining the case of the inconveniences caused by the operation of an open-cast coal mine in Barnsley, Yorkshire.

Little knowing what the future would hold, I raised all manner of objections. I was preoccupied by the European question, there was no time for me to carry out the considerable research needed into the Coal Board's policies, there were only two days of the week I would even be in the country. The

producer was not to be put off. A researcher would take care of all preliminary work. What, for instance, would I require? Thus challenged I did not
understate these requirements. All this, said the producer, would be taken
care of. All that would be required of me was that I turn up at a stated time
and platform on one of the days I would be in London and I would be met by
a production assistant equipped with the information. Would I not at least try
this first item and then see whether I wanted to do more? Out of curiosity I
said I would.

At the station platform I was handed a large dossier, in which appropriate
passages in speeches and reports to which I had referred appeared sidelined. I
settled down in a first-class compartment to give them the attention that ministers are supposed to give the contents of their red boxes. Arriving at Barnsley
I felt reasonably well briefed and left the train to gather my first, overwhelming impression of commercial, as contrasted with BBC, production. This was
that, plumb contrary to expectations, fed by Tory propaganda to the effect
that private enterprise was more sparing of manpower than its public equivalent, I was staggered by the number of people involved in what seemed to me
a rather simple operation. Being used to operating in Africa with two other
people or at most three, I found it astonishing that private enterprise should
require ten. However, not for me to reason why, I told myself, settling down
to an unstressful if slightly boring day. I was driven from place to place, receiving at each point dispatches from the front in the form of a written briefing
about the next interviewee. These were precise and detailed. One began, 'The
lady will have her hair in curlers and will say ... .' It remained only for me to
press the button and out would come the looked-for answer, which I supposed
had been carefully crafted by an unknown advance guard. The various brands
of *vox pop* (as interviews with the citizenry are described in the trade) were
there to yield the earthy, human element in the story we were uncovering.
There was the scholarship girl whose concentration was destroyed by the noise
of the explosions caused by the mining. There were the lovers who were no
longer able to walk in their lane which had been ripped apart. By the time I
could get to them they were word-perfect and, I suspected, those who failed
in that respect had fallen by the wayside long before I appeared. There were
quite long pauses during the day when I sat rather glumly with the camera
crew, who were wholly absorbed in reconstructing past exchanges with their
producer as if preparing witness statements for some form of summary court-
martial in front of their trade union.

At the end of the day everyone assembled in a piece of open-cast mine. I
did the principal interview with Roy Mason, the local MP, and then we all

relaxed. The producer asked me how I liked their method of production. I was politely positive, mentioning only that there had seemed little for me to do, but adding that I had been particularly impressed by the quality of the briefs I had received and would like to thank the person responsible. 'She's over there,' the producer said, indicating a pretty, slim blonde who was upside down in the course of executing a hand stand in the corner of the mine out of sheer *joie de vivre*. She was called Susan Harpur and a little over three months later we were married.

Suzy, who was 25 to my 37, was the eldest of four daughters of Canon Douglas Harpur, who was the vicar of the tenth-century St Michael's Church in St Albans, and Nan Harpur, headmistress of St Albans Grammar School and a dynamo in parish affairs. Suzy's parents, who were Southern Irish Prot-estants, had been missionaries in Ceylon, as Sri Lanka was then called. She herself was born in Dublin and still carries an Irish passport, but was brought up in Colombo until she was sent for her secondary education to an English boarding school. After graduating, she had worked first as an assistant to academics at Cambridge and then as a television researcher.

I reflected that I had been very fortunate, after a late start, in the various girlfriends I had had so far; their friendship had without exception been enjoy-able and my feelings about them remained warm but I had never met one that I felt ready to marry. I had come to think that I probably never should. I felt that out of no sense of arrogance, rather the reverse. I doubted whether anyone would want to put up with me on a permanent basis. 'You're not everybody's choice,' my mother had once said to me, referring no doubt to my infuriating absentmindedness and general impracticality about the house. Having learned to like the company of women since I had gone to live in America, I had never been certain that I had been really and totally in love with any one of them and of one resolve I was absolutely convinced: I would rather stay unmarried than consciously look for a wife. That was perhaps unwise of me as I might, with advancing years, require more looking after than most. But at the time I would have regarded any such consideration as being unworthy of me.

When the BBC's lady of iron whim, Grace Wyndham Goldie, after compli-menting me on the variety of female companions that I used to invite to the hospitality studio to watch my programmes, once asked me when I intended to 'settle down', I had replied that the answer might very well be 'never' but in any case not unless I felt a 'luminous certainty' that I had met the right person. 'Luminous certainty?' she questioned archly when I announced my engage-ment. 'Yes,' I replied. It turned out in all respects to be so.

Our marriage has worked at a time when so many apparently secure unions have come crashing down thanks, almost entirely, to my darling Suzy's combination of qualities – she is independent-minded but loyal, full of spark and initiative without being a dedicated feminist, and wonderful company too. But I hope I may be permitted to record that the most important decision of my life I got completely right.

When I proposed there were just three and a half weeks left before I had to return to Africa to film Ugandan independence. I had thought at first that, after announcing our engagement in *The Times*, there would have to be some delay while I was in Africa. But it was soon apparent that, with my marvellous in-laws, miracles could be performed. Since Douglas Harpur was a clergyman there was no delay about proclaiming the banns. There was then just room to fit in the service at St Michael's Church before we were to catch the plane together. My father-in-law was a remarkable man (alas, he was to die too young), genuinely devout but wholly unparsonical, immensely popular with his congregation, an inspiration by daily example rather than by mantra. Also, my mother-in-law was a great organiser. At bewildering speed the arrangements for the coming ceremony took shape. My own parents were, I think, overjoyed that I was going to settle down 'at last'. My father took a liking to Suzy and, as she told me much later, was very generous about me to her. He did, however, tell me that she was never as old as 25 and advised me to get a glimpse of her passport. 'You'll find she's not above 21,' he said.

It was 29 September and the weather was fine. It was a joyful occasion – on which I did not feel the slightest bit nervous. The service was conducted by Douglas (his elder brother giving Suzy away) and especially considering the shortness of the notice there was a very good turnout for the service and the excellent party afterwards. It was the beginning of a new and wonderful partnership. Afterwards we were taken to the airport and after a certain delay while the pistol was removed from the pocket of the Cypriot sitting next to us we took off for Athens and the two days which was all we could allow ourselves of honeymoon before heading for Kampala and independence for Uganda. My German cameraman Claus had been brought up from Salisbury and I had warned him by cable of my changed matrimonial state. He was kind enough to arrange that in the general hospital which had been turned over to the international press for the occasion the newlyweds should have a separate ward. That night the bed on wheels went skimming about the polished floor.

5. Wedding Day, September 1962.

CHAPTER 14

Tales of Africa

For all the balls, banquets, football matches, canoe races, military tattoos, state drives and ceremonial hand-over of documents by the Duke of Kent, representing the Queen, there was something of a wing and a prayer about Ugandan independence. As with my new bride I watched the gilded ceremonies pass by, the fragility of the new state was there before our eyes. Who, for example, was our host? Was it Kabaka Mutesa II of Buganda, or 'King Freddy' as the British tabloid press still loved to call him? Once exiled by the British he was now back in full uniform as the hereditary ruler of that part of the state where the ceremonies were taking place. Or was it his left-wing political ally, (Apollo) Milton Obote from the non-monarchical north, who under the terms of the most unnatural of political alliances was Prime Minister? Peaceful collaboration between these two seemed unlikely for long. My money would have been on Obote but this day seemed to belong to the Kabaka, who was letting everyone know that in the Brigade of Guards he outranked the Duke of Kent. For this once Obote was content to read out the noble and improving speech which had been written for him by a British civil servant. It drew, Sir Richard Posnett subsequently recalled, on Jefferson and Lincoln. It also included generous promises of career prospects for British civil servants.[17]

Happily for Suzy and me the opportunity of the presence of so much of the world's press had been seized upon to promote the country's potential for tourism. After all, Kampala was the terminus of the East African Railway, the famous 'lunatic line' conceived by private enterprise but built by the Foreign Office in order to open up the heart of Africa. Its original publicity had spoken of 'A Winter Home for Aristocrats'; a broader market might now be on offer. As Suzy reported to her parents we were taken up to Murchison Falls, where Speke had found the source of the Nile, and saw hippos, crocodiles, elephants and rhinos all feeding at the water's edge, while in the national park wild animals existed in profusion – elephants, lions, wildebeest, flamingoes and

other marvellously coloured birds. To round off the day we were flown to
Lake Albert. It was intensely hot and the prevalence of insects prompted us
to reflect on the remarkable powers of endurance of the early explorers. For
a newly wedded couple who had not yet had a proper honeymoon it was a
glamorous introduction to Africa. Ever a news junkie I still kept my eye on the
local press and could not help but observe the amount of apparently random
violence that was being reported there. John Kakonge, a friend I had made in
Tunis and a political supporter of Milton Obote, filled me in on the underlying
prospects in a manner that was not reassuring.

Since my next film was to be about Stanleyville, Lumumba's city deep in
the Congo's interior (unlike Leo and E'ville which are at its opposite edges)
and, since no one knew for certain who was in control of it, I left Suzy behind
with friends while I set off with Claus Krieger, the German cameraman with
whom I shared many adventures, for the city named after the great explorer.
When we flew low over Stan it seemed to resemble an island enclosed by the
thickest of African jungle and when we landed we were indeed in the midst
of a political and military thicket. It was my first direct experience of the
former Force Publique, the body which according to the Belgians was to hold
the country together after independence but had, on the contrary, at the first
opportunity mutinied. At Stan, after a period of anarchy during which there
had been brutal and disgusting slaughter, the soldiers of the renamed Congolese National Army (loosely loyal to General Mobutu on behalf of the central
government in Leo) were rather nervously in charge but their posture was not
reassuring. They lounged around in groups manipulating their privates or the
bolt actions of their guns or else they sat about dozily like the soldier in the
Fabritius picture. At the airport an officer objected to our coming *brutalement*
and ordered our camera equipment to be impounded. As we ourselves were
not under arrest and the impounded equipment was not guarded it presently
became possible to extract the latter and to proceed by taxi into the town.

We first went to the shop which was owned by Lumumba's brother and
began our enquiries about how the supposed leftists had lost control of the city.
We managed to film – rather surreptitiously in view of our ambiguous status
– around this largely deserted town and, guided by our cooperative driver and
the possession of a few names drawn from BBC Monitoring Service's daily
selections from the output of Stanleyville radio, we were able to track down
some interviewees. The man in apparent charge was Commissioner General
Joseph Ekombe, who had proclaimed a state of emergency, banned political
parties and meetings and imprisoned the Lumumbist burgomaster. 'Stanley's
statue has been put back on its plinth,' I later reported to the *Sunday Times*,

'while the authorities are still debating whether to remove the monument to Patrice Lumumba.' [18] We did not breathe at all easily until we were once more airborne with our camera equipment intact.

Only now was I in a position to drive Suzy from Nairobi across the border into Tanganyika for a proper honeymoon on the slopes of Kilimanjaro. It was getting dark and I had just remarked that the *twiga* (giraffe) was the chosen symbol of Tanganyika when one suddenly appeared in our headlights standing four square astride the Kenya–Tanganyika border. We stayed at a rest house owned by a German part way up Mount Kilimanjaro and, once I had filed a story on Stanleyville for the *Sunday Times*, our honeymoon could begin.

When, all too soon, it was time to leave we decided to do so before dawn to catch the fabled sight of the sun coming up over the mountain. We stopped near the Kenya frontier and left the car to sit in the open, observe the sunrise and consume our sandwiches. Presently we sensed that we were not alone. Two lions were seated only a few feet away. They had been sleeping and were in the process of gradually waking up, regarding us (if at all) through massive yawns. It seemed as well to return to the car. We had the same thought: to move very slowly and very quietly.

Our next task was to find a house we could afford in or near Nairobi. We looked at several places – one of them especially impressive – but, though tempted, we finally settled, as being more fitting to our modest estate, on a small tin-roofed bungalow in the grounds of a larger house in Karen, a village three miles outside Nairobi. The name had been made famous by the Swedish writer Isak Dinesen who had taken the *nom de plume* of Karen Blixen. In a grandiloquent gesture I christened our humble home Harpur Hall after my wife's maiden name.

In the 18 months of my second stay in Africa I followed three main stories – the coming of independence to Kenya, the break-up of the Central African Federation and the *coup d'état* in Zanzibar. But I was also frequently travelling to Uganda and the Congo. Conditions continued to be fraught in the former Belgian colony, where the UN finally asserted itself and forcibly ended the Katangese secession. During the second half of 1963 we lived in Uganda when Sir Bernard de Bunsen, the Vice-Chancellor of Makerere University College in Kampala, invited me to become a Scholar in Residence. Makerere is the oldest institution of tertiary education in East Africa, where many of the future leaders of the entire region were educated together. We occupied the house of the registrar who was away on long leave. This was many times more luxurious than our inaugural home at Karen but that home and our Luhya servant there, Javani, have a special place in our memory.

One of the odder characters that we met in Uganda was Bob Astles, an Englishman who liked to create the impression that he was the puppet master of the African political scene. I never thought that this was at all likely, though he regaled me with detailed gossip about the Kabaka who allegedly held the political future of the country in his hands. When I was next in Uganda a few months later I found that in the interim Bob had migrated to becoming a booster for Milton Obote. One day I ran into him in the rather elegant Kampala bookshop which doubled as a coffee house. He was drinking coffee with a huge silent African soldier, who was bursting out of the battledress onto which were sewn the chevrons of a brigadier. Bob introduced me to Idi Amin. My mind went back to an interview that I had previously had with Sir Walter Coutts, who had been made Governor-General of Uganda at independence and who, after having been a very active Chief Secretary in Kenya, did not conceal his unhappiness about being confined to the golden cage in which he was studiously ignored by his Prime Minister. Describing the alarm which had overtaken the British authorities when, on their concluding that independence was rushing in on Uganda several years sooner than they had anticipated, Sir Walter said that it had dawned on them that in the new Ugandan Army there would be no black officers. That had been precisely the problem with the Congolese Force Publique, with disastrous consequences. There were only two ways by which this could be remedied, either to train up at Sandhurst a bright young cadet new to soldiering or to promote a long-serving NCO. They had decided to do both. The long-serving NCO had been Idi Amin.

Idi Amin's main claim to fame had been his success in enlisting recruits, mainly from northern tribes. His favourite method was to demonstrate, with every muscle rippling in his outsize frame, his great physical strength. 'Join the army and you can have a body like mine.' Bob talked to me about Idi Amin in his presence with a proprietorial air, rather as if he were speaking of some tethered mastiff. Idi Amin, I was told, had been criticised unfairly for helping himself to the good things of life. In truth he had bought no luxury except a bed for his new wife. The Brigadier grunted assent. Wasn't a man entitled to have some little reward for his services?, Astles went on. Wasn't the acquisition of a new wife a fit occasion for some display? There was much more on the same lines. In increasing embarrassment I closely watched the silent giant as he bent and relaxed his enormous knuckles. I thought that he had only to extend one thumb and his presumptuous keeper would be crushed utterly. I did not, however, at the time guess that this would roughly be the fashion in which the Brigadier would subsequently rule Uganda, though it must be said that by then he would become anything but silent.

A year after independence Sir Walter Coutts was released from his golden cage by the proclamation of a republic. The new President was none other than the King of Buganda, the Kabaka, with Milton Obote remaining as Prime Minister. John Kakonge told me that he had learned that some of the Kabaka's soldiers had intended, in the course of the ceremonies, to swerve from their ceremonial stance and shoot Obote. (Later that idea sounded a good deal less unlikely when precisely this fate was to befall President Sadat of Egypt.) As soon as Obote's supporters learned about this, my informant said, it was made clear that his men would be tipped off to respond instantly by taking out the Kabaka. Under such auspices was the republic launched.

In the end, as far as immediate prospects were concerned, Kenya worked out well enough thanks, above all, to two men, Jomo Kenyatta and Malcolm MacDonald, who at the end of 1962 was at last appointed to take over from Governor Renison. Politics became more urgently competitive as the dates in May for the final election before *uhuru* approached. There were not many incidents but in the Kamba country I was given some direct evidence of the strong feelings that were just below the surface. The Kamba people, who are neighbours of and are after a fashion related to the Kikuyu, had provided in Paul Ngei one of the men who with Kenyatta had been imprisoned on a charge of managing Mau Mau. Ngei was a union organiser and a rough diamond whose relations with Kenyatta had been anything but cordial during their period of incarceration. He had again quarrelled with his party leader after they had been released, had formed his own radical party and had threatened to exclude Kenyatta's KANU from the Kamba country.

Kenyatta's people, anxious to show that there is nowhere where they can be denied a presence, bus 50 car-loads of supporters to a rally in Ngei territory. They are accompanied by a detachment of paramilitary police, who respond to the jeering from Ngei's partisans with ample use of their batons. Four miles away at Tula Market I am filming Ngei rallying his own supporters. The speakers are developing two main election cries: 'Down with Tom Mboya', who, it is said, will 'spoil' African political life in his drive to become dictator, and 'Stop KANU getting power at all costs' if they are going to keep the Cold War out of Africa.

The crowd, I note, roars its approval and begins to disperse. A man at the extreme edge of the crowd notices a small van approaching; it is flying a KANU party flag and has clearly come the wrong way. On a sudden whim the man picks up a jagged piece of rock and hurls it at full force at the van's windscreen. The peaceful scene is transformed; the whole square is sizzling with rocks (of which unhappily there are a large number to hand) lobbed with accurate force at the one van. The driver in a panic tries to turn it round; it crashes into one tree, then another. Someone from the van dashes for cover into an innocent baker's van full of bread and starts it to get away. The rocks then smash down on the baker's van; it crashes out of control into the back of the stationary lorry. A KANU man rushing across the road is smashed to the ground with sticks and kicked in the head.

I have been observing this sequence of events as they rapidly follow one another. I am a strong believer that a reporter should not get involved in the actions he is recording. On the other hand, can I just calmly witness men being killed, as they undoubtedly will be given the temper of the crowd? I step out into the middle of the scene and brusquely order the crowd to disperse. They do so at once and I am left alone with two injured men and a mass of car parts and spoiled loaves. I wonder what I should do next with the injured men and even more I wonder what has happened to my camera crew. To my great relief both questions are shortly answered. The camera crew have identified a nearby hospital and are bringing aid to the injured.

I thought back on what had happened. I felt that I had experienced something of what it was often like when the first white men imposed their will on large numbers of Africans. I was happy that I had saved lives and yet at the same time was rather ashamed of having behaved like a white imperialist. Then again there was the irony of having acted as an imperialist in the interests of Jomo Kenyatta. I took care to edit myself out of the versions of the Tula Market rally that I prepared for the *Tonight* programme and, on sound radio, for the General Overseas Service.

I covered meetings of the two main parties. 'In an arcadian setting under a huge spreading tree, with the audience squatting in semi-circle a group of KADU candidates ... urge their listeners to vote for their party. Their reasons: (i) Kikuyu take oaths at night; (ii) Kikuyu women have abortions; (iii) unity with a Kikuyu is unity with death.' At a KANU meeting, 'The oratory of Mboya swells on melodiously. His message: "tribalism is the enemy as much as colonialism ever was. There must be one Kenya and, soon after that, one East Africa."' [19]

It was the eve of poll and we wanted to film Jomo Kenyatta's speech in Nairobi. We seemed to have left it too late for when we arrived at the scene excited crowds were thick on the ground with no obvious way through them. 'Lumumba' Muigai, the chairman of KANU Youth, with his gang of stewards rapidly opened up a wide path for us to come up to the front. The 'Old Man' gave an inspirational address and as he ended the heavens opened, the monsoon arrived. Everyone sought refuge wherever they could and with some of the press I found myself for the first time inside the Muthaiga Club, then the symbol of white supremacy. It was already looking very damp inside. In the reading room the water had already soaked most of the carpet. One corner only was not yet saturated and in it was seated a very old man, totally absorbed in his newspaper and oblivious to events about him. This was Colonel Ewart Grogan, one of the original white settlers who had famously walked the African continent from Cape to Cairo. He was due to be 89 on Uhuru Day. When I caught sight of him the water was still rising.

On 11 December, the eve of Uhuru Day, I was taking my coffee in the outdoor café of the New Stanley Hotel when workmen appeared to remove the 'Delamere Street' sign, commemorating the most celebrated of the original white settlers, to replace it by a 'Kenyatta Street' sign. It was a fitting symbol of the passing of the colonial era. Robin Day had arrived to film the independence ceremonies for *Panorama* and I hastily alerted him in time for that moment to be recorded. Later in the day Suzy and I attended Malcolm MacDonald's garden party where all the diverse characters of the Kenya scene were represented, including four Mau Mau generals in khaki uniforms without insignia who stood shyly on one side until a few journalists approached them.

The Kenyans had expressed the thought that since Queen Elizabeth had been in Kenya at the moment when on her father's death she had ascended the throne she might want to officiate in person at the end of empire in Nairobi. Although not prepared to go that far, her advisers were agreeable for her husband, who had promised himself a holiday by Lake Rudolf (in the north of Kenya), to drop off on his way there, first at Zanzibar and then at Nairobi, to hand out self-rule to the inhabitants of both. Last-minute preparations were especially frantic because it had been unseasonably raining until just before the great day. But the dancers had well rehearsed the succession of tribal displays in front of Prince Philip lasting two and a half hours and representing each region of the country. Prime Minister Kenyatta and representatives of 80 foreign governments and a list of special guests who had over the years been on the Africans' side were there. Tribal priests poured libations of honey and oil on the earth. The mood in the racially mixed crowd in the stadium was upbeat and unprovocative. Some embarrassments had been feared. None occurred, although Kenyatta was quick to intercept a group of forest fighters who were headed towards the Duke of Edinburgh. At midnight a signal was received from one of the three summits of Mount Kenya from the flag party which was running up the new Kenya flag.

We stayed on in Nairobi for a few months after independence, observing the social and political changes that ensued from it. Superficially some things seemed to remain very much the same. The Nairobi races, which from the first years of the twentieth century had formed one of the great focal points in the white settlers' calendar, were held as usual in December, though, instead of the programme specifying that it was 'by kind permission of the Governor', they were held this time by kind permission of the Prime Minister. And Jomo Kenyatta was present in person to present the winning prize to Lady Delamere, a remaining symbol of settler power and of much else besides.

Unfortunately Suzy had not been able to come with me on many of my trips but, on the grounds of her television experience, I was at times allowed to bring her along and include her on expenses. Thanks to her help we were able to mount our most ambitious production. We were in Lusaka, the capital of Northern Rhodesia (Zambia). I had been concerned that our films were too heavily biased towards politicians (and, in the case of the Congo, brigands) and were not reflecting the concerns of the average African. When in Lusaka I thought I saw a solution in the 'Tell me, Josephine' column of the local English newspaper. Headed by a picture of a glamorous African lady whom I presumed to be the agony aunt in question, there followed a fascinating *mélange* of cross-cultural problems of a very human nature. I contacted the (British) editor and encountered the first snag – the glamorous African was not Josephine, who was in reality the editor's (British) wife, but was merely a fetching photo. However, we were able to find a black actress in exile from South Africa who was willing to be our Josephine. I had thought of trying to locate the actual writers of letters but this again proving too tricky we turned to the English-language announcers of Northern Rhodesia radio to voice to camera the pleas for advice.

This is where Suzy really came in. The announcers were not bad at reading a script but, unrehearsed, their intonations were not sufficiently modulated. This was the sort of challenge at which my wife excelled. By the time of filming they were very good indeed. We got each to read to camera one of the actual letters to Josephine calling for advice. Then our South African Josephine delivered the answer that the editor's wife had originally written. We had meanwhile rounded up another ingredient: a Congolese band which was in town and whose members cheerfully agreed to act as the chorus that separated the different appeals. In some ways this non-political report was the one which gave me most satisfaction. It was certainly my most ambitious effort at production.

When I made one of my periodic visits to Salisbury, Southern Rhodesia, in April 1964, I received a long telegram from Iain Macleod. I remember thinking at the time that he must imagine he was still at the Colonial Office rather than eking out *The Spectator*'s meagre resources as its editor. It was, however, very interesting in content, summarising the many reports from Southern Rhodesia that were reaching him. The political scene had changed since the days of Sir Edgar Whitehead, who had been defeated in an election by a more right-wing white party led for the time being by an Old Bromsgrovian, Winston Field, who thus gave my school the one head of government to which it can lay claim. Citing this link I had been invited down to the Premier's farm for a weekend. 'Some people say that if we declare our independence unilaterally they will take away our British passports,' my host had declared incredulously after dinner. 'Surely that can't be true?' 'I am afraid, Prime Minister, that it is.' There was a long pause, Winston Field swallowed hard and changed the subject. Now Iain Macleod's telegram told me that according to his information Field would be replaced by Ian Smith, a more resolute character, and that this would be the sign that white-ruled Southern Rhodesia was going for UDI (unilateral declaration of independence).

The editor recommended my seeing two individuals, one of them the Chief Justice, the other a former minister in the Southern Rhodesian government. I followed the advice and received information about the detailed preparations that were going on. Ian Smith himself, when I saw him, was giving nothing away but other contacts backed up what I had been told. I was just completing my enquiries when overnight the Old Bromsgrovian vanished through the trapdoor and Smith was duly enthroned.

I decided that I must break my story on the BBC. The camera was set up at Zimbabwe, which, though it is now the name of the whole country, was at that time the name of its Stonehenge. The word Zimbabwe means Stonehouse and refers to the ruins of a large seventeenth-century city built not of mud and wattle but of stone. It is the principal evidence that the empire of Monomatapa, though lacking in letters, had achieved a marked degree of organisation. For that reason it goes against the favourite argument of white settlers that the Africans never invented anything. That could only mean that someone else (Arabs?) must have erected the city of Zimbabwe. But this did not command much scholarly support. My decision to use Zimbabwe as the *venue* of my report was unquestionably provocative. I began the item with the bald statement that, 'In the self-governing colony of Southern Rhodesia Her Majesty's Ministers are today planning rebellion against the Crown.'

The degree of press censorship in Southern Rhodesia was such that local papers like the *Rhodesia Herald*, while alleging that the BBC in my person had scandalously slandered the colony, was barred from publishing any examples of my offence more serious than my statement that Zimbabwe had been

6. UDI 'scoop', Rhodesia, 1964.

constructed by Africans. With a straight face I responded by citing as my authority the official publication of the Rhodesia Museum but I was under no illusion that this would dispose of the matter. I was sent for by Clifford Dupont, the Minister of Justice. Dupont was physically a small man and when I was ushered into his presence he was flanked on either side by two very large and tough-looking characters whom I assumed to be policemen. What, I wondered, did Mr Dupont imagine I was going to do with him? The Minister said he supposed I had read the references to myself in the papers. Seeing no reason why I should assist him in his task, I said that I had seen the quotations about Zimbabwe and I had replied accordingly. Dupont beat about the bush for a considerable while, explaining why it had been necessary to impose press restrictions with rather severe penalties and that they also applied to foreign correspondents such as myself. He seemed too embarrassed to repeat what I had in fact said. As I remained silent he ended a little lamely by saying that I was not to repeat the (unspoken) offence and that I was to treat this conversation as being off the record. I replied stiffly that 'off the record' protocol required mutual agreement ahead of time and that I would certainly inform my colleagues about the restrictions that were being imposed. Thus the interview ended without either of us touching on the real content of my report.

The time had come to leave Africa, much as I might regret doing so. When Robin Day had been in Nairobi for *uhuru* he had reproached me for leaving the start of my political career so late. I was in my 39th year, had only recently joined the Labour Party, and had not even been adopted for, let alone fought, a hopeless seat. 'It's no use your staying here hoping to become Senator for Kiambu,' he had said with his typical bluntness. He was right. I was now married. If my future lay with British politics it was high time for me to put down some roots in my own country. I arranged to wind up my affairs in Africa and to see some new parts of the continent on our way home. We flew first to Léopoldville. Ironically, despite my fascination with the Congolese scene, I had never yet been in the Congolese capital. There were broad avenues and imperial-type buildings, most in the ragged state that must have prevailed in Britain with Roman buildings once the Romans had left. There were many Fabritius-type soldiers to be seen and others rushing hither and thither for some unknown purpose. Otherwise there was little activity in the streets. Suzy knew a senior member of the British Embassy, so we had an elaborate picnic by the Congo river meticulously laid out by the accompanying Embassy servants. It seemed a strangely defiant way to celebrate in a world that had fallen into chaos. I was able to contact a Congolese friend who, shortly after, went to Stan and suffered a horrible death.

We went on via Lagos, the New York of Africa with its extraordinary push-and-shove vitality, everything covered by outlandish slogans, and Accra, more like Washington, DC, where we stayed in the university suburb of Legon with the Vice-Chancellor, Conor Cruise O'Brien. Conor had moved on from the United Nations and had felt obliged because of all the controversy over Katanga to resign from the Irish Foreign Service. Then, being the formidable polymath that he was, he had accepted academic preferment from Kwame Nkrumah, who, very broadly speaking, was on Conor's side over Katanga. It seemed clear to me from the other leading expatriates who had enjoyed the patronage of *Osagefo* (the Redeemer, as Nkrumah liked to be called) that the Ghanaian President, who was also the University Chancellor, liked to employ men of acknowledged talent who had for some reason (preferably of a left-wing kind) made themselves unemployable elsewhere. Alan Nunn May, the nuclear traitor, was in charge of physics at the university, Geoffrey Bing, the able lawyer-politician who was on a red list of those not going anywhere in the Labour Party, was the Attorney-General of Ghana, and Hanna Reitsch, Hitler's pilot, was training the Ghanaian Army. Conor was evidently, according to *Osagefo*'s estimation, in this category on account of his role in E'ville. This proved to be a miscalculation.

When Suzy and I reached Legon, Conor Cruise was in the middle of a tremendous battle of wills between the Chancellor and the Vice-Chancellor of Ghana University. At lunchtime every day a dispatch was ceremonially delivered into Conor's hands from the residence of the President. It varied in degrees of peremptoriness, reaching a climax with 'I INSIST on [some candidate whom Conor considered unqualified] being appointed Professor of Philosophy.' As I remember, the African don's main qualification consisted in having ghosted *Conscianism*, the definitive statement of Nkrumah's political philosophy. Much of lunchtime would be taken up with suggestions for a suitable riposte.

It became time for Conor to deliver his Commencement Address and he showed me a draft. It plunged head-on into the matters at issue with the Chancellor. This seemed to me unnecessarily confrontational. I recalled to Conor at least two respects in which he had shown me in his previous conversation to be at one with his demanding patron in wanting to make Legon a little less a copy of Oxbridge. Would it not be more tactful without being untrue to himself to start off with those points of agreement before launching into his polemic? While temperamentally Conor is not one to lay much stress on points of agreement he in this case followed my advice. A day or so later I was talking to a couple of his African colleagues. I asked them what they thought of the Vice-

Chancellor's speech. 'We were very worried with the first two paragraphs when he showed he was going along with the Chancellor,' one said. 'But after that we knew it was all right.'

From Accra we flew to Rome, spent a weekend there, and then returned to England, resolved to set my sights on Westminster and to make a start on what I still thought of as my real career.

CHAPTER 15

Setting Sights on Westminster

R obin Day was right. It was high time that I took seriously my ambition to serve as an MP. I could until now say to myself that I was acquiring experience of the world. But if my purpose was political I ought not to spend all my time living abroad but should apply my mind to issues at home. My intention at first was to seek a Labour nomination for any seat, however hopeless, that was still available for the impending election. I soon had to face the fact that I had left things too late even for that. True, Sir Alec Douglas-Home, having acquired the premiership well on in the life of the Parliament, was leaving it as long as possible before seeking a popular mandate, but time was now running out on him. The election was held on 15 October 1964. In the Labour Party, my friend Hugh Gaitskell, whom I had hoped would be willing to assist my career, had died suddenly of a rare disease. As a political correspondent I had known his successor Harold Wilson but not nearly so well. My enquiries at Transport House (in those days the headquarters of the Labour Party) produced the information that there was only one seat left for which there was no Labour candidate. Did I wish to fight Jo Grimond in the Orkneys and Shetland? In view of my own political history, I quite definitely did not.

Since I did not want to be left out of the election altogether I volunteered for work in Transport House. I think I was mildly useful in helping with foreign visitors, including American Democrats, by ensuring that their expressions of ideological solidarity did not interfere with the serious work going on. I was less effective as a speechwriter. Not being used to speaking from a written text myself I found it difficult to ventriloquise one for George Brown. It was a relief when I learned that the BBC wanted to recruit me for its election team. The task I was assigned was to compile a profile of the existing Prime Minister to be used in the event of his winning the race. For this purpose I went up to the

Hirsel, a place which is fractionally north of the Scottish border.

One of Sir Alec's brothers, Henry, was a naturalist who made programmes for the BBC and was retained to brief us about the family. His house, which was quite close to the family seat, was full of live specimens, such as the mynah birds who were given to making loud wolf-whistles just as the ladies sat down at the dinner table. Henry told us pleasing stories of the three youngsters – Alec, William the playwright and prankster, and himself – at the Hirsel. An aunt had to be entertained. The three managed to assemble a stuffed crocodile which they wedged next to a bridge in the grounds of the estate. Alec was assigned to take the aunt for a walk. The others, at a suitable distance, were to mark the collapse of stout party. The walk commenced and the two were closely observed when they approached the bridge. Nothing appeared to happen. William and Henry eagerly got hold of Alec once he was free of the aunt and asked what had gone wrong. 'She noticed all right,' he said, 'but merely remarked, "I didn't know that they came so far north."'

William, it appeared, remained a practical joker in adult life. Once, Henry said, after his brother had become Prime Minister, he had sent in a House of Commons card to him with the Purpose of Interview question filled in as 'Assassination'. Probably with this in mind Sir Alec, on picking up the phone at the Hirsel and hearing a high-pitched voice say, 'I've got 1,000 women just longing to hear you,' slammed it down after snapping, 'Don't be a damn fool. You go too far.' Lady Home, the Prime Minister's octogenarian mother, received a call shortly afterwards. A plaintive voice said, 'This is the Provost of Edinburgh. I was hoping to speak to Sir Alec but I got a very rude man on the phone.' Lady Home herself received us most charmingly. She looked not a day over 60, which was the result I was told of her wearing brown paper next to the skin. I asked her what she would be doing during the election to help her son. 'You mean asking people if they were going to vote for him', she said. 'I don't think that would be proper; the ballot's supposed to be secret.'

On the night itself I was one of the constituency reporters and by the end of the night the Labour Party was just in power. Two of my friends, Dick Taverne (who had won a previous by-election) and Shirley Williams, would be on the backbenches. Both were younger than I and had been Labour supporters for much longer. But the margin of victory was so small that another election was bound to follow soon. I needed to bestir myself. Yet there was that in me that led me to hesitate before pushing myself forward and ballooning my own merits. My efforts to do so were at best embarrassed and at times, in appearance though emphatically not in intention, half-hearted. We were living for a while with my parents-in-law at the vicarage at St Albans. Because television was still a duopoly the fact that I appeared on the screen fairly often meant that I enjoyed a certain local fame, to the extent that I would be recognised by strangers in the street and in St Albans would be asked to address various societies, including the local Labour Party, as a guest speaker. One of my main themes was the misgiving I felt whenever Americans, in the climate of fear that prevailed there, would express envy of the copper-bottomed British enjoyment of human rights. That enjoyment, I used to reflect, was scarcely ever entrenched and depended precariously on the conventional restraint of the authorities.

One day, on reading the life of some nineteenth-century politician, I remarked unseriously to Suzy that it was a pity that the days had passed when a deputation would wait upon an individual to request him to contest a seat. That very afternoon a deputation from the St Albans Labour Party called at the vicarage and invited me to become its candidate. It was mentioned in passing that to satisfy party rules they would have to go through the routine of an open selection but I was given to understand that I need not fear the competition. In due course I became the prospective Labour candidate for St Albans. My chances were not brilliant but they were better than hopeless. The seat had been held by Labour in 1945–50 and after three Conservative parliaments it was permissible, though not all that plausible, to hope for a reprise. The incumbent was Victor Goodhew, who owned a chain of restaurants and had functioned as an opposition whip.

Having carried my wife off to Africa as soon as I had got married, one of my first obligations on coming home was to be shown to that part of Suzy's family and their friends who still lived in the Irish Republic. They belonged to the Protestant minority and were mainly to be found in County Leix, one of the two counties (Offaly being the other) which were the first sites (ahead of Ulster) of Protestant plantation in the island. I was duly passed round like a plate of cakes in one delightful drawing room after another. By one family friend, a substantial landowner named Fred Walsh Kemmis, I was asked along with a puzzled expression why the Protestants in the North contrived to have such difficulties with Roman Catholics. 'We have no such trouble with the Catholics down here.' I gently told him that the proportions of the population were very different. 'I believe that the Catholic Church is right for the Irish,' he remarked rather unexpectedly, 'because otherwise they would be entirely without discipline; but I am worried about Pope John XXIII. He seems to be set on breaking all the discipline down.'

My first priority while I was living in my father-in-law's vicarage was to try to finish my books. I had been commissioned to write one on the Congo on top of my personal project on East Africa, and it is still a matter of some shame that although work on both went on over a considerable period I completed neither. Looking back I can understand what went wrong. It was a mistake to attempt two books at the same time; even so, I would have done better, certainly with the East Africa project, if I had narrowed its scope. My trouble was that I was excited by the process of historical research and let myself be carried away, particularly at the Public Record Office, down too many corridors. There was also the question of my health. I have not referred to this for some time but the fact was that I was still liable to suffer from intervals of extreme lethargy and fatigue. In some undefined way these were connected with my eyesight and I still at times, after a period of reading, had difficulty in standing on my feet. My old habit of working late into the night would alternate with a languor arising from these residual symptoms of ME.

I took a part-time job with *Punch*, providing a weekly critique of the national press, and continued to supply articles to *The Spectator* about African affairs. Iain Macleod was keen to integrate me more closely with the magazine, but his particular suggestion – to take over Randolph Churchill's press column – did not appeal. Suzy went back to work with commercial television and I began accepting more radio and television work with the BBC. I tried to do as many domestic stories as possible, having in mind the need to prepare myself for political life. I remember doing a series on Britain's industrial winners and a critical examination of the traditional British budget, in which I challenged the need for pre-budget secrecy, with reference to the American example. (Rather to my surprise, the Permanent Secretary to the Treasury told me, but not on camera, that he agreed with me.) But I returned on various trips to Africa.

One of these programmes was about Nkrumah's Ghana and his ambition, very much like the propaganda of the Soviet Union, to create a New Man. This sent me to a party school to see African ward-heelers being instructed in English – a language of which many of them had an imperfect grasp – about the subtleties of Hegelian philosophy and its relevance for Nkrumah's ideology of Consciencism. I was also taken up in a glider by Hitler's pilot, Hanna Reitsch, who, as earlier explained, was employed by the Ghanaian Army to instruct its soldiers. The powerful sound of silence as we rushed through the air was divorced from any previous experience. I felt quite safe since a pilot who could have landed and taken off outside Hitler's bunker when German resistance in Berlin was at its last gasp could surely manage a Ghanaian field. I asked Frau Reitsch why it was considered so essential to teach African soldiers to fly gliders. Came the answer, 'Because what they lack is DISCIPLINE', with an immense guttural emphasis on the last word.[20]

When at home and not working I now spent as much time as possible in the constituency, filling up columns in the local press with my protests, pronouncements and petitions. I went to the annual conference of what was now a Labour government. I was able to perform a slight service for the Prime Minister by taking his father off his hands. Herbert Wilson had been a works chemist and a Scout Commissioner in Yorkshire, but above all he was a political buff, from whom Harold had evidently inherited his remarkable memory. David Butler, the Oxford psephologist who obviously knew him well, came up to him briskly and demanded to know the result in a particular constituency in the 1906 general election. Herbert effortlessly gave the names and votes of all the candidates. As a newcomer to the Labour movement I was glad enough to listen to him. Partly perhaps as a consequence the Prime Minister began to include me in the miscellaneous group of journalists and friends with whom he used to gossip late at night at the House or at Number Ten, until a member of his staff (probably Marcia Williams) would tell him that it was time for him to go to bed. At first I was excited and perhaps flattered by this, but I am bound to confess that the novelty soon palled. Wilson seemed forever preoccupied with petty parliamentary details and imagined intrigues. I soon found being with him a disillusioning experience.

In 1965 Nigel Lawson and I were both retained by the BBC as political consultants. Nigel ran a regular column in the *Financial Times* and was known

7. With PM Harold Wilson at the Labour Party Conference.

to be a Tory with political ambitions. The BBC was clearly set on covering itself on both flanks. When George Brown produced his National Plan and the two of us were required to pronounce on it in prepared pieces on *Panorama* we separately concluded that the targeted expansion was without a hope unless there was first a devaluation of the currency. I rather fancy that Nigel leaned towards making this a criticism of the plan, whereas I thought that it was one of its considerable merits. However, it was not this programme that brought Number Ten into collision with the BBC. Press briefings of mounting heat conveyed the impression that the Prime Minister was seriously concerned that the corporation was setting itself up in opposition to the Labour government.

The role which 40 years later was to be played by Alastair Campbell was in 1965 partially filled by an elected politician, Colonel George Wigg. Wigg, who had devoted most of his political career to matters concerning Armed Services' welfare, was what was known when I was in the army as a 'barrack-room lawyer'. He fastened with great tenacity on the pedantic, the trivial and the conspiratorial. He was precisely the wrong kind of influence to have in close proximity to this Prime Minister. Yet he had an office in 10 Downing Street, the title of Paymaster-General and easy access to Harold Wilson. The BBC was accused of anti-Labour bias because a notorious Tory, namely Nigel Lawson, was influential within the Current Affairs Department. I wrote to the Prime Minister, pointing out that, though a prospective Labour candidate, I had a similar position and offered to be helpful. I got a call from Colonel Wigg, who asked me to come to Number Ten but (typically) not to enter by the front door. I found him steaming over a Nigel Lawson column in the *FT* which referred to 'the egregious Colonel Wigg'. What did I think that word meant? Disingenuously (because I realised that the adjective was so frequently used with the word 'idiot' that it had acquired its disrepute) I replied, 'It means prominent or distinguished.' Out of the corner of my eye I had seen a copy of Chambers dictionary on his desk and was aware that these were the definitions it gave. Instead of exploding, as I thought he might, Colonel Wigg went for the dictionary. He looked at it, made no comment and the subject of Nigel Lawson was dropped.

In 1966 I was approached by the Forum World Service, for whom I had done some work in Africa, to go to the Sudan, the largest country of the continent and the first to be given its freedom by the British colonial power, to investigate the civil war which had been raging in the southern provinces for some time. This was to be the first time I had been to a country that had broken off diplomatic relations with Britain, but it was the first time that on the day of my arrival I was invited to dine with the Prime Minister.

After dusk on this, the last day of Ramadan, I seated myself at the banquet, which was overflowing with Arab delicacies, most notably kebabs. The Prime Minister, whether out of custom or for my benefit, was in full flow in his superb English. From time to time, without a pause, he broke into Shakespearian quotation, then asked me if I knew any Arabic. I replied that, having only had ten days' notice of the trip, there had been insufficient time. 'Ah,' Mohammed Ahmed Mahgoub replied, 'I think that I speak English perfectly. But Arabic! That requires more than one lifetime.' He warmed to his theme of the resemblances between Arabic and English poetry. 'You may not understand the meaning but you can get the resonances,' and then he launched into a spirited rendering of Arabian verse.

At Marakal the Governor of Equitoria, Mohammed Abbas Fighiri, a northerner but one who cursed government policy louder and louder as if daring Khartoum to dismiss him, put his personal plane, a small Cessna, at my disposal to be flown by his personal pilot called Sabry anywhere I wanted to go within his province. I chose to go to Akobo on the border with Ethiopia, where I had been alerted by Anya Nya supporters that there could be an interesting story to investigate. Sabry, a wiry, competent Arab of few words, flew me in to a reception brimming with Arab hospitality. I was told that a special party had been prepared in my honour. It was clearly going to take me quite a while to penetrate beneath all this cordiality. Relaxing for a moment I suddenly heard a soldier tuning his radio and picking up in passing the unmistakeable tune of 'Lilliburlero' that had for very many years heralded the BBC World Service. I got him to keep it onto the news, whereupon there came out the solemn announcement that Harold Wilson had decided to call a general election. Since I was a prospective parliamentary candidate I realised that I must get back to England at once. I told the commanding officer, who looked up into the sky and said, reflectively, 'Isn't that your plane flying away?' So it was. My general did not hesitate. It was too late to leave that night but at dawn 'we must mount an expedition to take you to Marakal'. I then realised to the full the extent to which the army garrisons in the south were cut off.

At dawn we left, an astonishingly large parade of vehicles, with myself in an armoured truck enjoying VIP treatment but facing a ten-hour journey with a distinct danger of ambush. We did not, as it happened, have to drive the whole way. We came to an airstrip on which was poised my plane, together with Sabry. The town clerk of Malakal was with him to see, so I was told, that he did not do anything rash. The town clerk briefed me earnestly. Whatever I did, he cautioned me, I was not to say a word to the pilot about his defection. Clutching the beaded ostrich egg I had been presented with by the senior chief at Akobo, I climbed on board the Cessna and we headed off for Marakal. The blotched and mottled countryside looked much more interestingly patterned than had appeared on the ground. But it was getting dark and my pilot observed, almost casually, that there were no landing lights on Marakal airport. Would he make it by dusk? No, he said. I could visualise in my mind the alarm of the Labour Party in St Albans at finding themselves without a candidate. It was a compensating thought that if I did come through I would surely make the front page of the *Herts Advertiser*.

It was indeed quite dark by the time we arrived, but the Governor had turned out every vehicle at his command and lined them up with their head-lights on. My pilot made a perfect landing. I was greeted at the foot of the steps by Mohammed Abbas Fighiri in person. He had suffered, since I had left him, a savage attack of malaria. He was in full uniform with the sweat pouring down his face and he was shaking terribly. He apologised profusely for what had gone wrong and as he took me to his car he said, 'You see my troubles. They don't even supply me with a proper pilot from Khartoum.' 'How long have you had Sabry?' 'Just five days. He's an adventurer, you know, went down to the Congo to fly for the anti-Tshombe forces and ended up flying for Tshombe. I like adventurers, so I gave him a month's contract. But I tell that boy, "It's no good, a pilot has to take care of himself." He was up all night and didn't have a proper breakfast, that's what makes a man nervous. But you know it's just struck me looking at his eyes I think he must be an opium – what do you call it?' 'Addict?' 'Yes, that's it, they can get like that in the Congo.' I caught the local airline to Kampala, where a *coup d'état* executed by Idi Amin on behalf of Milton Obote against the Kabaka was taking place. For once fleeing from a story, I caught the next plane to Heathrow and presented myself via the front page of the *Herts Advertiser* under the banner headline 'Election Dash Home'.

Nursing the thought that two battles had been fought in St Albans during the Wars of the Roses,[21] I quickly swung my campaign into action. I had once propounded in *The Economist* that 'the ideal rule for a politician is only to fight seats in which the result is a foregone conclusion – ones in which you either cannot win or cannot lose ... [T]here is no way of acquiring party merit quite so effectively as putting up a really great fight for a hopeless seat. ... But if at any time there is any doubt about the outcome you may be in trouble. If you win by a narrow margin you may be out next time with the national swing, no matter how good a member you are. ... [I]f you improved the vote and your campaign was beyond reproach, you may be under strong pressure and in honour bound to try again in the same place again – where the tide may still be against your party.'[22]

However, that was journalism and this was real politics in which the first rule must be to display buoyant confidence that one will win. 'I feel I have a good chance,' I was quoted as saying on appearing out of Africa. 'The issue here is clear-cut because my Conservative opponent is on the extreme right wing of British politics.' This, though true, was rather difficult to illustrate with recent examples because, as an opposition whip, Victor Goodhew had recently been playing a silent role. I was, however, able to point out that he had opposed his own party leaders over Rhodesia, though to be truthful I was not sure that my own views on that subject were foursquare with those of my leader. I had, after all, said that, 'The chances of compromise between Britain and the present Rhodesian government have always been nil, are nil now and always will be nil in the future.'

Since my adoption I had been trying, with some success, to fill the local press with items on controversial issues, mostly domestic, which were designed to place me in the 'extreme centre' of British politics, not far distant from the positions I had taken up as an *Economist* leader writer. There was not, I must confess, much reference to be found to socialism or public ownership. 'There was little in his manner or his words to remind anyone of traditional British socialism,' wrote the *New York Times*, whose correspondent spent a whole day with Suzy and me in the constituency, my loyal wife being recorded as bearing election literature in a shopping basket. He quoted me as saying that the Labour Party 'should become what the political philosophers call a party of movement' (which, come to think of it, is not a bad definition of twenty-first century Blairism). Of course I was hoping to carve off some liberal and liberal-conservative fragments of the electorate. My manifesto made housing the Number One priority, promised a fundamental overhaul of local government, a firm grip on public expenditure and a new defence review, but it also tackled the Europe issue about which my party was declining to speak. 'I favour British membership of the European Common Market,' I said, 'and if elected I shall work within the Labour Party group in the House of Commons which supports this policy.'

I found my first exposure to the business of canvassing highly stimulating. Not being an instinctively gregarious person, I enjoyed having a recognised mandate for intruding on the company of strangers. There were moments when I would forget myself and begin to recede into the background. Then I would take a hold, saying to myself, 'Remember you're a candidate' and thrust myself forward once again. It was the first time that I had systematically visited people's homes (or, more often, their front doorsteps). On St Albans's market day my oratory (quite unlike in the Oxford Union) had to compete with the

You know **'LABOUR GOVERNMENT WORKS'**

VOTE KYLE

TODAY

Thursday, March 31st, 1966

7 A.M.—9 P.M.

Published by H. J. Arnold, 28 Alma Road, St. Albans &
Printed by Albanian Press Ltd., 107 Camp Rd., St. Albans

ST. ALBANS

NEEDS

KEITH KYLE

at

WESTMINSTER

8. General Election, March 1966.

cries of salesmen as well as the jeers of opponents. I drew the line at kissing babies. As I confessed in the local paper, 'I looked one baby firmly in the eye and said, "Isn't he a fine-looking chap? I hope you [switching to the mother] will support me on the 31st." To which she answered – quick as a flash and witty too – "He's a she and I'm a Tory."'

A candidate experiences the full variety of responses. 'I voted for you,' said a lady constituent shortly after the poll. As I murmured expressions of gratitude, she went on, 'I could never vote for Victor Goodhew. His chain of restaurants all cook with sunflower oil.' At another door a lady said, 'We are Christadelphians here. We have voted already.' 'And for whom did you vote?' I enquired. 'We have voted for Christ.'

The day of the election approached. I had entered the contest determined to fight all out but not expecting to win. The seat was not exactly hopeless (it was represented by Labour from 1997 to 2005) but my strictly private thoughts were that for me to win the country must feel very emphatically the need to endorse Harold Wilson. Just before the poll, the *Manchester Guardian* came out with what purported to be a new method of matching public opinion polls to particular constituencies. According to this method I would emerge narrowly the winner by 1.1 per cent. My mood was therefore, if I may put it that way, enhanced when I stood on my soap box for the last time in the St Albans market. The competition being more formidable than before I was soon reduced to raucous shouting. A hefty black man put his arm round my shoulder and said, 'Don't waste your voice, son. Save it for your maiden speech. We'll carry you home.'

Thought of a maiden speech did, momentarily, flash through my mind. The historical examples – Disraeli's disastrous maiden, F.E. Smith's brilliantly successful one – were present. I thought I knew what I wanted to do. George Brown, who had been placed by Harold Wilson in charge of the economy and had produced a National Plan, in attempted imitation of the (successful) French example, had started his political life as Hon. Secretary of the St Albans Labour Party. One is always supposed in a maiden to start by making graceful references to one's constituency and one's predecessors. If given the chance it occurred to me that I could make the transition between this flummery and my serious purpose by recalling this episode in the Minister's career before saying that the price of attaining his economic targets was immediate devaluation. Such was the shock and awe surrounding this absolutely vital subject that I thought that my speech might make some impression. Meanwhile, my final 'Into Battle' call to my energetic and hard-working supporters ended with the cry. 'Go to it. You have nothing to lose but Victor Goodhew.'

On election day itself the candidate shows himself briefly at each polling station with the purpose of thanking the staff for their efforts and then joins in the last-minute drive to get the last laggards (or rather such of these as are alleged supporters) to the poll. At 15 minutes to electoral closing time, I drove into one area which was heavily postered in my favour and issued a final call on the blower. A man came out in a towering rage. 'I've voted for you already,' he bellowed. 'But if you wake up the children any more with that noise, I'll break your neck.' I humbly apologised but in the confusion forgot to turn off the loudspeaker when doing so. Thus, in embarrassment and confusion, ended my campaign.

When the votes were counted, I had shaved Victor Goodhew's majority from 5,391 in 1964 by not very much to 4,977. True, I had increased the Labour vote by 2,756 but the Liberal candidate's total had gone down by almost as much. I see that I remarked to the *Herts Advertiser*, 'Actually it went very much as I assessed it as a professional political commentator.' In fact the swing from Conservative to Labour in the constituency was 2.8 per cent, compared with a national swing of 3.0. So much for clever tactics. There was one footnote which for me was significant. At one of my meetings a constituent had asked what my view was on whether Britain should join the European Economic Community. I replied that, if the French objections could be overcome, we should join. 'Darn it!', the constituent said, 'that was the only thing I wanted to affect by my vote. The Tories and the Liberals are both for joining. Labour was the only hope. Now I can't be against the Common Market by voting for you.' Later the Returning Officer told me that one ballot had been most elaborately spoiled by being written all over with arguments against Europe. I from then on became a member of the smallest but ultimately the most successful groupuscule in the Labour Party, consisting of those who passionately wanted Britain to join but only if the people had first had their say directly in a referendum.

I had completed an important rite of passage in British politics and I could say to myself that I had done so creditably – or, at least, without discredit. There was no seat I would rather have represented than St Albans, but at 40 I needed to get a move on and must now look elsewhere. Things had come to me perhaps too easily so far; they would never come so easily again. With one eye kept open for impending by-elections I returned to the business of being an impartial reporter, sometimes at home but more often abroad. Before the general election I had been invited by Harvard University to be an inaugural Fellow of the Institute of Politics that was being set up in the John F. Kennedy School of Government as part of the memorial to the slain President. I had to decline at the time as no one knew when, with an almost hung Parliament, Harold Wilson would go prematurely to the polls. I was told that a place would be held for me for the following year. In the meantime I was asked by Amnesty International, an organisation whose establishment I had always supported, to undertake a mission to Turkey and Greece to follow up a number of individual cases of injustice and in the case of Greece to witness a political trial.

While in Turkey I called as requested on the Ecumenical Patriarch, the *primus inter pares* of the Eastern Orthodox Church. He was not very well and after exchanges of courtesies the conversation of substance proceeded with the archimandrite who was in attendance. My main purpose was to pass messages to them and to find out whether, since there had been talk of severe pressure on the small Christian population left in the former city of Byzantium, they were all right. It was clear from the archimandrite, echoed by the Patriarch himself, that they were both very anxious to be rated as good Turkish citizens. In a lengthy discourse the archimandrite spoke as though a thousand years were but as yesterday. 'The one mistake that Charlemagne made ...', as if referring to a speaker at last year's party conference. They were not, I concluded, in any imminent danger.

I returned to London to find that I had been selected to give a series of four fortnightly talks, 20 minutes in length, on the Third Programme, the thinking person's radio channel which has, like unwanted kittens, long since been drowned. The subjects were to be of my own choice and I was guaranteed that all my texts would be subsequently published in *The Listener*, the BBC's weekly journal, an indispensable (one might think) organ which somewhat later was consigned to the refuse bin. Though I came to be known mainly for my television work for which I later received an award, I valued this 'Personal View' series the most since it gave me a rare opportunity and the space to develop ideas of my own.

The first two talks really selected themselves. I had recently been spending some time in West Germany to make a television series with the British forces there. On camera I had probed with BAOR and NATO Commander General John Hackett the practical implications of the current NATO strategy, which as publicly proclaimed did not seem to me to make much sense. General Hackett made no bones about the fact that if there was a large-scale Russian attack using conventional weapons he would with his limited forces and absence of reserves have lost control of the battle within 48 hours unless authority had by then been received for him to fire his tactical nuclear artillery. I asked him whether he was confident that he would be given such permission. 'No', he answered, 'far from it. It is very difficult to suppose that there would be sufficient agreement between governments.' This exchange was at the heart of my Third Programme talk and *The Listener* article but I also had space to discuss ways in which the Soviet political position might be expected sooner or later to unravel and to point to East Germany as the most likely point of weakness.[23]

My second talk, headed 'Morality and Conscience in Politics', which arose partially from debates following the tenth anniversary of Suez, opened with a statement that would have sounded familiar enough to newspaper readers 40 years on. 'Politics, in my experience,' I said then, 'is not held in very high esteem among the public at large. There is a widespread impression that politicians are as a class quite exceptionally untruthful, evasive, given to doing the precise opposite in office from what they have undertaken to do at elections, thus making a monkey out of the people who have voted for them.' The bulk of my argument was an examination of the very real contradictions of a democratic society and specifically of one governed by a parliamentary system in which governments fell if serious enough splits were publicly acknowledged. If there were a free vote on everything and no collective cabinet responsibility, governments would be forever resigning, as indeed in the France and Italy of the day they were. 'Morality, if it is not a set of beatitudes, is a complex, arduous and at times tortuous subject. No man more strove within himself to discount unworthy motives and to be sure that he was right than Mr Gladstone. No man was so accused in his time of inconsistency, expediency and disingenuousness.'

It was therefore against a background of tolerance and understanding of ordinary parliamentary discipline that I criticised two very honourable people involved in the extreme case of the Suez crisis: Anthony Nutting, who had resigned as Minister of State at the Foreign Office rather than share responsibility for Anthony Eden's handling of the crisis but had left it for ten years before explaining himself, and Walter Monckton, who had stayed in the cabinet despite holding similar views. Both these dissenters declined to speak out at the time because it would have been disloyal and might have brought down the government. This meant that they had acted as if, 'for a responsible Minister to conclude from his inside knowledge that the government is going out of its mind is a mere personal matter to be solved by the personal self-effacement of the Minister who has made the discovery'.[24]

For the fourth talk I expanded the thesis which I had first developed at Oxford which questioned the idea that until fairly recently Britain had 'ruled the world'. Britain, I conceded, 'was for a while pre-eminent in that medium of power, namely the sea, and in those parts of the world in which others chose not to compete. In the nineteenth century she was never pre-eminent, though at certain times and in particular circumstances she did have some influence, in that sphere in which others did choose to compete, namely the central forum of world diplomacy, the continent of Europe.' Palmerston was 'tremendous at upholding England's honour in two circumstances: when the country to be chastised was very weak and had no means of replying to the force which Britain could bring to bear and when the defaulting state had a capital city or some possession of value on the sea coast within range of British naval guns'. I concluded that, 'exaggerated notions of Britain's power and wisdom in the past have induced exaggerated despair about possibilities of her effectiveness in the present'.[25]

This left talk Number Three and about that there is a more intricate story. I have already referred to my feelings of revulsion at my father's attitude to the Jews. This may have been subliminally responsible for the fact that, especially in America, I tended to be attracted mainly to the company of Jewish people. This was not deliberately so; indeed I often suppressed in myself any tendency to identify people by their religion. Once, in the course of a congenial discussion among friends in California, my colleague Paul Jacobs called out, 'Keith is the only Jew in the room,' and it was only then that I noticed with surprise that I was the only Gentile. This may well explain why I had been psychologically resistant to studying the affairs of the Middle East at all closely. Without much knowledge of the local situation I had as an undergraduate been strongly in favour of the independence of Israel. But I must have been afraid that if I examined too closely what was at issue between Arabs and Jews I should discover facts that were to the disadvantage of Israel and of my Jewish friends. When therefore I was approached by the producer of the Third Programme series with a special and, as he admitted, an irregular request to devote one of my talks to Arab–Israeli relations, I realised that I was being faced with a major moral and intellectual challenge.

Conceding at once that under the terms of the 'Personal View' series I was entitled to complete freedom in my choice of subjects the producer confessed the embarrassment of the Talks Department that a major crisis was approaching in the Middle East without the BBC having made a sufficient contribution to the discussion of the background. Would I oblige them by devoting one of my talks to the subject? I swallowed hard, slept on it and decided that it would be moral cowardice to refuse. This was to have a major effect on my future career.

There being luckily a gap in my television work I was able to spend three uninterrupted weeks in intensive study in the London Library and in Chatham House, the famous international affairs think-tank of which I had been a member for the past eight years. The climate within the media in 1967 in relation to the Middle East was quite opposite from what it was to become 30 or 40 years later. Comment and coverage were heavily biased in Israel's favour to the degree that sympathetic examination of the Arab point of view was only to be found in the rarest places. This fact prompted me to argue in my talk that Britain was 'the sole inventor and progenitor' of the calculated ambiguity of the promise of a Jewish National Home in Palestine at a time when Palestine was a territory in which (except, as I should have said, for the city of Jerusalem) Arabs were in an overwhelming majority. 'The most appalling moral dilemma which the West as a whole faces in the Arab–Israel dispute is this: the Arabs are in the right but our collective sense of guilt about the Jews is so enormous that it is out of the question that we should act in accordance with our realisation of this moral truth.'

I agreed that, having a good case, the Palestinian Arabs did not over the years handle it at all well. I blamed the rapidly deteriorating situation on disproportionate Israeli retaliation against Syria and Jordan and on the irresponsible

Syrian, Jordanian and Saudi taunting of Egypt's Gamal Abdul Nasser for not taking a strong enough stand over Palestine and for instead sheltering behind the skirts of the United Nations. Consequently the Egyptians had ordered the UN away but, 'in blockading the Straits [of Aqaba] President Nasser, however, is running a severe risk'. The Arab armies were by no means fully prepared for another war; the rivalries among the Arab states were 'creating a competitive display of brinkmanship'.[26]

The broadcast created considerable controversy in the letter columns of *The Listener* (and elsewhere) with some writers vigorously disputing the 'preposterous statement' that 'Palestine was an Arab country'. In reply I quoted Arthur James Balfour, who was responsible for the 1917 declaration about the Jewish National Home and who wrote in 1919 that in the case of the independent nation of Palestine 'we do not propose even to go through the form of consulting the wishes of the present inhabitants of the country'. Balfour summed the whole matter up by saying that 'as far as Palestine is concerned the Powers have made no statement of fact that is not admittedly wrong and no declaration of policy which at least in the letter they have not always intended to violate'.

Although to read my piece today one would see little remarkable about it, it stood out at the time as being unusually sympathetic to the Arabs. Very shortly afterwards the Six Day War was fought and the Israelis, defeating the combined forces of Egypt, Syria and Jordan, occupied the additional territories which (except for Sinai which was later returned to Egypt) are the subject of today's disputes.

For the first time I had found myself involved in discussions about the Middle East. I was asked by an Oxford contemporary, Colin Jackson, to take part in a panel discussion that occurred just after Nasser's defeat at a time when his resignation had been announced but before it had been withdrawn. The atmosphere in the room was tense and there was throughout a potential for rowdyism. The rest of the panel was inclined towards sympathy for the Arabs; some of its members including Jackson went on to form CAABU (the Council for the Advancement of Arab–British Understanding). When at one point I made remarks very critical of Nasser's judgement, there was a wave of dissent through part of the audience with cries of, 'Who let that Zionist in here?'

CHAPTER 16

Harvard, Ireland and the Middle East

arvard University, founded in 1636, is older than all universities
in England except for Oxford and Cambridge. Its second graduate, George Downing, came to England, built Downing Street and
became an ambassador, being described (by Colbert) as 'the greatest quarrel-
ler among the diplomats of his time'. Thus when one enters Harvard Yard, as
the campus has always been known, one is treading history as much, or almost
as much, as when approaching the ancient centres of study on the other side of
the Atlantic. As an Oxford man I felt it a privilege to be able to spend a further
year in the USA in this setting. The Institute of Politics, of which I was now a
Fellow, was the newest part of the university – it was grouped administratively
under the renamed John F. Kennedy School of Government as a memorial to
the murdered president. Its aim was to perform a pioneering role in mixing
the academic and the practical study of politics. All of the other Fellows in my
year were American and all had hands-on political experience, whether as a
member of the White House staff under Eisenhower, as members of Democratic and Republican Congressional offices, as political correspondent of a
national weekly or, as in the case of Barney Frank, as a young aspiring (and, in
the event, long-serving) Congressman. I suppose that I was there to represent
the intention to give the Fellowship an international flavour and because of *The
Economist*'s reputation for American political coverage. There was an academic
staff, headed by the Director, Professor Richard Neustadt, who had been in
Truman's White House and whose book *Presidential Power* had a subtlety and
depth that put all practitioners and academics in his debt.

We discovered an 'efficiency apartment' in the town of Cambridge, which
was in fact one very large room on a quiet street very near the university, and
settled down comfortably enough for the duration. The Institute's premises

in the little yellow house on Mount Auburn Street consisted of a conference-and-coffee area on the ground floor as well as room for secretaries and, on the upper floor, individual offices for the Fellows. For much of the time we were free to do our own thing – Steve Hess, for example, was writing a history of political cartoons. He had been a White House staffer and shared with us the news that Checkers, the puppy which had notoriously been given to Vice-President's Nixon's daughter (for which Nixon, in the course of rebutting the charge of being in the pocket of rich donors, had creepily declined to apologise) had never been successfully house-trained (but could not, of course, be destroyed). The two Congressional aides – one Republican and one Democrat – worked together in drafting legislation to set up fresh enterprises in city centres of high unemployment. I tried both to consolidate my knowledge of how American politics worked and to make progress on an African book that only finally surfaced in print some decades later.

We were invited but not obliged to offer undergraduate courses and, having as yet had no experience of teaching, I decided to run a class on nationalist politics in Sub-Saharan Africa. This attracted a fairly small but very keen group of students, the subject feeding into the fashionable interest in African-Americans' continent of origin. I was entitled to join the joint Harvard–MIT seminar, which held weekly sessions on arms control and was moderated by Henry Kissinger. One day the guest speaker was Ralf Dahrendorf, then a professor at a German university who afterwards became a minister in the West German government and a European Commissioner and then changed into an Englishman and was in succession Director of the LSE, Warden of St Antony's, Oxford, and a member of the House of Lords. When he had completed a brilliant paper in his perfect English, he was followed by the American moderator in his heavy, joke Central European accent. Later when Henry Kissinger was Secretary of State a colleague of mine interviewed him in depth for a major profile and, on being about to depart, remembered that his subject had arrived originally in New York as a teenager with his elder brother. What had happened to the brother? He, it seemed, was president of a medium-size firm in the Mid-West. My colleague went to see him and after having been with him for a time remarked that he had been speaking without a trace of Henry's Germanic accent. 'Ah!' he replied, 'I am the Kissinger who listens.'

The years 1967 and 1968, during which I was at Harvard, were years of great social tension on account of two issues: the war in Vietnam and race relations. Harvard itself was not one of the main scenes of violence which often centred on university campuses but after a while our students felt that they ought not to be left out. Honour required that this *doyen* of American universities should also have its demonstrations against what was being done in America's name in Southeast Asia. The chosen target was Dow Chemicals, the makers of napalm, the fiery substance that was creating so much devastation in Vietnam. As with many leading firms Dow was in the habit of dispatching a team to Harvard in the hope of recruiting the most promising students. This year they got in but were prevented by a large crowd from getting out, all of which caused considerable heartburn among certain members of the faculty who had been liberal veterans of the McCarthy battles. What price freedom of speech now?

Senator Robert Kennedy came to the Institute to consult the Fellows about his course of action during the coming presidential election. Lyndon Johnson had withdrawn from the battle. Hubert Humphrey, as Johnson's Vice-President, was committed to Johnson's conduct of the war in Vietnam, while Eugene McCarthy had courageously stepped out first into the arena to articulate the mounting opposition to it. A quirky senator from Minnesota, he did not, for all his merits, sound like a man who could win the Democratic nomination against the officially backed Humphrey. Should Bobby Kennedy, with all the glamour that still adhered to him as the right-hand man of his slain brother, risk appearing to be muscling in at this relatively late date on what had hitherto been McCarthy's stand against the war? As the only non-American present I held my peace while the issues were tossed about the room in lucid but unemotional fashion. Bobby himself took little part but was listening intently. I noticed two things about him: he was beginning to turn grey behind the ears (this shocked me as I had always been in the habit of thinking him so young) and he appeared very tensed up, as if living on his nerves.

Later I interviewed Bobby Kennedy for half an hour in a special BBC series which featured established interviewers choosing their own subjects. He was very positive about the rights of African-Americans, but what was perhaps more impressive was the fact that he took the initiative in speaking also about the plight of Red Indians (or Native Americans, as they are now known), people who were not much accustomed to voting in presidential elections. In East St Louis I saw him give to a largely black crowd their first news of the death of the black hero Martin Luther King, and do it as only he could in such a way as to avoid a riot. And I watched on television the moment in California at which he was gunned down just at the moment of winning a vital primary election.

As Mort Sahl had been the satirist who had epitomised for me the election year of 1956, so that role was played for me in the election year of 1968 by a mathematician teaching at Harvard with a raucous voice and an aggressive way of punishing a piano – Tom Lehrer. His talk was of 'sliding down the razor blade of life' and of 'Dr Gall, inventor of the gall bladder, who specialises in the diseases of the very rich'. But above all he sang daring, cynical ditties that took apart the sacred truths of American orthodoxy.

In the summer Suzy and I crossed over to Canada, where we stayed with one of her relatives and I made a film for the BBC about the remarkable phenomenon that was Pierre Trudeau. Here was a politician who managed to make himself into an icon for the young, so much so that posters and postcards displayed his cool, youthful figure alongside those of Martin Luther King and Che Guevara (both of whom, one could not help remarking, were dead). It was not that he had anything very remarkable to say and what he did say was rather academic. Yet in a huge open-air meeting in Toronto it was really only necessary for him to appear. He was a megastar.

We spent Christmas amid the snows of New Hampshire at a lodge at Franconia. When the weather warmed up we spent our weekends exploring the New England coast and in the Easter vacation went out west with an able and charming Irish friend, Denis Corboy, an official of the European Commission who was spending a year in America as an Eisenhower Fellow. Like so many visitors to the States we enjoyed the generosity of American friends. In particular, Bill Shannon, by now with the *New York Times* and married to a beautiful and lively Texan called Liz, made us welcome in their summer home at Woodstock in New York State and lent us their temporarily vacant Washington residence. This enabled me to introduce Suzy to the city in which I had spent such a formative period of my life.

My continued interest in a political career, stimulated rather than the reverse by my Fellowship, made long-term career choices very difficult. Fortunately the BBC offered me a freelance contract, so that would keep me going for the time being. I came back to an unhappy country whose Labour government had achieved little of what it had promised and appeared to be reeling from one crisis to another. That I was still not thrilled by my party leader is apparent from a letter to my parents on New Year's Day 1968 when I wrote that 'H.W. is rather a disaster to the party, but we're stuck with him now and it's something that Roy Jenkins, who since Gaitskell's death has been my favourite politician, is at last sufficiently powerfully placed to have a major impact on the overall strategy of the government.' By May I was writing gloomily that, whereas I had been hoping to get a safe seat within a couple of years, 'Now it is hard to see what seat can be regarded as safe. It looks as if I shall have to be content with the BBC and journalism for quite a while ahead.'

Before taking up my BBC position I was in Beirut on a free trip. I knew that *The Economist*'s stringer in the city was Rosemary Sayigh, the English wife of Dr Yusuf Sayigh, the Palestine Liberation Organisation's resident intellectual, and had alerted her in advance of my visit. They were both extremely helpful in organising contacts, the most significant of which took place at a party at their house. I had asked to meet a range of opinions within the Palestine resistance and my hosts had been as good as their word. There was considerable discussion about the wisdom or otherwise of the hijacking of aircraft belonging to the Israeli airline El Al by Palestinian gunmen, which had happened twice recently. The aim was to get the world talking about the Palestinian cause, of which at the time very little was heard. It was clear that there was no consensus in the room about the advisability of this tactic and I was asked what impact the two instances had had on public opinion in the West. Acknowledging to start with that these dramatic occurrences had pushed the Palestine question for a while to the top of the news agenda, I said that the Arabs had been very lucky in that so far there had been no casualties. But I strongly urged them to quit while they were ahead; next time somebody would get killed and then any gain in publicity would go rapidly into reverse. I was promised that those who favoured this tactic had agreed to go ahead only three times, after which the whole PLO would take stock. I concluded from this that there would be an 'El Al 3', though understandably I was given no idea of when and where it would take place. I made no use of this information at the time but it was to have an important effect on my later involvement with the Middle East.

I continued to handle political stories although it was no secret that I was a past Labour candidate and might very well be one again. I was quite widely used on lower-level political stories and I can honestly say that the conflict of interest that might be thought to arise never did so. Or rather perhaps unconsciously it did but was always resolved in favour of responsibility to the BBC and its viewers. I remember once travelling back by train from taking part in a Brains Trust with a Conservative MP, Patrick (later Lord) Jenkin. In the course of a conversation about broadcasting and politics I said that I was grateful to the Conservative Party for not making a fuss about my working for the BBC. He replied, 'It's not people like you who have respect for the parliamentary process that we are worried about. It's those people who have no regard for it.'

Nineteen Sixty-Nine was the year in which I first became deeply involved with two issues that were to play a major part in my career – Northern Ireland and the Middle East. And it was the year, too, in which I was to come closest to achieving my ambition of becoming a member of the Westminster Parliament.

On 4 January 1969 I found myself instantly whisked off from the Lime Grove offices of the *Tonight* programme to Luton Airport and a BBC plane to Belfast. A civil rights march calling itself non-sectarian, heading for Londonderry, had been intercepted at Burntollet Bridge by a Unionist crowd which included off-duty policemen. Many of the marchers had been badly beaten by bottles, sticks and iron bars. Those Irish Troubles which historically had intruded so often into British politics had revisited it with a vengeance. The local Belfast office of the BBC was overwhelmed by a sudden switch from the national network's habitual indifference to Ulster's affairs to a mood of intense interest and I was one of the relatively few correspondents with some acquaintance, thanks to my *Economist* days, with the Irish political scene north and south. For the next five years in which I was frequently in the Province and also, though less often, in the Republic, I came to feel great affection and pity for men and women on both sides caught up in the conflict while never ceasing to sense that I was caught in a time warp, of having been posted to an earlier century.

The superficial archaisms were less important – the fact, for example, that the press in Ulster regularly called the police 'peelers', in reference to Sir Robert Peel who had started the modern police force, even though the term had not been used in England since the 1930s. What seemed utterly out of time was to find religious affiliation at the cutting edge of political division with types of feeling associated in England with the Catholic Aggression crisis of 1850 or, even worse, the Gordon Riots of 1780. The Revs Henry Cooke and 'Roaring Hugh' Hanna[27] had raged without limit against the Catholics in the nineteenth century and the Rev Dr Ian Paisley was following their path in the twentieth. Nor was his spleen limited to the Catholics themselves: anyone who appeared to be conciliating the Church of Rome came within the compass of his abuse. A big man with a big voice he was, like Hanna, a formidable orator. In 1958 when the Queen Mother and Princess Margaret visited Pope John XXIII in Rome, he denounced them for 'committing spiritual fornication and adultery with the Anti-Christ'. And when Pope John died Paisley's audience was assured that, 'This Romish man of sin is now in Hell.' I felt that this was a man I must get to know.

I went to his Sunday service in the Free Presbyterian Church, which he had founded and of which he was the Moderator. The hellfire sermon was followed by an invitation to the congregation to join him in alfresco refreshments. There were several tables laid out in the grounds of his church and, as my purpose was to meet Paisley, I moved towards the one where he was standing. 'Only Free Presbyterians here,' he roared, striking the table with his fist. Fortunately I happened to know that Kyle was his middle name and with a matching gesture I cried out, 'Only Kyles here.' Dr Paisley is not with-out a sense of humour and I was invited to sit down beside him. In the next few weeks I got to know him fairly well. The paradox was that while he was totally unreasonable theologically he talked raw politics very much as, *mutatis mutandis*, a Boston Irishman might do, in striking contrast to the oddly remote remarks of the Anglo-Irish landowners who had been accustomed to handling on a part-time basis the affairs of the Province. The charming Prime Minister, Terence O'Neill, who started his political career as the son and nephew of two leading politicians in his county of Antrim, had, for the 20 years since his first election, been without an opponent in the constituency he had inherited from his aunt.

I was challenged by one of the few working-class Ulster Unionist MPs, a docker named John McQuade, to spend an evening in his sitting room in the Shankill Road, the core of militant Belfast Unionism. I readily agreed and found myself in a small space that was absolutely bulging with fiery voices excoriating Roman Catholics in terms strikingly reminiscent of Southern-ers in the United States talking about Negroes (who did not wash or weed their gardens, avoided work and had too many children) and being hardly more complimentary about the British government and the BBC. This was on account of the BBC giving equal time to government and opposition in the Province without taking into consideration the fact that the former were loyal and the latter disloyal to the British Crown. To these Unionists this was plain evidence of false equivalence.

When I subsequently interviewed John McQuade on camera and asked him why he was so anxious to evict Catholic tenants from the Unity flats, a block which had deliberately been planned as a social experiment in encouraging integrated living, he said it was because Catholics had insulted the Union flag when it was being paraded in front of the flats. 'It's your flag as well as mine,' he replied. 'How would you like to see your flag spat at?' I observed that I did not believe in involving our flag in political demonstrations. 'That's where we are different from the mainland. Our colours, as I say and shall maintain, are not kicking the Pope but are shown to us and our children as the victory of good over evil, of King William over King James.' In common with many journalists now pouring into Ulster,[28] I had been brought up in the classroom to assume the same attitude towards the events of the seventeenth century. Moreover this historical prejudice was reinforced by the present-day associa-tion of the Catholic Church with regimes that were reactionary politically in Spain and Portugal and culturally in Italy and the Irish Republic. I started off therefore with presuppositions, mildly held, that were broadly favourable to the Ulster Unionists. The manner in which they expressed their 'loyalty' to the British Crown soon placed such sympathy under severe strain.

A rich example was provided soon after I arrived by a vast demonstration that filled all streets leading to Belfast City Hall. The most colourful speaker among a gallery of Unionist names was Dr Paisley, and one noticed through all the speeches the glaring contradiction between repeated declarations of loyalty to the United Kingdom and equally repeated references to Dublin in terms that in Britain itself would only be used of Moscow. This was a case if ever there was one of the tail demanding to wag the dog. But a day or two later there was another contrast – between the fervent response of the previous audience to Ian Paisley in the streets and the extremely meagre turnout at a well-advertised meeting at which the same Ian Paisley was deploying theological arguments that were supposed to show that one could not at one and the same time be a Roman Catholic and a Christian. The lesson I drew from this was that, while the two tribes were for historical and cultural reasons labelled Catholic and Protestant, this was not, as in the time of Calvin, primarily a dispute over transubstantiation.

Meanwhile the British public, mainly through the media in which I (with others) was working, were being exposed for the first time to the visual impact of what was for them an almost unbelievable situation. Now, getting on for 40 years later, television viewers have become inured to the colourful but grotesque political graffiti of the Northern Ireland struggle. But in 1969 it beggared belief that in our own country as opposed to other less happy lands there should exist beliefs (and historical references) both threatening and ludicrously anachronistic. At this date IRA militancy and its accompanying graffiti had not yet reappeared on the scene. The IRA and its political wing Sinn Fein were still given over to a socialist, abstentionist (from all institutions arising from partition) and non-violent ideology. The aggressive street signs were still only those showing King William III proudly riding a white horse across the River Boyne to defeat King James, oblivious of a few facts such as that the Pope was on King William's side and ordered the *Te Deum* to be sung in celebration of his victory, that the horse in question was not white and that, caught by a rising tide in the Boyne, it was led on foot with some difficulty across the ford by a King dismounted and breathless, wracked with coughing and propped up by a dragoon. The artwork was repeatedly directed against Dublin, against the Catholic minority in Ulster and increasingly against the 'soft' Prime Minister, Terence O'Neill.

I went to Londonderry and witnessed the local council in action. Its mainly Protestant members were only too visibly out of synch with the by now numerically dominant Catholic community. Having associated since schooldays the name of Londonderry (and Enniskillen) with heroic Protestants making a valiant stand for liberty, I could not but note that the area inside the castle walls was more solidly Catholic than that outside, so that the triumphalist Unionist march round the tops of the walls, which was an annual event, was an especially provocative symbolism. Yet because of the narrow franchise in the city as a whole the Unionists remained in charge. I stayed at the City Hotel which was destined later to be blown up. There had been some ugly clashes in the streets and the manager was downcast. 'Things were just beginning to look up,' he said mournfully, 'and more tourists were starting to come to the city so that we had planned to upgrade the hotel. We had even thought of hiring a stripper.' As Marlon Brando said in *On the Waterfront*, 'I could have been a contender.'

A member of the not very powerful or united Northern Ireland Labour Party, but an admirable man and one well attuned to the wrath to come, advised me to be particularly careful about what I said on television 'because it is our lives that you are treading on'. He added, 'we shall be here when you have gone off to the Lebanon'. On returning to London, I was indeed posted to Beirut. One reason why the BBC decided at this moment to mount an extended series of reports from the Middle East was that its processes of internal self-criticism had drawn the conclusion that its reporting of Arab–Israeli matters since the 1967 war had relied excessively on Israeli sources. One reason was that Western public opinion in general had blamed the Arabs for that war and had admired the dramatic response of Israel to extreme pressure. As the Israelis often said, the Arabs could fight and lose war after war but Israel could not survive a single defeat. But a further reason was that too many of the Arab states had been shooting themselves in the foot by banning the entry of Western journalists. I was sent partly because it was thought that my previous trip under Arab auspices might give me some priority of access. As it happened the Arab Ministers of Information had just jointly reached the conclusion that their previous policy was not a good idea and I was one of the first beneficiaries of this change.

While the subjects of the individual films were left largely to me and my producer, a personable and engaging young man called Tony Summers, we were asked, while doing nothing to compromise the BBC's reputation for fairness, to bear in mind the alleged unintended pro-Israeli bias of previous reports. (There was the additional complication that the resident BBC correspondent in Israel was an Israeli citizen. I formed a high opinion of his work when I was there but I knew that the Corporation was feeling vulnerable on this account.) I accepted this brief but with the understanding that as well as giving Arabs a fair chance to put their case I would be free to investigate the questionable treatment of the remaining Jewish minorities in Syria and Iraq.

For the next seven weeks Beirut could be regarded as our home base, the place we went back to when we wanted to relax. This was before the terrible years of the Lebanese civil war. The city gave the superficial impression of being vibrant, multicultural and wealthy without any very obvious signs of possessing a government at all. In those days the Lebanon was often pointed to as a model (as with Switzerland) of how a mosaic of diverse communities could be held together peacefully by consociational institutions (meaning, broadly, power-sharing and off-setting vetoes). It was known, for instance, that the president was always a Maronite Christian, the prime minister a Sunni Muslim and the parliamentary speaker a Shia Muslim. Other elements, such as the Druze, also had their recognised roles in the cabinet. The potential for violence in the country as a whole, of which I was at the time slightly aware, was mainly evident in the fact that any political leaders worthy of the name seemed to regard it as essential to be backed in their constituencies by armed paramilitaries. (The analogy of the Scottish Highlands before the Jacobite rebellion occurred to me.) The Lebanese Army, on the other hand, was a strictly non-fighting force, though that did not stop its generals from dabbling in politics. Those who wanted to make money seemed to be making it with little interference from a political system that to all appearances was revolving quietly on its own axis according to its own arcane rules. Although there was plenty in Lebanon worthy of investigation we did not investigate it but took advantage of its ample facilities to investigate the affairs of others.

In Beirut many situations were to be viewed at one remove, unlike in many of the other Arab states. There was a lively and varied press, with individual papers known to be attached to most tendencies throughout the Arab world, and there were also influential individuals who for a variety of reasons preferred not to live in their own countries. For that reason – and not normally for the coverage of Lebanese affairs – there was a large presence of the foreign press and, since no aspect of life in the Lebanon was not commercial, there was a sophisticated industry in existence to service that press. As most journalists there, including myself, did not know Arabic, this included an efficient translation service, to which the BBC subscribed, so that I received over breakfast every morning in the press hotel a thick file in English of the leading articles and main political news reports from the day's Arabic newspapers. By comparing them one could tell what the Saudis had to say, what the Syrians, and so forth. The English-speaking taxi driver whom we hired for the duration of our stay would know the personal habits of the person we wished to interview and would take one to the café or eating-house (or girlfriend's flat) where he was most likely to be found. While we had lunch he would on his own initiative switch his radio to the BBC World Service in order to tell us of any relevant news when we rejoined him.

Our first task was to locate Arabs from Palestine who were students at Lebanese universities or exiles in Beirut. We met quite a number but the one who stands out in my memory is Hanan Mikhail, better known now by her married name as Hanan Ashrawi. She was in her early 20s, completing her graduate studies at the American College. Her thesis, as I recall, was about the travels in the Middle East of two seventeenth-century Englishmen, one of them the illegitimate son of Archbishop Sandys of York. She was at that time slim, beautiful and bubbling all over with life and aspirations. She had an extraordinary knack of producing on the spot English blank-verse translations of Arab poetry. It was really Hanan, with the aid of some of her compatriots, who first interested me seriously in the proposition that there was a separate Palestinian nationality with its own customs and culture rather than simply Arabs who happened to have lived in Palestine. This seems so obvious 35 years later that it is hard to recall that my television reports are credited by many

9. With Hanan Ashrawi in Beirut, 1969.

Palestinians with being the first time that this had received any public recognition in Britain. But this was all the more unwelcome in Jewish circles in that the Israeli Prime Minister, Mrs Golda Meir, had publicly committed herself to the proposition that there was no such thing as a Palestinian people.

Before we were to go to Israel, for which purpose we would have to leave the Middle East and change planes at either Cyprus or Athens, there was work to be done in Syria and Iraq. Damascus, still containing 'a street called straight' to which I thus returned, was largely under water, not very much water to be sure but enough to require duckboards along most of the pavements. Politically Syria was in the early stages of one of the most prolonged *coups d'état* in history, with the President, a dentist called Nour Al-Deen Al-Attasi, and the regime's strongman, the reclusive General Salah Jdeed, at one end of town and the Minister of Defence, Air Force General Hafez Assad, at the other. The two elements glowered at each other for 18 months before Assad was ultimately to prevail. Jdeed was transferred to jail, from which he was only released when he was dying.

In addition to reporting this unusual political situation, my interest was in the fate of the remaining Syrian Jews. We entered the ghetto and attended a wedding. We were told that most Jews would have liked to leave either for Israel or the United States but that they were not allowed to go. However, it was said that life was a little easier in Damascus than in Baghdad because the existence of a ghetto in the former city enabled the Jews to bunch together, though they knew that they were being constantly watched. The watchers at the Damascene wedding were pointed out to me. But Baghdad, I was told, was worse because there was no ghetto.

When we arrived in Baghdad there was an urgent message for us to contact the British Ambassador, Glencairn Balfour Paul, archaeologist and poet as well as diplomat. Tony and I presented ourselves at the impressive riverside Embassy. The Ambassador had bad news for us. The Foreign Office had been warned by the Israelis that my presence in Israel would not be welcome, though the consequences of ignoring this were not spelled out. As I absorbed the news over drinks, Balfour Paul remarked that the Foreign Office would like to know what I planned to do. None of my films had yet been transmitted but it was apparent from the official message that the government of Israel had taken exception to reported remarks I had made on screen in London about the hijacking of El Al planes. What had happened was that I had been in the green room awaiting transmission of the *Tonight* programme when the news came through that a third El Al plane had been taken. I said immediately that this must be the 'El Al 3' to which reference had been made in Yusuf Sayigh's drawing room when I had previously been in Beirut. The editor urged me to repeat this on air at the head of the programme, which I did while deleting the location. From this had sprung stories in the Israeli press that the BBC's Keith Kyle had admitted being present at a planning session of the Arab hijackers and that, knowing these plans, had failed to alert the authorities. I had also been mistakenly identified as a member of the Council for the Advancement of Arab-British Understanding (CAABU), a body I had deliberately steered clear of as being incompatible with my role as a reporter. I told the Ambassador that I would go ahead to Israel as planned. The Israeli government would have to make up its mind what it was going to do with me but my guess was that it would be sufficiently concerned about its reputation as the only democracy in the region not to do much. I was more concerned than I let on for two rather personal reasons: that being fascinated to discover what Israel was really like it would be frustrating not to be allowed in and that I particularly regretted that what appeared to be a personal breach had opened between myself and the Israeli Foreign Minister, Abba Eban, whom I had regarded as a personal friend.

Eban had been the Israeli Ambassador in Washington while I had been living there. A man of remarkable intellect – he had a Triple First from Cambridge and once, when visiting Singapore, had tactfully removed this detail from his c.v. on learning that the Prime Minister of that city state was immensely proud of having a Double First from the same university – he had served as a major in the British Army and had been the first head of the Middle Eastern languages school in Jerusalem. He was equally fluent in English, Hebrew and Arabic and invariably spoke in whichever language in complete, well-rounded paragraphs.

However, for the moment I had to forget about Israel and concentrate hard on what I was doing in Baghdad. Never, not even in the Soviet satellites I worked in later, did I sense such an atmosphere of fear as on that trip to Iraq. There had been a murderous overthrow of one section of Ba'ath Socialism by another and the army was everywhere. I opened a wrong door in the Ministry of Information and found myself in a barrack room full of soldiers. The Ministry official who received me (once I had found the right office) was silkily welcoming. He had clearly got the new Pan-Arab message that foreign correspondents were to be encouraged. Two other journalists, a male and female French pair, were just leaving as I was admitted. Expressions of incredulity were coming out of them at the ease with which all their requests to travel in the Kurdish north had been granted. As for me the official was more than anxious to aid the BBC's filming; for our use there turned out to be still photographs and videos aplenty. Since the new regime had been notoriously employed in the public execution of its enemies I at first sought to raise this topic by indirection. My scruples were quite misplaced. After a moment's genuine uncertainty about what I was on about, the obliging official reached into a drawer and poured out before me samples from his large collection of public enemies hanging from a rope. I had mentioned Jews. He had here a video, which we were at liberty to use, of the Chief Rabbi of Baghdad confessing all his sins. Did we want to talk to a Jewish psychologist of international reputation who would be perfectly ready to explain how he pursued his work with complete freedom? Then there was a flourishing Jewish school which we could film. As for the university, of course, it was not true, as had been wickedly alleged, that Jews were excluded. We could go there and see for ourselves. In the meantime the Minister of Information (who was, I was led to believe, a key figure in the regime) would like to receive us. The conversation with the Minister was on roughly similar lines and ended with an invitation to the races, at which we were told the leading figures in the 'revolutionary command' would be present.

Next day we appeared at the racecourse and were presented to Saddam Hussein. I had been told beforehand that this was the strong man of the Ba'ath Socialist Mark II regime, although he only bore the title of vice-president. He was in his early 30s, which was considered too young for a head of state. That title was borne by General Hassan Baqr, who was not present on this occasion. He was usually described in Iraqi publicity as 'Struggler Baqr'. Little was known about him. He struggled for a full decade and then disappeared when Saddam, having now apparently attained years of discretion, was proclaimed President. Saddam passed some compliment about the BBC and offered me a nut. I took it and broke my front tooth on it, which is an unfortunate accident for a television reporter. The thuggish entourage by whom the Vice-President was surrounded did not make a reassuring spectacle.

The next day, accompanied by our minder, we went to see the Jewish psychologist. I have never in my life been in the presence of a man so obviously scared. The filmed interview was an intensely painful one, as the poor man squeezed out the briefest of assertions that he was living and working with total freedom. I brought the meeting to an end as soon as I decently could. The video of the Chief Rabbi on very grainy film carried an impression not dissimilar to that created by the broadcasts of hostages in Iraq in 2004 and 2005. I realised that I must find some way of operating apart from the Ministry minder. We were taken to the Jewish school. I took advantage of the interest created by the television crew and camera to slip off out of sight of the man from the Ministry. Parents and teachers were not slow to take advantage of my tactic. They briefed me in person or passed short written messages to me. Told of my hotel number one or two of them ran the considerable risk of contacting me at night. The picture that they conveyed was one of a fearful existence. We also managed to visit the university without escort. But the Ministry of Information had evidently not had time to think through the implications of its new policy of openness. We had been invited to verify the presence of Jews on the campus, and when we went there we were told blankly that no Jew had been seen on campus for at least five years.

We returned to Beirut to script and edit our material away from the clammy atmosphere of military government. Tony and I were both eager to increase our background knowledge of the Levantine world. As I have said, as well as being a supremely capitalist city in a world of so-called Arab socialism, Beirut was a city of exiles, those Arabs thirsty for free speech and uncomfortable in their own countries. I became friendly with a Syrian poet who had a very independent line on what was happening in his country and who, admiring Arnold Toynbee immensely, entrusted me with a copy of his poems to pass on to him.

My Syrian friend had hoped that I would endorse the then current PLO policy of calling for the abolition of Israel as a state. I told him why I could not do so, because I was a European, because the Europeans had horribly betrayed the Jews, because it was therefore morally impossible for me to deny them the only thing that they believed would prevent this happening to them again. I said that I had called for the creation of the state at a time when Britain had been reluctant to grant it and that, however much I might now sympathise with the situation of the Arabs, I could not and would not go back on that. I spoke with some passion and, grasping me by the hands, the poet declared with emotion that I was an honest man.

The BBC, having, it appeared, liked the first batch of films that we had sent, extended our period in the Middle East. This would involve a change of camera crew while we were in Israel, because of which Tony Summers was able to negotiate for us to have a week's local holiday over the period of the changeover. Suzy being due some leave from her television job, it was arranged for her to join me in Jerusalem. There was, however, a snag: I had not yet passed through Lod (now renamed Ben Gurion) airport. Because Israel was not then recognised by any Arab state, we could not fly direct from Beirut, so that we went by way of Athens. After the drama at the Embassy in Baghdad the actual arrival in Israel was something of an anticlimax. No obstacle at all was placed in my way at the airport and we moved off along the road to Jerusalem, which in those days was still lined by burned-out tanks and other souvenirs of the tense battles which had marked the birth of the state of Israel.

The first sight of Jerusalem which Richard Coeur de Lion either did or did not manage to see (and, if he did, it was his only sight of it) is one of life's great experiences. My mind conjured up all the medieval maps of the world with Jerusalem at their centre. We made our way to East Jerusalem where we put up in the famous 'American Colony' hotel which dates from Ottoman times. We rather rapidly discovered the extent of the fallout from my brief studio appearance. Mrs Meir was not going to be interviewed by me and, what was personally more painful, my friend Abba Eban had cancelled the interview which I had arranged. It had been ruled that no minister should speak to me.

Our first stop was at the British Consulate General. The Consul-General could not have been more helpful. He escorted us round the eastern part of the city, showing where new buildings were being planned as the first part of what he explained was designed to be a Jewish-owned screen breaking the links between the city and the West Bank. We filmed scenes from the Wailing Wall, which is a sacred place for Jews as being the only relic of the Temple of Herod (at any rate above ground) and from which Israeli Jews had been excluded during the period (1949–67) of Jordanian rule. The opportunity for Jewish worship, which had been guaranteed under the British Mandate, had at that period given rise to chronic friction between the display and apparatus of Jewish worship and the closely surrounding Muslim premises. This culminated in 1929 in violence and a League of Nations committee of inquiry. I had read its proceedings and the picture which they drew of a cluttered ceremonial being thrust into a narrow alley-way were partially confirmed by the crumbling multi-storey buildings that were still overhanging part of the site. These were, however, in the process of being demolished and from an upper window an Arab resident, seeing us with cameras below, was shouting down in English that their homes were at that very moment being destroyed. I must confess that, sympathetic though one might feel about the predicament of individuals, I saw the Israelis' point of view. Even if their intention was to withdraw eventually from most of the occupied territory, they would surely not withdraw from the Wailing Wall, in which case it was arguable that creating an open plaza in front of the Wall was the least bad solution available. It was something that the British Mandatory had talked of doing under the heading of slum clearance; it was a pity that it had not done it.

The collective punishment being imposed on the West Bank was an altogether different matter. A large house which was owned by an American citizen of Palestinian birth and which was home to several branches and generations of his family was about to be dynamited by the Israelis because one of the young men living there had been accused (not convicted) of having been involved in an act of sabotage. In researching this story I got information not only from the IDF (Israeli Defence Forces) and the Palestinians involved but also from the Americans and, most significantly, from the International Red Cross. Its representative, who could not be publicly cited, supplied me with an extensive briefing on the international law affecting military occupation, much of which had been updated in 1949 to take account of German practices during the war. I had the feeling that Jews of all people should be exemplary in upholding such rules. The contrary argument which was put to me was that the decree under which the IDF was acting was held over from the British Mandate. It had been introduced in order to punish refractory Jews. There was also a contrived argument that, as Jordanian sovereignty over the West Bank had been recognised only by Britain and Pakistan, the Israeli occupation was not an occupation in the sense of the international rules. An IDF officer, who turned out to have been a Polish Jew, put the point to me rather more brutally, 'They claim this is bad treatment. They are lucky not to have been Jews in Poland.'

The house was blown up. In the film which we made of this the vision of the explosion and the distress deliberately created was accompanied by my reading out off-camera the appropriate clauses of the Geneva Conventions which outlawed this action. In my piece to camera I quoted the words of the man who was now Israeli Minister of Justice, written when he was struggling against the British, to the effect that this emergency legislation was a barbaric procedure. I interviewed an official spokesman from the Ministry of Defence, who at the time was the most senior Israeli I was entitled to see in view of the complete ban on politicians in office talking to me. He was later quite unfairly criticised in the Israeli press for not administering an adequate political refutation. It was this film more than the others which obtained for me at the time a reputation as an enemy of Israel.

But this was not the only report which when transmitted in Britain fed the hostility of Israeli correspondents. There were films from the West Bank demonstrating that, despite Golda Meir, the Palestinians as such did really exist. We had received from Hanan Mikhail in Beirut a letter of introduction to her parents in Ramallah. Her father was a successful doctor who lived in a comfortable middle-class home which in itself was a refutation of the impression among many British viewers at the time that all Arabs were unshaven and lived in tents. The Mikhails being Orthodox Christians, I sat down with them on the Orthodox Easter Sunday to eat the special patisserie (not hot cross buns, but cakes decorated with a cross) that goes with the occasion and to conduct a relaxed conversation under the television cameras about the

10. Filming in Israel.

evidence of Palestinian nationality and possible ways of resolving the problem of living next to Israel.

As planned, Suzy arrived at the halfway point of our stay in Israel. For the first few days we still had work to do and I was able to arrange for Palestinian friends to guide her round some of the historic places in Jerusalem. Then we were free to be tourists and set out in a hired car to see as much as we could in the Holy Land. We were by the Sea of Galilee, which at this point was so low that I speculated that I might perhaps be able to walk upon its surface, when a dispatch rider on a motor bike tracked us down. He brought a message from Abba Eban, inviting me to the Foreign Ministry and reinstating our interview. I was relieved both from a personal viewpoint and also from a professional one since I did not wish to return without a proper examination of the Israeli position. When I reached the Ministry I was warmly greeted, Abba showing me the innocuous text which he had by then acquired of my actual remarks about 'El Al 3'. He dismissed the fuss that the press had made and we had a civilised exchange, with the Foreign Minister expressing impeccable views about Israeli readiness to discuss major concessions (provided that there was a similar response from the Arabs), while I pressed him by quoting the very much less forthcoming opinions and deeds of some of his ministerial colleagues. He sought, a little too easily I thought, to brush these aside, creating an impression that, regardless of all the talk about annexation of 'liberated' *Eretz Israel*, Arabs had only to show interest in negotiation to be amazed at the generosity of the Israeli response. Shortly afterwards my more controversial films about Palestinian nationality went out in Britain and the full force of Jewish reaction to them hit the Israeli press. Our further efforts to interview Golda Meir hit a brick wall.

A few days after I returned to London I was taken ill with a condition called Tropical Sprue and from the Hospital for Tropical Diseases observed the anti-Kyle campaign achieving headline status in the Jewish press and seeping into the gossip columns of a few national papers. I was regarded, according to the *Jewish Chronicle*, 'as one of the most extreme pro-Arabists among British journalists'.[29] My previously strong pro-Jewish leanings were somewhat tempered by my recent exposure to the realities of the Middle East but they were far from being reversed; and on what was at that time the basic point at issue between Israel and the PLO – whether there should be one secular bi-national state between the Jordan River and the sea – I remained on the side of Israel.

A Labour MP, Reginald Freeson, for whom I had once spoken politically, had acquired a copy of one of my shooting scripts, the one which included the demolition of the Palestinian house. Against almost every line of my commentary he had scrawled a question mark and the word 'source'. As the report was in fact very well sourced, though a television report is unable to carry footnotes, I had no difficulty in answering very precisely every one of the queries. Lord Hill of Luton, the 'Radio Doctor' who was now the BBC's chairman, had my 'footnotes' in front of him when he received a deputation from the Jewish Board of Deputies who asked that I be banned from the screen as a biased reporter. The doctor was in consequence not disposed to give them that satisfaction.

By the time I left hospital the criticisms had built up a considerable head of steam and I was asked if I were willing to appear with my critics on radio. I was so willing. The editor of the *Jewish Chronicle* started off by basing his case on the assumption that I was a member of CAABU and therefore as *parti pris* should not have been sent to the Middle East. Since the assumption was wrong the rebuttal was not too difficult and I was considered to have acquitted myself sufficiently well for the BBC to be prepared to expose me to a full-length challenge on television. This was a very early experiment in providing for a talk-back programme. My only stipulation was that Yusuf Sayigh, who happened to be in London at the time, should also take part. I had it in mind that 'El Al 3' would be cited, so that he could confirm the circumstances of the party held at his Beirut home, but, more importantly, he could be relied on to establish the wide divergence between my outlook, such as it was, and that of the PLO.[30] A different editorial writer from the *Jewish Chronicle* was the chief prosecutor, but other people, including a Labour MP and a visiting Israeli intellectual of moderate views (who got into serious trouble with his colleagues for his expression of such views on the programme), also took part, under the efficient chairmanship of Robert McKenzie of the London School of Economics. I was, I think, conciliatory in manner but firm in defence of my programmes. The television critic of the *Jewish Chronicle* thought that I became 'more heated' as the discussion proceeded, but there is nothing incompatible between vigorous delivery and inner calm.[31] The experience of being at the centre of controversy was reassuring in that it satisfied me that I was well able to take the heat. I retained friendships with Jewish people (though socially there was some strain while the press offensive was on) and I returned to Israel seven or eight times, first as a journalist and later as an academic. I was very sorry to have come into conflict with Jews, whom in general I continued to admire, but I did not regret having played a small role in the recognition, which 38 years later is universally accepted, of the Palestinians as a party in their own right to the perennial and agonising conflict with which the British Mandate had endowed the Middle East.

CHAPTER 17

Islington, Ireland
and Europe

S uddenly an opportunity to quit being the unelected reporter of events
and to start being entitled, by virtue of having been elected, to play some
part in creating them seemed to be opening. The much-loved Labour
MP for Islington North, a constituency with a considerable Irish population,
died of cancer. I put my name forward and was short-listed for the candidacy.
With a little bit of luck my Irish plan would be the theme of my maiden speech.

The Labour government was not in 1969 in good shape in the eyes of public
opinion and, one year off from an expected general election, it was vital that
such a normally Labour seat as Islington be held. There were rumours that
Irish groups were considering running a candidate of their own if six demands
for a change in Northern Ireland policy were not met. This very much worried
the local Labour Party, which had been so obsessed with the dangers of entry-
ism from the left that, as a number of people complained to me, it was very
difficult for an outsider to secure membership. The party members now feared
that the threatened loss of Labour's traditional Irish vote, combined with the
Labour government's current unpopularity, would wipe out their normal
victory margin. My approach was that, while it would be illegal and in any
case wrong to make a deal with another party in return for its withdrawal, any
constituent or group of constituents was perfectly entitled to ask a candidate
for his views. My views on Ulster not only encompassed all six of the points
raised, including the suppression of Stormont, but went beyond them since I
was then prepared to try for a power-sharing government. With no question
of a deal (to prove the absence of which I envisaged inviting the local press to
any meeting with the Irish), I felt confident of being able to take care of the
threatened intervention. A local official of the General and Municipal Workers
Union, which I had joined in my capacity as a 'general worker' some four years

11. 'Mr Keith Kyle, one of the five men on the short list from which the
North Islington Labour Party will select its by-election candidate on Sunday,
interviews the late Senator Robert Kennedy for the BBC Television "Personal
Choice" programme. Forty-four-year-old Mr Kyle has travelled widely for
the "24 Hours" programme and from 1967–68 he was a Fellow
at the John F. Kennedy Institute at Harvard.'
(*Islington Gazette*, 5 September 1969)

before, interviewed me at his house and came down strongly in my support.
But not being a 'time-server' (i.e. I had not been a union member for at least
seven years) I was not eligible for an official endorsement.

On account of my presence on the screen there was some publicity in the
press, especially in *The Times*, about my candidacy, and the *Islington Gazette*
carried a picture from BBC publicity of my interview with Senator Robert
Kennedy. This was in no way instigated by me, since I had noticed before that
individuals given exposure in advance of selection conferences normally bit
the dust. I had four competitors of whom the most serious, I was told, was Vic
Butler, an official of the London Co-op whose wife was already in Parliament.
There was also an Irishman, Michael O'Halloran, who was an office manager
for Murphy's, the Highbury building contractors which relied on labour from

Ireland, and who was also the party secretary for the constituency.

The postulants at a selection conference are herded into a small waiting room off the hall in which party members are gathered. They are summoned one by one before the meeting to give a ten-minute speech and submit themselves to ten minutes of questioning. As rather stiffly we introduced ourselves, Michael O'Halloran observed amiably, 'There is only one thing about politics that I don't like and that is making speeches.' An adoption speech is in fact very difficult to organise because its target is uncertain. Is one setting out one's qualifications before potential employers or is one providing a sample of how one would address the wider world? When it came to my turn I supplied the best mixture I could, trying to balance my Irish expertise with my (much more recently acquired) interest in the constituency. The questions were not difficult, but rather to my regret no one took up, as I had hoped, my invitation to supply details of my policy for Ulster to which I had referred. As we waited in the narrow waiting-room for the party to give its verdict Michael O'Halloran confided, 'There is only one thing about politics I don't like and that is answering questions.'

The result was victory on the second ballot for O'Halloran. What I had not entirely realised was that, whereas for most people membership of the Islington North Labour Party was a difficult hurdle to cross, for friends of the party secretary it could be arranged quite extensively within the rules. Just after the previous MP's death 21 new members were admitted on the secretary's motion, many of them Irish and most of them from affiliated unions such as the Transport and General Workers which had hitherto not paid enough dues to have their full voting rights. All this was accompanied by a campaign to mark the launching of a new newspaper for the Irish community in Britain by calling for Irishmen to seek election as MPs from suitable constituencies. The result was that when the usual party members assembled to make their choice they were surprised by the presence of strangers. There were subsequently serious allegations of fraud and, according to an account by an American journalist based partly on a *Sunday Times* 'Insight' investigation, two of those who voted for O'Halloran and supplied his victory margin were impersonating absent committee members, while a third, not residing in the constituency, was ineligible to vote. Fifteen party members appealed to party headquarters at Transport House and I was asked to take up the cudgels. I declined to do so. As I explained in a letter to *The Times* I had no personal evidence of impropriety and no desire to create public scandal. 'All candidates for nomination have in common a belief that their party ought in the public interest to win a by-election. This really is, and ought to be, a consideration more important than which of them is entrusted with the opportunity of being the standard-bearer.'

Thus passed, though I did not then know it, my best opportunity of pursuing my preferred career. At the time I accepted it as the kind of rebuff one must expect in politics. What I regretted was the chance to speak my mind about Ireland. Michael O'Halloran won the by-election though by a much reduced majority. The Irish had got their man in and did not hear from him again. In 1999 his obituarist in *The Times* wrote, 'He was not a memorable MP. He rarely spoke in the House ... and held few public meetings. It was genuinely agreed, however, that he was a first-class constituency member.' As for me, I went back to Free Derry, where I was greeted by my new friends with a cheerful shout, 'Thought you were going to go to Westminster.' 'I would have done if I had not been run over by a bunch of Irish bus drivers.' 'You should have told us you were up against Murphy's man. We would have come over and smeared Murphy's with the Irish all right.' It would not have been my way but the spirit did me good.

It would be tedious to refer to every effort that I made at this period in advance of the 1970 election to secure nomination for a safe seat. The trouble was that at this period the only safe Labour seats, other than those in London, were in the Midlands or the North and, quite understandably, the selectors were disposed to prefer someone from their region. I was determined to be involved actively in politics if at all possible and in May 1970 I had a go for a seat that had been held by Labour but could not be labelled as safe. A vacancy had occurred in Lichfield and Tamworth, the spiritual and the political capitals of the Kingdom of Mercia. (Lichfield once, for a short time, had a third archbishopric.) I was again short-listed, or rather long-listed, since the local party had decided to choose between seven aspirants. As my train pulled up at the station I was immediately buttonholed by a local journalist who, being a member of the Labour Party, had taken it upon himself to orchestrate the selection process. Breathlessly he explained that the party was desperate to get its man into the field because they were now without a Member and a general election was expected any day. There were, he said, only two serious contenders, myself and Terry Pitt, who was in charge of the Research Department at Transport House; we should not wait for the selection but should each immediately go through the process of being interviewed, photographed and prepared for the plucking that an endorsed candidate might expect. I challenged my interlocutor's assumptions. 'What about the others on the list? There is Betty Boothroyd. She's a formidable personality and orator.' 'That's as maybe,' came the answer, 'but this is not a constituency for a woman candidate. The contest is between you and Terry Pitt.' How fortunate it was to be that some years hence the Commons was to take a different view of the suitability of a woman to be Speaker.

I went through the routine that would normally have followed a candidate selection, after which I appeared before the selection conference. One of the issues raised was whether Britain should become a member of the European Economic Community. This had once more become a live issue because General De Gaulle had resigned the presidency of France and had been succeeded by a man thought to be more favourable to British membership, Georges Pompidou. The Wilson government had sent off positive signals and had gone so far as to appoint George Thomson as official negotiator. The issue, however, was very controversial within the Labour Party and several of the trade unions had come out in opposition. There was no way in which I was going to fudge this issue. When questioned about it, I expressed myself firmly on the side of British membership. The verdict, as predicted, came down to a choice between Pitt and me. I got a narrow majority of constituency votes but was outvoted by the affiliated organisations. Several of the union delegates came up to me afterwards to say that they were sorry they had to vote that way but they were mandated to oppose anyone who wanted to go into Europe. In the event the by-election was overtaken by the general election, in which Terry Pitt lost – as no doubt I would have done; later Lichfield and Tamworth returned to the Labour fold.

Meanwhile in a single week in October 1969 I had sustained two personal losses. My father had throughout his 79th year shown signs of faltering health. My mother gallantly supported him, though her own health was threatened by multiple causes. The country doctor who made it a practice to call in on them as he was passing told me he half expected that one day he would drop by to find them both dead. My father's 79th birthday passed. While I was snatching a short break from Northern Ireland to spend a few days with Suzy at Auntie Omy's Cornish cottage I was told there was a message for me at the village telephone. The three of us rushed there, all fearing the worst for my father, only to be staggered by the completely unexpected news that Suzy's 61-year-old father had had a heart attack. Over the next few months he seemed to be responding to treatment and recovering well enough.

The time came when at the family doctor's urgent advice I had to decide that for my mother's sake my father should go immediately into a home. Fortunately an enquiry at the local retirement home showed that there was a vacancy. The move had only just been made when the news came that my father-in-law had had a second heart attack and had died. This was a terrible blow for his family and for all who knew him. Canon Douglas Harpur was a man deeply loved and admired, a good man in every sense of the phrase and for me a real friend. While doing what little I could to support my wife, who was devoted to her father, I was acutely aware that I must take the first opportunity to find out if my own father was settling in and, if not, to reach an alternative solution. But time had run out. Three days after my father-in-law my father died.

I have often reflected whether I could have done more to make my relations with him warmer. I was after all his only son. There had been several occasions after I left home when I had decided to make a fresh start with him and there were short periods when I had seen a glimpse and perhaps more than a glimpse of a proper father–son relationship. They all seemed to end in bad feeling but there was never any formal breach between us as there would have been if his anti-Semitism had not gone into apparent abeyance. Probably my mother had convinced him how much it offended me. He had many fine qualities which I tried to convey in an obituary notice for the local press. But for me it was a sorrowful coincidence that the week in which he died had begun with the premature end of the man on whom I had come to look as a substitute father as much as a father-in-law.

My own political career was evidently going nowhere and I had to spend the 1970 election on the sidelines, with a walk-on part in the BBC's results programme. I had liked Ted Heath since covering him during the 1962 Common Market negotiations but I was led to speculate when he was chosen to lead the Conservative Party as to which of the two images both on display in 1962 would come to the fore once he had reached the top – would it be the jolly, shoulder-shaking Heath or would it be the wooden, jowly, tin soldier Heath? It turned out to be the latter, on television at least, and the box was becoming the most powerful determinant of the nation's attitudes. In the Commons, too, there were doubts in his own party, held at bay so long as the Wilson government seemed lost in the doldrums but becoming more apparent as fortune seemed at last to be smiling in Labour's direction. Wilson seized the moment, thinking perhaps that it was too good to last, and went to the country. To the surprise of most observers, the outcome was that Heath was in and Wilson was out. 'The people have just carried out a peaceful revolution,' I was able to pronounce on screen when the constituency from which I was reporting proved to be the one which confirmed the Tory victory.

Heath almost immediately launched the new application for Britain to join the European Community. Anthony Barber was appointed Chancellor of the Duchy of Lancaster to take charge of the negotiations. I was delighted to be asked to cover them. I remember the first encounter when Barber and his delegation were not to be moved from the metronomic answer that their task was simply and solely to collect facts on the basis of which Britain's negotiating strategy would be determined. Foreigners were intrigued by Barber's title and some, historically minded, wondered aloud if it was connected with the Wars of the Roses. In the press quarters the usual messages requesting mislaid objects – including copy – to be returned festooned the notice board. There was also, I noticed, a blackboard, with chalk, that had up to now kept its pristine condition. I waited until no one was looking and then wrote on the board, 'If anyone has found any facts, will he please return them to the British delegation.' This, which was subsequently quoted in the House of Commons, could be said to sum up the initial encounter between Barber and Europe.

I did not give up on Ireland. Indeed there were times when all I saw of England would be Heathrow airport when crossing over from Belfast to Brussels and back again. But these were also important days for our family, as, not being able to have children ourselves, Suzy and I adopted Tarquin in 1970 and Crispin in 1971, each shortly after birth. In 1971 we acquired our terraced house in the neighbourhood of Primrose Hill, which has proved to be a marvellous synthesis of town and country living. It is in London and within easy reach of the West End, but there are trees on both sides of the house, a small garden on the sunny side and also swift access to Regent's Park, Primrose Hill and Hampstead Heath. The house has a garden flat, the former 'downstairs' quarter for servants, which is below street level but leads out straight into the garden. Here we installed my widowed mother, thus enabling her to return at the end of her days to her natural habitat as a Londoner. In a diary found after her death she had written about her situation, 'I glow'.

Despite vague historic memories of Londonderry and Enniskillen, Ulster was for the bulk of the British people emphatically no Kosovo. When Stormont was finally prorogued and Heath had relieved Reggie Maudling from the need to see again that 'bloody awful country' by appointing William Whitelaw to the new portfolio of Secretary of State for Northern Ireland, a truce was arranged to find out if the Provisionals were in a mood to compromise. I was filming in the rather bleak Creggan housing estate in Derry, which had been one of the no-go areas from which the security forces had allowed themselves for a while to be excluded. I came across a young man twirling a car tyre on his finger. I had met him before and knew him to have been active with the Provisionals. He did not look happy and greeted me by asking how long I thought the truce was going to last. I told him that that depended on his people as I thought the British were prepared to go quite a long way. This did not seem to lighten his spirits. 'You've seen me before,' he said. 'Then I was in command of a body of men. If this truce succeeds I shall just be a member of the unemployed, twirling a tyre on my finger.' He spoke with some pathos; what he said was moving and terrible and could, I suppose, be replicated in many parts of the world.

While I was thus engaged I had to keep in mind what was going on in Europe. The negotiations were clearly advancing in a different spirit from that which had prevailed when I was covering the earlier attempt. There was one absolutely critical meeting on 20 May 1971 in the Elysée Palace in Paris between Ted Heath and President Georges Pompidou. The international press, I remember, were cunningly diverted by a special exhibition to show the relationship between different wines and different types of cheese. We were cordially invited to sample both. Nor was this the only occasion on which my part in the affair was facilitated by French wine. The *Tonight* editors had prepared a table setting on which were displayed a pitcher of wine and two glasses. I was seated opposite a French journalist called Edouard Sablier and we rehearsed the neuralgic points of the negotiation. At last, in January 1972, it was time to sign the Treaty of Accession in Brussels. After an agonising internal debate, because the Labour Party was officially opposed to accepting membership on the terms negotiated, the BBC decided that the whole ceremony should be shown live. Alan Watson (later Lord Watson of Richmond) and I were invited to do the running commentary but were firmly told that we should make clear that this was not a 'national' occasion because of Labour opposition.

This was exciting for me, both because I believed passionately in British membership and because I had never before done a running commentary. As I arrived to take up my position I was given two pieces of information. The first was that I was not going to see (directly) the events I would be describing. The picture selected by the Belgian director would be fed into the long line of boxes containing the commentators. The second was that Alan's plane to Brussels was delayed. I could go on alone or a substitute for Alan would be provided. I told the bosses who were present in some strength that I would do it alone.

I was told that I would be expected to speak for five minutes, after which the ceremony (including the interpreters) would take over. I spoke for 55 minutes. The difference was caused by a young lady who threw red ink over Ted Heath as he paused at the head of the marble stairs of the Palais d'Egmont. This was done in protest not against the Common Market, as one might have supposed, but against the Heath government's decision to remove the vegetable market from Covent Garden. Since this incident was not shown on the screen in my box I should have remained ignorant of the reason for the prolonged delay if a BBC boss had not settled himself beside me. A scribbled note set him doubling out and a further note when he returned enabled our viewers to know why their leader was being scrubbed down and fitted out afresh. How, nevertheless, to fill the 55-minute gap? I seized on the point that most of the audience would be unlikely to be familiar with the Community's institutional structure. There they all were in front of their very eyes – the Commissioners, the Council of Ministers, the European Court of Justice and the (still appointed) Parliament. The Belgian director was taking slow, broad sweeps over this ensemble.

I knew most of the names and anecdotes about many of them, so the lecture-with-slides, as it were, was kept running. But there was one physically prominent figure who defeated me. Who was the enormous man spread out over three chairs who was caught every so often in the camera's lens? During the latter section of my talkathon, Alan Watson arrived. The object of my bafflement was once more holding centre stage. I passed a scribbled note to Alan and he took the microphone to identify Joseph Bech, who had been Prime Minister of Luxembourg for ever and who had in Alan's presence received the annual Charlemagne prize. For the final minutes Alan was able to alternate with me until, with a flourish, the newly kitted-out Heath arrived.

As the Prime Minister bent over to sign the document the screen went to close-up and, with professional pride, since the truth about the Labour Party that I was uttering was for me an especially bitter one, I clearly spelled out the caveat that I had been instructed to deliver. I felt nevertheless a tremendous surge of spirits. For Britain the Second World War was going to have a worthy sequel after all. From London came warm congratulations and instructions to order a bottle of champagne on the Corporation.

For two things – my coverage of Northern Ireland and my coverage of the EEC negotiations – I received at Broadcasting House from the Lord President of the Council, Robert Carr, the annual 'Best Political Reporter on Television' award for 1972 at a ceremony presided over by the Director-General. This was recognition by my profession. Paradoxically, I felt that it would soon be time for me to quit the small screen.

CHAPTER 18

The Candidate

In British political life the role of 'Europe', by which I mean what was successively known as the Common Market, the EEC (European Economic Community), the European Community and much later the European Union, has been markedly odd. Time and time again the opinion pollsters have rated the subject low in the list of issues on the minds of voters. Yet first the Labour, then the Conservative Party came within measurable distance of being totally wrecked by it as effective organs of opinion. 'I wish to devote my whole political life to keeping Britain out of political union with Europe,' declared a Labour backbencher to me solemnly as we returned from a party conference.

During this period I had continued to look out for opportunities of launching my own political career. I had in any case decided that my career in television had reached a natural peak and that I should try to negotiate a shift. As had already been the case at Tamworth, I had by now given up the idea of only competing for a seat with a substantial Labour majority since such seats (they had included Bolsover, where to the surprise of few, Dennis Skinner was preferred) quite evidently did not accord with my profile. Hence, when the Essex seat of Maldon was split up, I put my name forward for the new constituency of Braintree. Though the old Maldon had been a Tory seat, the Braintree half was thought to be leaning Labour. It would go, it was said, the way the country went. This did not at all accord with the advice that *The Economist*, through the voice of its anonymous political correspondent, had offered to aspiring politicians, but time was rolling on and this seemed the best bet available. There was going to be a special feature about this candidate selection. Until very recently this crucial part of the democratic system had been invariably conducted out of sight of the public. One Conservative constituency had invited in the television cameras, but this had not hitherto happened in the case of Labour. Part of the reason for this was the fact that Tories nearly always had presentably filmable premises while this was not generally the case with their opponents. In Braintree, however, Labour had a smart, up-to-date headquarters, most capably run by the party secretary, Doris Oliver. When Rex Bloomstein, the talented producer of *All in a Day*, an occasional series of in-depth documentaries for the BBC, and a man able to command resources which other producers could only dream of, was looking around for a willing Labour selection, Braintree fitted the bill. Some of the five members of the short list were not too happy at the prospect of this intrusion of cameras but Doris disposed of them briskly. 'This is the media of the day and they would very likely have to appear on TV if they became a Member anyway,' she said. The BBC is a large organisation and Bloomstein's operation was not connected with *24 Hours* and no official obstacle was put in my way. Nevertheless I was warned informally that it might damage my authority as a commentator if I were shown seeking the nomination and losing it. My mind was quite made up: I would risk it.

I made my pitch before a group largely drawn from the two main towns, Braintree itself and Witham (pronounced Wit'm), a place whose origin is recorded in the Anglo-Saxon Chronicle under the year 912, when the King (Edward) camped in Maldon 'for the time the borough was worked on and built at Witham'. But also represented were the suburbs of Chelmsford and a considerable number of delightful Essex villages such as Finchingfield, Cogge-shall, Great Bardfield, Hatfield Peverel, Black Notley and Good Easter. In the chair was a hereditary landowner, John Tabor, who spoke for Labour in the County Council. To my relief I this time won. Before long I was to be seen shouting through a microphone in a local election, 'People of Tabor Street. Vote Tabor at the Tabor High School next Thursday.' One political promise I took immediate steps to fulfil. I had been asked whether I would acquire a home in the constituency. Suzy and I had for some time been thinking of having a country cottage where our young children could at least partly grow up in rural surroundings, but we had decided to wait to see whether I would get a constituency and where. With the nomination under my belt, we set off to explore every stick and stone of the Braintree division. Stopping for a picnic we looked round and saw, arising from an area of desolation and neglect, what appeared to be our dream house. 'What', we said, 'is that?' It was an aban-doned farmhouse, lath-and-plaster, with beams and thatch and with a curious appendage that was suggestive of mystery. Above the door was inscribed the date 1663 and alongside it a death-mask. There was also a large barn and an orchard that was in reasonable shape. This was Tinker's Green.

We made enquiries at once, found that the owner had not got round to putting it on the market, and, helped by a legacy from my aunt, we met his reasonable price. The house was every bit as exciting inside as out. The appendage turned out to be the remains of a workman's cottage, of earlier date than the mid-seventeenth century, with every beam crooked, which had been incorporated into the main building. It was to be approached, on the upper floor, only through a three-foot high passage – which made it an exciting bedroom for my younger son. The house, we were advised by our surveyor, had scarcely any foundations – 'But it has stood here for over 300 years and I see no reason why it should not stand for another 300.'

Thus we were established on the ground; indeed, Tinker's Green is the only physical possession of which I have ever felt unashamedly proud. It took some time to lick into shape. But we found a builder who was not only a Labour supporter but who was as eager as ourselves to strip out Victorian adaptations and restore the old fireplace, and to expose every covered beam and the ancient lights and the original bread oven. The work, appealing to all Suzy's historical instincts, was completed under her careful supervision. We kept the name – Tinker's Green – together with the death-mask for historical reasons, but after a while discovered that they had rather grim associations. One owner in the mid-nineteenth century had taken a wife from the gypsy community. This did not make for harmony between him and her relations and the Romanies resolved to raid the house. The owner was awakened and emerged with his shotgun. The adult raiders faded away but the owner managed to shoot dead poor little Moses who had insisted on tagging along. It was his death-mask that was preserved by our fine vigilante who collected the congratulations of his peers at quarter sessions for ridding the district of a nuisance. It was not a very happy tale but then this could be said of much of history that is commemorated.

With two children growing up, a constituency to nurse and two houses to live in, I concluded that I should be doing less television and not be out of the country so much of the time. I applied for one job and as a result got another. The job I applied for was that of editor of a monthly publication put out by the Fabian Colonial Bureau. I did not get it, but the news that I was interested in employment outside television reached the ears of the Royal Institute of International Affairs. I was offered and accepted a part-time job as head of the Meetings Department at the Institute, which was popularly known by the name of its St James's Square location as Chatham House. The highly talented Director, Andrew Shonfield, I had known since he had called on me at my office in the Washington Press Building. Very much with his approval I continued for the time being to do some work for the BBC, mainly for *The Money Programme*.

Until 1923 the RIIA had occupied one room in the Institute of Histori-
cal Research, but in that year No. 10 St James's Square, at the time a private
house that had been owned by the late Lord Kinnaird, came on to the market.
It had been built in 1736 and boasted that it had been the home of three Prime
Ministers – Lord Chatham, as William Pitt (the Elder) from 1757 to 1761, the
Earl of Derby from 1837 to 1854 and Mr Gladstone in 1890. Never mind that,
strictly speaking Pitt was not during those dates the Prime Minister or indeed
Lord Chatham, that Derby was there for only the first and shortest of his three
administrations when he did not move into Downing Street, and that Gladstone was there (as a tenant) for only one session of Parliament. The building has since 1910 proudly born the plaque of the London County Council
proclaiming, 'Here lived Three Prime Ministers'. In many ways the substantial mansion would ideally suit the Institute. It was also strategically placed
in relation to Whitehall, academia, journalism and the City – not to mention
a high proportion of the gentlemen's clubs – which made up its cocktail of
membership. The only snag was the purchase price which soared well above
the RIIA's resources. But to this too there was a solution. A Canadian, Colonel
R.W. Leonard, was on a hunting holiday in Ontario when he saw an item in
the press to the effect that this difficulty existed. He cabled his London banker
to acquire the property on the Institute's behalf. Since the Commonwealth
prime ministers were coming to London for a conference it was decided that
they should all be present at Colonel Leonard's handing over of the deeds. The
Institute received its royal designation and the Prince of Wales, having been
created Visitor of the Royal Institute for the occasion, received the deeds 'on
behalf of the Empire'.

It is a membership organisation and I had not only been a member since
1959 but had been invited to address several of its meetings on both American
and African affairs. According to Marion Gain, the historian of the Chatham
House Meetings Department, 'unusual gales of laughter' had accompanied one
of my talks on 'Personalities and Powers in American Politics'.[32] To the outside
world it is best known for its 'Chatham House Rule', which provides that those
present at a meeting should feel free to use the information received but are
forbidden to disclose the identity of any participant or where he was speaking.
It was a form of what was known in Washington as 'compulsory plagiarism'.
Originally almost all meetings were covered by the rule, but to me this seemed
at odds with the aim of 'educating our masters', and in any case many of the
speakers, especially overseas visitors, wanted to publicise their views. I therefore limited the use of the rule to meetings where it was strictly necessary,
when for example the speaker was a civil servant; this has had the paradoxical

result of the 'rule' being much more liable to be cited outside Chatham House than within it.

At first much of my time under the new arrangement was taken up both for the BBC and Chatham House with examining the implications of our having joined the European Community. To this end I organised for Chatham House a series of joint seminars, commissioned by the Foreign Office, with French, German, Italian and Benelux institutes, to go into the economic and institutional consequences, while the nitty-gritty of the practical outlook for trade and commerce were examined in my televised reports. The European project, however, was never in my view confined to what Gladstone, dismayed at his first ministerial assignment to the Board of Trade, described as 'a matter of packages'. It surprised me that even the Director of Chatham House seemed to have overlooked the message of the 20 October 1972 meeting of the Heads of Government of the European Six plus Edward Heath and the Prime Ministers of Denmark and Ireland held in the lavish ambience of the Hotel Majestic in Paris in anticipation of the entry of the three newcomers. In their declaration they undertook to enter into an economic and monetary union by stages that would be completed not later than 31 December 1980 and in Article 18 they went further, setting themselves 'the major objective of transforming before the end of the present decade' the existing treaties 'into a European Union'. How so much of British opinion could have thought we were merely entering a rather elaborate trade agreement puzzled me then and still puzzles me now.

In a number of published articles I supported political union but opposed the Werner Plan for economic and monetary union, which I thought, as I was subsequently to argue about the euro, was approaching the project in the wrong sequence. A common currency should be a topping-out event when all the remaining features of the system were in place, not an engine for advancing that result. 'The requirement that the problem of how to avoid regional imbalance would have been essentially solved by 1980,' I wrote in the June 1973 issue of New Europe, 'is a little like American legislation requiring that a clean, non-polluting car shall have been invented by 1975.' [33] Writing about the European Parliament in Chatham House's monthly magazine, The World Today, I argued that the growth of that Parliament's functions and prestige 'is inevitably limited by the fact that it is not confronting a real government. In reality the Community's reputation for being a technocracy is the direct consequence of the opposition in member states (and pre-eminently in Britain) to the notion of federalism. The main democratic dilemma arises from the builders having been told to avoid central issues as "academic" and "dogmatic". ... [H]ybrid institutions, with their attendant problems of locating democratic

12. Representing Chatham House in Israel.

13. Meeting HM the Queen at Chatham House.

responsibility, are the consequence.' [34]

Looking back more than 30 years on at what I was writing just after Britain joined 'Europe', I can see that the same issues that were to bother politicians and writers in the early twenty-first century were to the fore from the start. It was already apparent in the articles I wrote then that as the system of financing the Community from 'own resources' was to come into effect Britain would be contributing disproportionately if not compensated by a share of regional funds that would seem likely to be too large to be feasible. The devil, as now, lay in the Common Agricultural Policy and I see that already Jacques Chirac, at the time French Minister of Agriculture, had been caught in my cross-wires. 'What was new about the controversy unleashed by an interview with Jacques Chirac,' I wrote in *The Listener* on 30 August 1973, '... was not the crude violence of the Minister's language ..., there have been such tirades from French Ministers before, but the extremely robust nature of the German response.' Chirac was being rude to everybody – rude to the British (whose Commissioner Sir Christopher Soames was said to be acting as spokesman for Tate and Lyle), rude to the Commission and even rude to Herr Ertl, the German Agriculture Minister, whom I used to characterise as 'Europe's marginal man'. He was marginal because he belonged to a minority faction of a minority party (the FDP or Liberals) who spoke up for the marginal (part-time) farmers of Bavaria. The FDP held the balance in the Bundestag and, as at the time I was quoted as saying, Ertl, like the German Foreign Minister, symbolised the difference between the British electoral system and the German, between the Liberals never being in power and the Liberals always being in power.

Besides television and Chatham House, I began in 1972 to contribute a weekly column on international affairs to *The Listener*. I had been a regular reader of the output of the BBC Monitoring Service for many years. It was remarkable, considering the controlled nature of most of the media in the countries that the Service covered, how much interesting material could be derived from the output. The prolonged struggle between the Albanian majority and the Serbian minority in Kosovo, for instance, was a regular feature for years, despite the broadcasts being all in Communist hands. It was possible, through daily study, to get accustomed to the operating code of such alien cultures – to one who was not a trained sinologist – as that of Communist China. In a way my proudest moment on the *Tonight* programme ought to have been in 1965 when I pronounced that the publication in a Shanghai paper of Yao Wenyuan's polemic against Wu Han's historical opera *The Dismissal of Hai Rui* was perhaps the most important foreign story of the year. I had hoped that this apparent paradox would be sufficiently startling to arouse interest among my colleagues who were in the middle of an exercise in self-examination to decide the direction in which the programme would develop. Instead a senior BBC official closed off any further discussion with a sneer, implying my total absence of reality. Yao's article was the opening round in the Cultural Revolution.[35]

Domestically by 1973–74 Heath's regime was rapidly unravelling, as the coal miners openly confronted the government's wages policy in naked battle. After a damaging period of hesitation, Heath plunged the country into a premature election on the issue of 'Who governs Britain?' This instantly made me not a journalist but a candidate, in the midst of a political battle to start my political career at the rather advanced age of 48. My opponents were Antony Newton, the head of economic research at Tory Central Office, and the Liberal David Scott, who was a sports writer in one of the local papers. The *All in a Day* television programme, holding *The Candidate* to have been a success, decided to film as a sequel the fate of the winner of the Labour nomination at Braintree.

14. Family with Herod.

15. Photo for the local newspaper.

The constituency has a fine weekly paper called *The Braintree and Witham Times*, but the fact that it was a weekly rather than a daily helped to shape the campaign. There was very little sense of debate between the candidates. No one organised a joint session. 'The candidates,' I wrote, 'ploughed through their planned programmes in isolation from each other.' A parliamentary candidate has to issue a manifesto, which is delivered by the state. In it I was, as convention required, photographed seated while a most fetching Suzy stood behind me with one hand lightly poised on my shoulder. My two little boys, looking in opposite directions, are neatly framed in front of us and lying in front of them is the dog. 'CONSENT and FAIRNESS are the themes of my campaign,' I pronounced controversially, and then, 'KEITH KYLE asks: Do you Sincerely Wish to be Poor?' There are sections on fighting inflation, the social dividend, an emergency energy policy and further sections on local issues. Finally, with tongue in cheek, I say that in the interest of fairness I am going to yield part of the address to three leading Conservative spokesmen, two of whom in fact say disobliging things about Heath or his government, and the third, Edward Heath himself, is saying things in 1970 which look distinctly odd in 1974.

16. Suzy on the campaign trail.

As before in St Albans I enjoyed the canvassing because through it I made contact with ordinary, that is mainly non-political, people. One theme that came through was an often-expressed wish to get rid of both Ted Heath and Harold Wilson. The first time I heard this I reacted as a political correspondent – 'Oh, Ted Heath's not a bad chap really' – then I realised I was now supposed to be a politician and curtailed that line of reasoning. Then there was the first of two notable responses. 'I will give you my vote if you can tell what the name on this door means.' Knowing the answer, I took care to ask the housewife, 'Will you pledge your husband's vote as well?' 'Yes.' 'It's Proinsias, which is Irish for Francis.' That was two votes to send me on my way to Westminster. I ended the campaign on the eve of poll with a short and rather emotional speech from an agricultural wagon drawn up in Braintree market square to a large and responsive crowd which had turned out for me in the bitter evening cold. 'We should have elections more often,' said Chris, the agent's son, when he heard it. 'They radicalise the candidates.'

Braintree was one of those seats which was not counting the votes on the night of the poll. Nevertheless I stayed up late and witnessed on television how extremely close the race was becoming. It was becoming much too close by my reckoning, since I thought that Wilson needed a convincing win if Kyle was going to be pulled across the winning post as well. When Suzy and I turned up at the count the next morning, Rex Bloomstein had me fitted with a radio mike, a small and highly sensitive transmitter enabling me to record impressions unobtrusively while I agonised through the morning's work. Shortly after noon my wife and Chris compared notes and quietly concluded that I had lost. The Liberal candidate told me cheerfully that my majority would be 1,800. 'He's been wrong about everything else,' said Chris when I told him. 'What makes you think he would be right about this?' About one o'clock I thought it was time to record through the radio mike that Tony Newton was too far ahead to be overtaken. 'Your film sequel,' I told a member of the BBC team, 'can't now be called *The Member*. It will have to be *Son of Candidate*.' At 2.20 the Town Clerk gave the figures: Newton 20,797; Kyle 18,796; Scott 15,201. I had not made it.

The next day Rex wanted additional shots for continuity and sound effect. I pulled on my sheepskin campaign jacket, grasped my clipboard and crawled into the car festooned with my name. While the new MP for Braintree was settling down to his first official engagement, the dead slogans from the dead campaign boomed for the last time over the Essex countryside. I was told, when I came to say farewell to Rex and his crew, that the members of it had said privately at the beginning of the campaign how they felt inclined, were

they Braintree citizens, to vote and had done the same at the end. At the start
the votes were spread among all three candidates; at the end they were united
in my favour. I was deeply moved; it was the nicest thing anyone ever said to
me in politics.

In October Harold Wilson dissolved Parliament and the year's second struggle was on. Though I had been feeling rather tired beforehand, the adrenalin of
politics worked once more and I hurled myself wholeheartedly into the fight.
As there had been a change of Liberal candidate, perhaps, I thought, some of
their total could be won over. There was the argument that a new government deserved to have a working majority. And there would be the strategy of
concentrating on the ranks of last time's no-shows. I was much more familiar
with the constituency now and, especially after the second instalment of *The
Candidate* had gone out, the constituency, I hoped, was more familiar with
me.

Since I was going to spend the bulk of my time this time in the towns I
decided to begin with a fairly noisy swing through the villages so that it could
not be said that they had never heard from the Labour candidate. We set off in
a procession of cars and had just finished a short, sharp and, I hoped, stirring
blast on the microphone at one quiet, rural spot, with my helpers giving out
leaflets to anyone who stirred while my agent drove me on to the next target.
I suddenly felt rats running through my brain. Winding down the window I
asked my agent to stop the car. 'Have you got a headache?' he asked, anxiously.
'I'm afraid it's worse than that,' I answered. By the time he had pulled over I
was on the floor of the car, desperately struggling to get up, not succeeding,
unable to speak. Four days later I came to in a hospital at Black Notley, one
of the neighbouring villages. My wife, in the car behind me, had taken charge
and had insisted on my being given priority treatment. The Russian-trained
Sri Lankan doctor at Black Notley turned out to have just the right skills for
handling a stroke. He told Suzy that I must be kept quiet until I had had a
second attack; he could tell after that whether I was going to recover. A second
opinion was sought, which entirely endorsed his diagnosis.

For this purpose there was some advantage in the local paper only being a
weekly, in that there were no daily bulletins on my condition, but of course
rumours spread. Small knots of Labour supporters began to appear outside the
hospital. Four days later Suzy received the news she had been waiting for: the
second stroke had happened. I was to recover totally or almost so but it would
take time. My agent was allowed in to see me. I was not in a very presentable
condition and was only just conscious. I had, it seems, already made enquiries
about my parents (who were both dead). The photographer from *The Braintree*

and Witham Times was pressing for access. It was settled that Suzy should take the bedside photo instead. I was carefully propped up on the pillows with my best side to the camera and my agent was placed next to me. The caption in the next issue said that I was recovering from a slight stroke and was already instructing my agent on the next phase of the campaign.

With every incentive to do so I did in fact recover sufficiently fast for the doctor to discharge me on the eve of the election. Suzy and some of my good friends such as Ben Whitaker, the former MP for Hampstead, had been campaigning for me and I appeared at a final meeting. I even made a short speech, striving not to garble my words, to the effect that I had been assured by my doctor that I would shortly recover my health and be able if elected to discharge my duties as an MP. I had made up my mind that in that event I should have to put off my maiden speech for six months, during which I would concentrate exclusively on constituency work to make sure that the people of Braintree should not miss out. Helped by Suzy I was present at the count, which as before was conducted on the day following the poll. The tally over-night showed that Wilson was getting a larger but not an outstanding major-ity. Braintree was one of the last results to come in. As the count progressed Tony Newton was showing signs of stress. Labour was, so far as he could see, persistently ahead. Suzy, with her sharp journalistic instincts, knew better. She advised my rival, who had been most courteously solicitous about my health throughout the campaign, not to worry, because the village returns were not yet counted and the Labour lead in the towns was insufficient to put him out. She was right, of course. I had kept very quiet during the count, reserving my strength for the traditional remarks of the defeated.[36] Once they had been delivered I left the hall no more a candidate and unlikely to be so ever again, feeling that I was lucky to be alive but fearing, all the same, that a lengthy period of rehabilitation lay ahead.

CHAPTER 19

Struggling Back

For the second time in my life I had to pick myself up from ground zero. The NHS was there (the President of the Royal College of General Practitioners, Dr John Horder, was thankfully my GP) and, above all, Suzy was there. My employers were supportive. I had a great deal on my side. But nonetheless my stroke was a major setback. While never giving way to despair, I saw that my life would have to be permanently scaled down. Whereas my first reaction to ME at Oxford had been in terms of dramatic, despairing renunciation of everything I had hitherto aimed at, this fresh bolt from the blue produced a gentler and more resigned mood. I expected, because I had faith in the Black Notley physician and in John Horder, to recover eventually the use of most if not quite all of my faculties. But my use of them would have to be more restrained, my ambitions toned down, my expectations from life reduced. All thought of politics would need to be abandoned, likewise the writing of scholarly books. I would have quietly to live out what remained to me of life. Up till now, though in fact approaching 50, I had still thought of myself as a youthful man – I had been so described at election time in the press. Now abruptly I felt that I was an old one.

Although I had managed to force out a few intelligible remarks at the end of the Braintree count, I soon realised that I was talking mainly babble most of the time. I could also hardly walk. There was evidently a long way to go. Ironically it was just at this point that I received an invitation from the Oxford Union to speak in a debate about Ireland. I had returned to the Union as a guest several times since going down; it was something I particularly enjoyed doing. This time I had to explain that I could scarcely get two words out coherently. I was never to revisit that scene of past triumphs as a speaker again. Inch by inch, yard by yard, I was walked by Suzy a little further each day along the country road which went by Tinker's Green. I attended a clinic to be taught to use again my limbs. I began, painfully at first, to begin again to read. Derwent May, the literary editor of *The Listener*, sent me a book by Lord Devlin about

America coming into the First World War to review and told me to take as long over it as I liked. Very slowly at first, I worked my way through it, lucidly though it was written, and the effort was unquestionably therapeutic. Then I caught mumps from one of my young sons (I had never had it myself when young) and for weeks lost all sense of taste, except only for soup. It came back to me suddenly on Christmas Eve.

I returned after six months to work at Chatham House, doing at first only the basic administrative functions of my job and avoiding public appearances. But the cause of Europe pulled me, perhaps prematurely, out of retirement. The 'renegotiation' of the British terms of entry, which changed little of substance, having been proclaimed a success by Harold Wilson, the Labour government was proposing to carry out its pledge to hold a referendum on continued British membership. Anti-Europeans, predicting victory, were pleased by this; pro-Europeans bit their lips and prepared for trouble ahead. I marked one milestone in my recovery by publishing an op-ed article in *The Times* explaining why as a pro-European I was in favour of a referendum. This had the immediate result of my being invited to speak from the platform at a packed meeting at Central Hall, Westminster, as part of a debate for and against a referendum. It would be my first attempt to place the stroke entirely behind me and as such it turned out to be a little premature. I managed to get to the end of my contribution but at one point when there was some barracking from one section of the large hall I found myself possessed intellectually of a quick retort as of old but physically estopped from uttering it. More than once I caught myself searching for words. I was to get better, much better, as time passed, but the carefree spontaneity on which I had hitherto always been able to rely was now for ever beyond me.

Other people who have suffered strokes have regarded the extent of my recovery as an ideal they might hope to emulate. Therefore one should not complain. But having already had certain difficulties to overcome in life it did seem to me a little hard that others, however relatively slight, should be added to them. Handwriting was for most purposes no longer possible. I can now manage a signature and a sentence but not more if I am not to lapse into unintelligibility. Although on certain limited occasions and for fairly short periods I am still capable of speaking without notes, this now requires careful preparation in order to make certain that I am not going to run into aphasia, or inability to pull certain words at will from the brain. Instances occur in conversation when, embarrassingly, words escape me which I would obviously be expected to know. (Later on, for a while one such word was Coleraine when this was the site of the university at which I was teaching.) I cannot speak as fast or as fluently as I used to but I admit that some may have found that an improvement. Yet to the world at large I did seem to have made a quite remarkable recovery and most people, meeting me for the first time, would not write me down as a stroke victim.

Steadily I went about piecing together the elements of my life. My wife's love was the rock on which everything else depended. She was doing a full-time job in television and also bringing up two small children. To my surprise the BBC, for which for a while I had been able to do nothing, suddenly asked me to go to Dublin to report on a European summit meeting. I went with some misgivings but determined to try. I remember being shown around Dublin Castle, where, having been invited to sit on King William III's throne, I found that I, a tall man, was left with my feet dangling in the air – leading me to remark that the King evidently expected to rest his feet on the necks of his Irish subjects. The following day I summed up in a live insert into the *24 Hours* programme the (very modest) achievements of the summit. My rehabilitation could be rated as only partially a success. I received a letter from the political correspondent of *The Braintree and Witham Times* congratulating me on having reverted to normal. But when I next went on to Belfast I was required to write a report for another correspondent to voice and I was never again employed in live reporting into camera. I had to accept that things would never be quite the same.

It soon appeared that for the referendum on Europe there was no consensus inside the cabinet, with the result that ministers were quite exceptionally to be allowed to figure on either side of the debate. Benn, Foot and Castle, for example, campaigned quite actively for 'No'. There had never been a referendum before in British history. In one respect its introduction by a Labour government was curious in that in the past the device had been mainly advocated by conservative writers such as the great constitutional guru A.V. Dicey as a means of checking abuses by the 'elective dictatorship' of a party enjoying a safe majority in the House of Commons. Since popular majorities had been generally thought to abhor innovation it was a widely held assumption that a referendum would be fatal to British membership, though, since Britain was technically already actually in the Community, a 'Yes' vote could be represented as favouring the (very recent) status quo. The opponents of British membership started the campaign confident that they were ahead. I decided that I would concede nothing to my status as a convalescent and accepted invitations to speak on a great variety of platforms for almost every night of the referendum campaign.

There were always several speakers so that I did not become too exhausted.

But one impression predominated: the audiences came alive whenever I reached beyond the merely commercial merits of the arrangement and portrayed European union as a unique political advance whose stature was commensurate with the challenges created by the war. Thirty years later it is often argued that the British people, when they had a choice, were misled, especially by Ted Heath, into believing that they were merely being offered free trade. A replay in 2005 of the television coverage of the 1975 referendum result which in all regions (except Orkney and Shetland) endorsed British membership, showed Enoch Powell, one of the European Community's most implacable enemies, volunteering the fact that during the campaign Ted Heath (no longer, of course, Prime Minister) had made no secret of the political content of the 'ever closer union' envisaged in the Treaty of Rome.

Confident at having withstood well enough the strains of the referendum campaign, I gradually extended the range of my activities, writing book reviews for *The Listener* and feature articles for *The Times*, taking a more proactive role in Chatham House and working my way back into television. In 1976 I received a chance of tackling a major project for the screen. The 20th anniversary of the Suez fiasco was approaching; two of the major figures involved – Christian Pineau, who had been the French Foreign Minister, and General Moshe Dayan, who had been the Israeli Chief of Staff – had written books which, Dayan accurately and Pineau not so accurately, had filled in much detail about the crucial tripartite meeting of the conspirators at Sèvres. The opportunity seemed ripe for a reappraisal of that pivotal point in the closure of the informal British Empire in the Middle East. My former producer Christopher Capron had taken over the editorship of the nightly current affairs show, now once more called *Tonight*. He was willing to devote three successive editions (in the event we stretched it to four) to an investigation of Suez. Peter Hill was to be the producer. Would I be researcher, writer and reporter?

Contrary to what has sometimes been written or spoken about my interest in Suez, it is not the case that I had been obsessively occupied ever since the event in finding out what exactly happened. Of course, having been exposed to the American fallout of this affair and also, to a lesser degree, to the political consequences in Britain, I had given them much thought at the time. But life had moved on and, except for having read with the utmost interest Anthony Nutting's *No End of a Lesson* when this came out at the time of the tenth anniversary, I had not focused on the subject again until offered this fresh chance of making a contribution to television's treatment of history. In this I could not have had a more congenial and talented collaborator than Peter Hill, whose main line of work had hitherto lain in the exposure of individual instances of miscarriage of justice. The reconstruction of what had happened in 1956, using film of the time and interviews with various participants, was a fascinating experience though frustrating in certain respects because some material was still being withheld. Enough, however, was already available to make clear the nature of the fraudulent collusion between Britain, France and Israel. The actual Protocol of Sèvres, by which the three, meeting in the utmost secrecy, bound themselves to strike at Egypt, was still inaccessible but we filmed the secluded Bonnier de la Chapelle villa at the end of the rue Emanuel Giraud, which was where the three met. One of the key aides who had been present, Louis Mangin, then attached to the French Defence Ministry, described what had happened there.

The villa itself had quite a history, having been a safe house for the Resistance during the war, which was a reminder of the fact that the Mollet cabinet at the time of Suez was exceptionally full of Resistance figures. This made it seem natural to them to proceed by 'underground' methods. One of the Bonnier sons had been in Algiers at the time of the American landings in 1943 and, having drawn the short straw, became the man assigned to assassinate Admiral Darlan, a hated Vichyite leader who at the last minute had made a very rewarding deal with the Americans. Young Bonnier, having discharged his task, had been hastily executed. His room in the villa had been kept ever since exactly as he had left it. One irony of the filming was that, whereas the villa's merits as a safe house for Resistance fighters and for politicians had lain in its quietness and isolation, big changes had taken place in the two decades since the signature of the Protocol. A raised motorway had been built alongside the villa's grounds and the remorseless, incessant rumble of heavy vehicles, most of them stacked with cars, presented very tricky problems for our sound engineer. The lady from the Bonnier family who was then the chief resident explained that to have a picnic they needed to get up between two and four o'clock in the morning.

There was one other notable report that I made for Chris Capron's *Tonight* in March 1977 which involved me in considerable controversy. The Troubles in Northern Ireland had continued during the 1970s with mounting violence. With my Chatham House responsibilities I was going there much less often and the story I went over to cover this time was no earth-shaker. I was merely expected to report on the operation of the new local councils which, with a bare minimum of powers, were to be a first delicate experiment in getting local politicians of various parties to work together. We had just wrapped up a sequence with the new Enniskillen Council when I found myself being vigorously lobbied by a councillor from the SDLP (the constitutional, mainly Catholic party). He wanted me to talk to a constituent called Bernard O'Connor who had a grievance against the police. We were in a hurry, the television equipment was being packed up and delay over a matter not strictly within our remit would not have been a popular move. The constituent, it then appeared, was right on hand and I was prevailed on to give him five minutes. He used it well to supply me with a short, eloquent and highly specific version of his experience under interrogation by the RUC (Royal Ulster Constabulary). Allegations of abuse were becoming commonplace, mostly sponsored by Sinn Fein and for that reason usually discounted. I realised at once that O'Connor, if let loose on the screen, had the personality and the plausibility to make a strongly positive impression on an audience, a factor which must add to our responsibility if we were to give him the opportunity. Then in a London taxi I heard on the car radio a statement by the Attorney-General, Sam Silkin, to the effect that interrogation practices in use in Ireland five years before, which had been condemned by the European Commission of Human Rights in a case brought by the Republic of Ireland against the United Kingdom, were no longer practised. O'Connor's highly specific allegations, if true, would indicate that, on the contrary, they were continuing. This convinced me that we must pursue the case journalistically.

We went back to Northern Ireland. We carried out research about O'Connor's background and spent altogether some seven hours talking to him (not on camera) in various settings. We decided to go ahead with a recorded interview. Chris Capron, with our full support, decided to alert the Director-General, Sir Charles Curran, about what we were doing. There was a tendency among some current-affairs people to regard 'the hierarchy' of the BBC as the enemy of proactive journalism and in some instances there was perhaps anecdotal support for this view. But I thought that in sensitive matters it was only fair that if the DG was going to be in at the crash landing he ought also to be in at the take-off. We returned from Enniskillen with two hours of material recorded.

Bernard O'Connor in 1977 was a slight, energetic man (5ft 6ins and nine stone), 35 years old and with a wife and seven children ranging in age from ten years to two months. They lived in a roomy, elegant house near the centre of Enniskillen. Besides being a teacher in the Catholic primary school, he ran, with a partner, the only driving school in town. He was once a salaried youth officer at the community centre but had given that up for voluntary youth work including that of being a Scout Commissioner, as well as being a leading figure in the choral society. In short he had every appearance of being a model citizen in a community that is about 50 per cent Roman Catholic. The security services, however, had come to the conclusion that this was but a cover for his activities as a 'godfather', that is, one of the sinister figures who did not themselves dirty their hands in carrying out terrorist actions but were responsible for organising those who did. There was considerable reason to believe that such godfathers existed and it was very likely that they would hide behind a veil of civic activism. The questions to be asked in O'Connor's case were whether he was such a person and how far it was permissible to go in order to find out.

Bernard would call himself a Republican, since he believed strongly in a united Ireland, but he did not belong to a political party, though he had been extremely active in promoting Republican unity in elections, since differences between abstainers and non-abstainers had had the effect in the past of allowing a Unionist to be sent to Westminster for the local division of Fermanagh and Tyrone. He had also at the height of the civil rights movement edited a magazine, which at times poked fun at the local officers of the Royal Ulster Constabulary. Since Enniskillen is very close to the border, it was no surprise to learn that, in pursuit of his various activities, he frequently crossed it. In the perspective of some Unionists that amounted to a suspicious liking for hostile territory. Bernard doubtless contributed to that impression by his habit of cheeking members of the security forces at border roadblocks. He did not, however, behave to authority in general in the manner of many a dedicated Republican, finding for example no difficulty about dealing with the local uniformed RUC police in ordinary day-to-day life or with other institutions of provincial government.

At 5.30 am on 20 January 1977 there was a loud bang on Bernard O'Connor's front door. Outside were a number of soldiers who had come to search the house, accompanied by police who arrested him under Section 12 of the Prevention of Terrorism Act, which permitted him to be held without charge for two days, which could be extended for a further five days. Handcuffed he was taken to the Castlereagh Holding Centre, which was a notorious place of interrogation. One characteristic of their latest suspect about which the RUC may well not have been fully briefed in advance was that Bernard O'Connor possessed a remarkable memory which, when allied to considerable powers of observation and of self-expression, would in the long run make him a formidable opponent for those who for seven days had him totally in their power.

The first day and a half in Castlereagh O'Connor described as very rough indeed. 'For some three or four hours,' he said, 'I was made to stand on my toes with my knees in a bent position and my hands out in front of me.' Each time his heels touched the ground and every time he refused to give the answers that were required he was slapped in the face. Following the 'hard' man before lunch there came the 'soft' man after lunch who tried to convince him of the merits of a confession. In a play-acting scene, one interrogator screamed that he was going to kill him but was restrained by another. He was kicked in the legs as he was made to run on the spot and was hurled across the room between two policemen until one got out of the way and he crashed into the wall. He was punched below the ribs and made to do press-ups. 'When I wasn't lifting my knees high enough they then told me to take my trousers off. They kept screaming, "higher, higher". I was then told to take my underpants off.' One of the interrogators 'caught me by the back of the neck and kept pumping my neck up and down in front of the radiator'. Then he was hooded by his underpants. One police officer, by O'Connor's account, began by punching him in the stomach; then he lifted him up, spun him above his head and threw him onto the floor. Another poured the contents of a waste-bin over his head and then made him 'pick up each cigarette butt in my mouth and put it back in the bucket like a dog would'. There was much more of this for hour after hour and all the time he was being asked to accept responsibility for all acts of terrorism performed in the Enniskillen area over the years, which amounted to four murders and 23 other acts.

After a day and a half the physical violence ended and was replaced by psychological tactics. Friendly talks alternated with crude threats and with a religious approach. O'Connor said that his Roman Catholic faith was alternately subject to ridicule and appealed to as a reason to confess. A bogus confession from an unnamed witness was produced incriminating him and confessions to two separate conspiracies to murder were prepared for his signature. On his refusal he was told that it wasn't going to stick in the interrogator's throat to stand up in court and give evidence that he had made these statements verbally in custody and had then refused to sign them.

Bernard told me that one of his interviewers went so far as to allege that the mere fact of his having been taken in for interrogation would make him a target for assassination by the UVF (the Loyalist Ulster Volunteer Force) if, coming to the end of the seven days that the police were allowed to hold him without charge, he were now to be released. Therefore, for his own safety, he should select one of the offences alleged and by confessing to it gain the safety of a prison cell. Getting nowhere with this elegant suggestion, one of O'Connor's interlocutors is said to have speculated that, if they were compelled to let him go, they might assassinate him themselves or, alternatively, tip off the UVF about where they were going to release him. At the end of the seven days Bernard O'Connor was released and at his solicitor's office registered a detailed complaint about his treatment for submission to the complaints division of the RUC.

According to Bernard's calculations he was questioned 20 times for a total of 51 hours by 15 detectives. Despite being subjected to extreme stress, he appeared capable of being surprisingly precise about the personalities and appearance of his individual interrogators, the sequence of their tours of duty and even the timing of the phases of his examination. (He said that, being a scoutmaster, he knew how to read wristwatches upside down.)

We took the material back to London and showed it to two senior BBC executives, one of them with experience of Northern Ireland, who had been designated by the Director-General. They told us after seeing the film that they believed O'Connor, that we were to return to Ulster to get on film as much as possible of the background research which was in our notebooks. I should record an into-camera piece putting the case into perspective, including the pressures on the RUC, and the painful casualties they had suffered. I had always envisaged that the RUC should be given a chance to comment. One entire 40-minute edition of *Tonight* was to be given over to this item.

We went back to Enniskillen where we encountered the strong belief in the Catholic community that the interview had been quietly buried. I gave them my word that this was not so, but they could be excused for not believing me. Bernard himself was still cooperative and we managed to record an interview with his family doctor, who had been allowed to see him in the middle of his stay in Castlereagh. He confirmed that he had found that his patient 'had been assaulted while in police custody'. The person that O'Connor was most anxious that we should see for a character reference was his priest.

The Father, who had been supplied in advance with the transcript of the unedited version of my interview, was invited simply to place on record a brief statement about the reputation in the community of his parishioner. Much to our surprise he proceeded to prevaricate. I naturally pressed him hard as to his unwillingness to act. He said eventually and after repeated evasions, 'Well, the police would not have taken him in without some good reason.' Independently of the police, I pressed him, would the good Father have any reason from his own knowledge to doubt O'Connor's good faith? The priest, sweating profusely and obviously wrestling with himself, called out in his agony, 'You are not a Catholic, so you could not know.' I suddenly grasped what was troubling him. Bernard had said (in a passage that did not appear in the broadcast version) that on the Sunday he had asked to see a priest to perform the Eucharist. This was denied to him, so, using an egg-cup that was to hand, he had administered the sacrament to himself. 'You mean, the Miracle,' I said. It was for the hard-pressed priest as if the sun's rays had appeared at the end of a storm. With immense joy he clutched at the revelation that I had some idea of the massive extent of the heresy implicit in O'Connor's usurpation of the priest's role. Later I was to take advantage of a meeting with Cardinal Basil Hume to recount the circumstances to him and to invite his opinion. He said then that if he had been asked for guidance about the matter he would have said that Bernard was simulating and not attempting to conduct the real ceremony.

Before the conversation at Enniskillen ended, the priest had protested that lives might be in danger were he to be seen endorsing Bernard's reputation. I, still having, I suppose, a residual assumption about the essential saintliness of a man of God, was mildly shocked. Rather naively I said that I had supposed that the fact that the priesthood was celibate relieved its members of family pressures. Not at all, he replied. He had a sister who was on an exposed farm next to the border who would be in acute danger if he took a controversial position.

Despite this experience we brought to London sufficient evidence for 'the hierarchy' of the BBC to authorise *Tonight* to go ahead. The RUC had been contacted and had issued a short statement which was of course included in the programme. I provided the introduction which, while giving credit to the RUC's work as a whole, referred specifically to the European Human Rights Commission's finding and to the Attorney-General's statement. It so happened that James Fawcett, the former Director of Studies at Chatham House, was Chairman of the European Human Rights Commission. After consulting him I felt justified in saying that O'Connor's allegations would, if true, show Britain still indulging in the 'cruel and inhuman treatment' which, though one stage less than 'torture', had likewise been condemned by the European Convention.

All accounts of the Northern Ireland story describe the O'Connor broadcast as a milestone. It had a far greater impact than anything else that I have ever done. The reactions of the British press were almost entirely hostile to the BBC as an institution and to myself as a reporter; the Irish press and the Republican press in the North were more understandably totally supportive. The most extreme example of the former was the cartoon in the *Evening Standard* of 16 March which showed a cameraman filming a body lying spreadeagled on the pavement while a reporter chasing two departing IRA men with smoking guns shouts, 'I'm from the BBC – could we have your side of the story?' The *Daily Telegraph* had a story of angry television viewers calling the paper to complain about the BBC putting out 'bash Britain' programmes. The claims, it said, were unsubstantiated and unjustified. 'At what stage does a part of the

State establishment provide the IRA with a platform from which to put their view?' demanded the Ulster peer Lord Brookeborough. The Vanguard Unionist Party, whose publicity was then entrusted to David Trimble, declared that 'one can only feel utter revulsion' at our programme, adding that 'The Province's majority will remember the same biased type of programme by this particular commentator in the earlier days of our troubles.' Further, Trimble's statement expressed his 'amazement' at 'the fantastic memory of the alleged victim, who despite terrible suffering was able to memorise every single event, including the actual length of each happening'.

In a relatively nuanced leader ('The BBC's Irish Troubles', 16 March 1977), *The Times* first criticised Airey Neave, the Tory opposition's Northern Ireland spokesman, for his demand that as Britain was at war with the IRA the BBC should shape its whole output to assist in the war effort, but then argued that the BBC should have held our film over until the results of the official complaints procedure had become available. I wrote a detailed reply on the Letters page, relying heavily on Sam Silkin's assurances and saying of our interview, 'If this account is correct, Mr O'Connor's experience is in direct violation of the directive of 1972, cited in the British Government's pleadings before the European Commission of Human Rights at Strasbourg that "under no circumstances must there be resort to physical violence, blindfolds or hoods, standing or other periods of stress for long periods to induce exhaustion. … [Prisoners] must not be threatened, insulted or subjected to torture or cruel, inhuman and degrading treatment."' If, I wrote, the interrogations had been carried out in the manner described it would mean that 'practices declared in February 1977 by the Attorney-General to be five years out of date were in use in one of the main holding centres in January 1977'.

I was sent for by the Attorney-General. His chambers consisted of the type of panelled, book-lined, comfortably furnished room one would most wish for oneself. Sam Silkin, whom I had hitherto met occasionally but hardly knew, projected a friendly nature, while expressing himself very slowly and very ponderously. It was immediately apparent that he was seriously worried by my references to his Strasbourg speech. What he said to me amounted to the giving of his professional advice to Bernard O'Connor through my agency to sue the Chief Constable of the RUC if he felt so strongly and was so sure of his case. He spelled out for me at some length the different hurdles to be cleared by a criminal prosecution ('beyond reasonable doubt'), which had resulted in the prosecution service not taking up O'Connor's complaints, and the lesser ones called for by a civil action ('the balance of probabilities'). He said he had read a transcript of my interview; in the course of our meeting he did not voice any criticism of our having transmitted it.

A fair amount of criticism was, however, coming in to the BBC, either instantly on transmission or inspired by a hostile press. I was told one evening that the Board of Governors had it on their agenda for the following day and that they had asked to have my written account of the preparation and background of the programme. Having had some experience of this over the Middle East, I worked at it through the night. I set down every stage in the originating, development and checking of the story. The minutes of the Board's discussion included the observation that 'DG said that in all his time as Director-General he had never seen a more impressive statement by a journalist working for the BBC'. The BBC issued a statement affirming that 'we do not do such things lightly' but that it felt that this programme was in the public interest. It added, accurately, that 'Mr O'Connor's allegations were not directed against the RUC as a whole'.

One additional factor added to the strain of these proceedings. Shortly after the broadcast an 18-year-old policeman, Constable William Brown of Strabane, became the 100th member of the RUC to be killed since the Troubles began, being gunned down in an ambush of his patrol car. The Provisional IRA took the opportunity to state that this marked the start of a new campaign against the RUC 'following the exposure of police brutalities'. The *Daily Express* splash-headlined their issue of 15 March, 'BBC accused after assassination "MURDER BY TV"'. The Police Federation of Northern Ireland issued a statement that 'The *Tonight* programme bore all the hallmarks of trial by TV. There could be little doubt in anyone's mind, at the time and since, that the BBC has returned a verdict of guilty against the RUC. The sentence – a cowardly bullet in the back – has now been carried out by the Provisional IRA.' This was of course the most painful aspect of the whole affair, although the bishop who conducted the funeral of the slain constable was thoughtful enough to send me a message that I must not blame myself for the event, whose linkage to the broadcast was only a trick of IRA publicity.

As to the question of whether we had correctly identified the public interest, two subsequent judicial decisions are relevant. In January 1978 the European Court of Human Rights, reviewing the previous findings of Fawcett's Commission, concluded that not only was Britain to be condemned for the 'five special techniques' defined as torture, in respect of which Britain had pleaded 'no contest', but that in some (though significantly not all) of the cases which the court heard, it was established beyond reasonable doubt that, for example, 'despite the absolute denials given in evidence by witnesses from the security forces' in the cases that the court was considering, four men had been

severely beaten and that 'the beating was not occasional but it was applied in
a sort of scheme in order to make them speak'. The court noted that, as the
Attorney-General had told me, it was open to the victims to bring a civil suit.
This Bernard O'Connor, who was not directly covered by the Strasbourg finding, proceeded to do.

The hearing of his case did not occur until the end of June 1980. It was
before a Diplock or judge-only court, jury service in Northern Ireland having
been suspended since the outbreak of the Troubles. The judge considered that
O'Connor was not justified in claiming compensation for brain damage as
the result of his experiences, but in all other respects he found in his favour
and awarded him exemplary damages 'by way of punishment of the police'.
Bernard's case was greatly assisted by his solicitor's use of the procedure of
discovery to gain access to the work chits of the police. These proved that
the victim's memory, which had seemed to some to be too good to be true,
was remarkably accurate. As can be imagined, this outcome came as a great
relief to me. I had been reasonably confident in my judgement, but I am not
a lawyer and moreover I had to accept the possibility, however small, of the
RUC or someone else, given the publicity that the broadcast had generated,
producing some irrefutable evidence that I had been mistaken in my assessment of Bernard O'Connor. Moreover, without waiting for the slow pace of
judicial decision, an administrative inquiry had been set up in the immediate
aftermath of the broadcast, whose findings resulted in a thorough overhaul of
the system of interrogation.

I was at this time feeling much restored in health; having to outward
appearance thrown off the effects of the stroke I began to get the feeling,
perhaps mistakenly, that there was nothing that I had done or had aimed at
doing before which I could not now do. In 1977 a by-election was to be held
in Great Grimsby and my name was put forward for the Labour candidacy. I
thought that this would be my last chance to pursue my chosen career and I
took special trouble about preparing my ten-minute speech, which because
of the after-effects of the stroke required committing to memory. My main
competition came ironically from the *Tonight* programme. I used to think that
Austin Mitchell, who is a man of great fun and resource, met the modern ideal
of the television presenter because his curriculum vitae embodied so many
apparently opposite characteristics. You could represent him as an intellectual, the possessor of a doctorate of philosophy, the author of a learned work
on the Whigs in opposition, 1815–30, a senior lecturer at a New Zealand
university. On the other hand you could describe him as a folksy humorist
with a pronounced Yorkshire accent, author of books on Yorkshire jokes and

the Half-Gallon Quarter-Acre Pavlova Paradise. I threw everything I had got into the speech but, perhaps inevitably, Austin won. 'Oh, your speech was marvellous,' said a cheery, ample lady at the conclusion. 'It was like listening to Churchill all over again. Of course,' she added hastily, 'I didn't vote for you because it is very important that we should win this election.'

CHAPTER 20

Another Election and At
Last a Book

It turned out, however, that I had not yet said a final farewell to elective politics. I had been a couple of times to the European Parliament at Strasbourg, to which the British members were at first nominated from among MPs and peers. I could not help thinking that the British bench rather resembled an old people's home, around which former Foreign Secretaries like Lord Gordon-Walker and Lord Stewart of Fulham were slowly but repeatedly moving. Surprisingly quickly, however, Britain came round by 1979 to the idea of electing its members, largely, I suspected, because it needed something positive to offset the long list of proposed reforms which it planned to reject.

The idea of serving in the European Parliament, especially now that a conventional political career seemed denied to me, had great appeal. My name went forward to the short list for the part of London in which I lived and I flattered myself that my familiarity with the European Community's institutions and procedure might tell in my favour. I was much mistaken. It turned out that my most formidable opponent was Alf Lomas, who was the author of *The Common Market: Why We Should Keep Out*. I was told (because, of course, being a candidate I was not present at the other speeches) that his line was simple and that the loudest cheer came when he declared, 'I don't know anything about the European Parliament, I don't think we should belong to the European Parliament, I think we should get out of the Common Market.' He and not I became an MEP.

On 26 March 1981 the Social Democratic Party or SDP was launched at the Connaught Rooms in London. It claimed to have broken the mould of British politics by bringing about a complete realignment of party allegiances. It let loose tremendous energy and enthusiasm among those who looked for policies that were socially progressive but not socialistic. Realistically, I thought,

259

Conservatives will always be with us and it was to them that the new party was supposed to provide a more credible alternative. The Labour Party could be driven back to its industrial strongholds but it did not look as if we were going to replace it there. Still the liberating thrill of striving for the kind of social policies that I had always advocated without having to pretend to believe also in the Clause Four commitment to common ownership prompted me to shout aloud, 'I've belonged to the SDP all my life.'

It was another matter to contemplate myself fighting a general election once again. In my own mind I had reluctantly, but I thought completely, given up any ambition to serve at Westminster. Yet it was a measure of the extent to which, with so many other people, I was caught up with the SDP spirit that I allowed my name to go forward as the result of which I was once again adopted as a parliamentary candidate, this time for Northampton South. This, I felt, was oddly appropriate, since it was to Northampton that I had come in wartime to be recruited into the army.

The local political scene was that each of the two Northampton seats, North and South, was linked to a substantial rural area and, although Labour had at one time represented the city, both seats in the 1979 election returned Conservative members. Nevertheless the longstanding civic leadership had been in the hands of Labour councillors who had moved over as a bloc to the SDP, confident that their personal standing would be sufficient to carry the city with them. Came the municipal election and the councillors so used to victory found themselves coming third.

The sitting member for Northampton South was Michael Morris, a marketing accountant, who had held the seat since 1974. He was a quiet, conscientious, unpretentious Member who was subsequently to become Deputy Speaker. There was a Labour candidate, John Coleman, the leader of Brent Council, and it became a matter of honour for my leading supporters, still sore at their own electoral humiliation, that I should end up at least ahead of him. I very nearly did not start at all because the local SDP had exhausted its exiguous financial resources in the disastrous municipal campaign and there was talk of abandoning the parliamentary struggle. Only when Lord Sainsbury signed a cheque was it possible to proceed. When I had first resolved to stand, the tidal wave of popular support for the new party had still not entirely receded. By the time that I had moved to Northampton to fight the campaign, it had seemed highly probable that Michael Morris would be returned. Nevertheless I was determined that there should be nothing in the least half-hearted about my Last Hurrah.

There was a great scarcity of troops on the ground, so I decided from the

17. The family on the campaign trail again.

outset that I would make no attempt at a complete canvass with the elaborate lists that were conventionally compiled for calling out supporters on the day. Fortunately, however, there was a daily local paper and local radio, neither of which outlets I had had in my previous campaigns. Also there were many civic organisations which, during the period of the campaign, would feel it their duty to invite all three candidates as speakers. I determined to have fun in riding on other people's publicity and to an extent I succeeded. Nationally, for instance, our campaign was fought as an Alliance of SDP and Liberals under the leadership of Roy Jenkins, the former Labour Chancellor and also former European Commission President. He made the massive renewal of Britain's Victorian sewers part of the package of measures that would stimulate the economy and help tackle unemployment. It so happened that an important section of Northampton's streets was already torn up for a major repair operation. Thus I was photographed emerging with a hard hat from the bowels of the earth to claim that our Alliance was fighting its campaign in the sewers.

Since we hardly had the resources to organise many meetings on our own – though we had one very successful rally at which Jo Grimond urged all Liberals to come to my support – I took maximum advantage of exploiting those of others. Thus, all three candidates were invited to a Hunger March in imitation of the famous march from Jarrow in the 1930s. As well as the Labour man I too turned up but not the Tory. A new local Chamber of Commerce was being opened: this time it was the Tory and I who were there and I contrived to be specially generous with my promises of action, provided only I should be the next MP. A meeting provided by a pressure group about pensions, to which only the Labour candidate and I came, turned into a lively, almost heated debate which anticipated many of the arguments taking place 20 years later. My opponent, being entirely opposed to means tests, was in favour of a steep rise in the level of all pensions. I, acknowledging the actual and psychological drawbacks and anomalies of any means-tested system, nevertheless argued for the line taken later by Gordon Brown and New Labour, namely that anyone serious about wanting to lift large numbers of pensioners out of poverty soon had to bite the bullet of the means test. Otherwise there were simply not the large amounts of money needed to take swift and effective action.

Canvassing, as I have said, was out of the question on a wholesale, systematic basis, but I did it nonetheless in a random, spot-check fashion. As I had hoped, this disclosed a sufficient number of people who could be quoted as saying that this was the first time in an election that their opinions had ever been sought by a candidate. It was thus that I hoped to give an impression that the SDP was everywhere. I had thought there would be curiosity about the party's policies since they were brand new – and some of them, quite frankly, were invented on the hoof – but I was questioned about only one of them. What line did I take over the banning of foxhunting, a policy to which Labour was already committed? My answer was clear: hunting was a traditional country sport and it had nothing to do with government.

There was one very tragic episode. A civic body had organised a brains trust, with the three candidates taking part. When a question was asked by an elderly gentleman about the Middle East I foresaw for myself a certain advantage through possessing more specialist knowledge than my two rivals. I was called on last and gave what I thought was a balanced and informed reply. Immediately I finished the questioner gave out a short groan and died. He slumped to the floor and was immediately certified dead by a doctor who was present. The meeting was adjourned. The next morning, in the house where I was made most welcome, which was just across the boundary in the next constituency, I was completing a letter of condolence when the Tory candidate for Northampton North turned up to canvass my support.

At the end of an enjoyable campaign in favour of what might be described in anticipation as a Blairite programme while Tony Blair was at the same time running for Sedgefield on a manifesto calling for unilateral disarmament and

18. With Crispin and Tarquin in 1986.

leaving the Common Market, I achieved the minimum requirement of my candidacy: I beat Labour for second place. But Michael Morris won.

Thankful to have withstood a vigorous campaign with no damage to my health, I was at long last compelled to recognise that chances of a political career were precisely nil. Not only had there been no electoral breakthrough by the SDP but the bulk even of SDP MPs in the last Parliament had been swept away. The mould had not been broken. Yet I shall never regret the creation of the SDP and its subsequent merger into the Alliance (with the Liberals) because this had at last identified the political space into which a progressive party would have to move if it was ever to replace the Tories in office. This in my opinion was more important than the conclusion of Crewe and King, in their history of the SDP, that 'the wholesale recasting of Labour policy [under

Kinnock and Blair] owed almost nothing to the SDP'.[37] Without ever losing my fascination for politics, I abandoned, not for the first time, the ambition to achieve things politically and resolved to be content with what was going well with my life. My sole role would be that of a commentator, but I could say to myself that I had made repeated efforts in good faith to take a share of responsibility for public affairs.

There was much to be thankful for – I had escaped almost unscathed from a major illness, I had regular work at Chatham House, which was interesting if not in the normal run of things terribly exciting, and I had the greatest joy of all in a hugely successful marriage, with the rewards and trials of helping to bring up two sons close in age. I had besides several literary outlets, in the opinion columns of *The Times*, in the long essay-type reviews of the *London Review of Books* and in the pages of *The World Today*, a publication of Chatham House. I had joined the International Institute for Strategic Studies and I find among my cuttings more than I had remembered of writing on strategic subjects. All of this, however subtle or insightful I might think myself to have been, is not worth recalling, and this for the happiest of reasons, namely that the Cold War is over. My strategic views seem as remote as if written in cuneiform. The one impression which does remain with me is of the United States competing with itself, that is that no sooner was an American breakthrough in weapons production achieved than it was automatically assumed that the Russians would arrive there soon afterwards, so that an antidote must immediately be worked on.

In 1983 came a new interest. A seat on the council of the Minority Rights Group had the unexpected result of landing me on the island of Cyprus. MRG's main activity takes the form of publishing a series of monographs describing inter-ethnic issues in complex societies. Cyprus, an obvious case for an MRG study, presented special difficulty. One possible text had been held to be pro-Greek, another to be pro-Turkish. I was invited by the Director, Ben Whitaker, to take on the task of writing an impartial account and I thought that, semi-retired as I was beginning to think of myself, I was yet up to taking on one more subject.

Over the years I would often come back to Cyprus. My MRG report was more or less accepted on both sides of the Green Line as being fair and I would be invited back either by Turkish or Greek Cypriots to take part in some academic event connected with the Cyprus problem. I went to two of the fairly rare events when people came from both sides of the line to take part in bi-communal discussion. One was an attempt by the Norwegian Institute of International Affairs to facilitate a compromise. On the second occasion I was invited by the British Foreign Office to take the chair at a bi-communal gathering of businessmen. Political matters, I was instructed, should be ruled out of order. All went promisingly, with Greek Cypriots showing themselves willing, provided the politics was settled, to enter into business partnerships with their Turkish Cypriot compatriots, but danger loomed as soon as one eloquent Greek Cypriot lady, with obvious backing from her side, insisted on making it clear that working with Turkish Cypriots was not in any way the same thing as working with Turkish 'settlers' who had been brought in from the mainland. Though I managed without too much difficulty to steer the discussion back to more positive channels, I had then a glimpse of the intensity of feeling that could be instantly generated. I kept up my interest, belonging in London to the Friends of Cyprus and to the Association of Greek, Turkish and Cypriot Affairs and taking the chair at a number of Cypriot occasions. In 1997 MRG published my second monograph, called *Cyprus: In Search of Peace*.

For the first time since 1947, I returned to India with a delegation headed by Roderick MacFarquhar to take part in discussions with Indian academics and some others. Two speeches, neither as it happens by an Indian, left on me a particularly strong impression. One was by an Afghan professor from Kabul, who entreated us, in an intensely emotional address, not to take advantage of the Russians leaving the Afghan capital to bring about the overthrow of the man who had owed his position to them, President Najibullah. He was, we were told, the only leader who could maintain order in the city and permit intellectual activity to continue there. If the West attempted to remove him we would live to regret it, because the capital would be wrecked by competing warlords and civilised life would become impossible. One could not be unmoved by a man speaking with the eloquence of desperation and, speaking for myself, however much I might have been inclined at the time to discount words spoken in favour of 'a Soviet puppet', those words haunted me during the appalling succession of events that followed.

Even more dramatic in a different way was the speech in excellent English given by the Counsellor of the Soviet Embassy in Delhi. Although it was clear that Gorbachev intended to make some important changes in the Soviet Union it was not at this point at all certain how far he intended to go. Bearing in mind that major pronouncements were not to be expected on the personal initiative of a counsellor, I found it highly significant that this speaker felt able to open his talk by saying bluntly, 'Hitherto the Soviet foreign policy has been decided in accordance with ideological considerations. We have concluded that this has not been successful. We are therefore from now on intending to decide policy in accordance with our national interest.' This formulation might in particular cases be deemed equivocal, but there could be no question that a sea-change was intended.

We were staying in Poona, as I have in a previous chapter related, and, as two of our Indian colleagues were involved in social work in a neighbouring Punjabi village, some of us rose at 5.30 to go with them to the scene of their endeavours. The village, it was clear, was divided in two parts, the part of the caste Hindus and the part of the Untouchables, who were mainly leather work-ers. There were two wells, one of which contained water the year round, the other of which functioned for half the year. It was not difficult to guess which of them was reserved for the Untouchables. We were told of the immensely painstaking work that was involved in trying to bring about accommodation in this and other matters. My standing with the Untouchables was established when in a flash of my Indian past I walked into a hut and was able to iden-tify immediately the dimly seen photograph on the wall as being that of Dr Ambedkar, the Untouchables' hero.

At some point in 1985 I was approached by Peter Hill, who had produced the four-part series about Suez which had gone out on the BBC ten years before. Peter, I learned, had got a commission from BBC 2 for a one-hour documentary on the 30th anniversary the following year. Would I come back to television just to research and write this one programme? It was Peter's idea that in addition the two of us should co-author a book that would be brought out simultaneously. Attractive though I felt this prospect to be I could see that there was one major snag. The television programme would have to go out on the actual anniversary at the end of October or the first week in November, but the only real justification for a fresh book in addition to the rather good books that were already in the field would be the use of a major new documen-tary source – and that would be the British official records which, under the 30-year rule, would be released only in January 1987.

This difficulty was eventually overcome by the decision that there should be a book but that it would not be a BBC publication and would be written after the programme. Peter then proposed that the book's authorship should be solely mine and he was kind enough to arrange that his own literary agent should place it with publishers. Three of them bid for it and I decided to go for Collins, mainly because the able historian and biographer Philip Ziegler would be my editor. For research in the field I was greatly helped by the fact that Peter used his discretion as producer in scheduling research work for the film so as to assist me in my work for the book.

Although the British primary sources would not be available until 1987 there was much material to absorb in anticipation. I was able to arrange with

Chatham House to have Friday of every week free so that I could spend time in the Public Record Office at Kew. In those days the building containing records was not so large, nor its grounds so landscaped as it is today, but associated with it were the remains (now removed) of a factory with a tall, thin chimney. I used to think of the research rooms as the History Factory and even to fantasise about the chimney, from which a thin trail of smoke could sometimes be seen emerging, as belonging to a crematorium for the disposal of ultra-secret papers.

At the end of 1985 and throughout 1986 I was building up evidence from primary sources of how the eventual crisis was approaching both in the Middle East and, critically, in Anglo-American relations, as well as absorbing what had already been published. I spent part of my annual leave in the United States in Princeton, where I became the first customer, much fussed over, on the opening day of the brand-new Seeley G. Mudd Manuscripts Library which housed some of the papers of John Foster Dulles, Eisenhower's Secretary of State, and a large collection of oral history interviews with many other Americans involved in the Suez and other crises. Then I went on to Abilene, Kansas, the birthplace of Dwight D. Eisenhower. It has been a twentieth-century American custom for a president after his retirement to deposit the vast proliferation of paper (and other memorabilia) that he has acquired in office in a purpose-built library funded by his admirers, at times at rather obscure locations to which scholars dutifully trek to carry out their researches.

Abilene, a real 'back of beyond' where the cowboy trail used to end, is the place 'Ike' Eisenhower came from. The locals have made as much of this as they can. Besides the fine modern building of the Eisenhower Library, the process had begun of restoring some authentic reminders of old Mid-Western ways. No expense had been spared to house Ike's papers – and some of Dulles's and those of other close associates – in a worthy memorial, and I noticed with regret that the modest Eisenhower residence, with the drawer in which he had been parked as a baby, had since my last visit been stripped of its context of connecting houses to leave the relic naked and freestanding. The library staff were aggressively on the side of the researcher, ready to do battle to secure the declassification of material that was still withheld; they continued to mail relevant items to me long after I had gone home.

In America there is no fixed term like the 30-year rule governing the release of documents, so the practice was uneven and the existence of multiple collections offered extra opportunities. I was, for instance, able to come across in Abilene a record of telephone conversations between the Dulles brothers, the Secretary of State and the Director of the CIA, at the moment when an

Anglo-American intelligence plot to bring about regime change in Syria was unhorsed by the startling news of an Anglo-French ultimatum to Nasser. I subsequently noticed with some amusement that the conversation had been withheld in other official releases. When I left Abilene it was with a large portfolio of notes and photostats covering the whole course of the Suez crisis.

I was lucky, too, about the timing of the visit. Not being a person who is at his best in very hot weather, I had had to nerve myself for a journey to Kansas in mid-August, which is normally punishingly hot at this season, but it was when I could best get away from Chatham House. It was a huge relief to find Abilene in the summer of 1986 exceptionally cool. Moreover, so far from the evenings being boring as well as hot, there was a wealth of Western-type entertainment. There was for one thing the Wild Bill Hickok Rodeo Show, which offered spectacular mastery of spectacularly unfriendly steeds, and then there was the Demolition Derby, which consisted of a large number of cars being driven into each other with lethal effect (though not, surprisingly, on drivers) until only one was left mobile. These might not be the most refined of pastimes but in the atmosphere of small-town America they made a welcome break from long hours of scholarship.

My work was much advanced on my return to England by an academic conference at St Antony's College, Oxford, an internationally minded post-war foundation for graduates, funded in the first instance by a Lebanese trader in frankincense and myrrh, of which I later became a Senior Associate Member. Arab, Israeli and American scholars and participants as well as British ones were gathered to speak of the background to the Suez crisis. The whole was orchestrated by Wm Roger Louis, of whom I had heard much but whom I met for the first time. He was to become a firm friend, as was a remarkable Israeli called Mordechai Bar-On, who had been General Moshe Dayan's top aide during the preparations for and the execution of the Sinai War (as Suez is known to the Israelis) but who subsequently became an MK (Member of the Knesset) for the 'Peace Now' party and after that an academic.

Wm Roger Louis is a splendid scholar who operates with extraordinary effectiveness on both sides of the Atlantic – in Austin, Texas, where he presides over the most important centre of British Studies in the United States and at St Antony's College, of which he is a Fellow. My first encounter with him was in print as the author of a book on Ruanda-Urundi and, given the subject and his surname, I had taken him to be a Belgian. Now he was organising this conference which preceded the publication in 1989 of a volume of essays entitled *Suez 1956: The Crisis and Its Consequences*, and, since he turned out to be an American born in Oklahoma, I got to pronounce his name as if it were

19. Researching *Suez*, 1986.

spelled 'Lewis'. His major work so far was on *The British Empire in the Middle East* – I had reviewed it in the *London Review of Books* – but he was also becoming known for his extraordinary skill as an editor and an essayist. Certainly my own experience as a contributor to the 1989 volume on Suez was that he had a phenomenal talent for assembling a broad spectrum of academics and participants and, what is more unusual, getting them to produce on time. He was to repeat this performance time almost without number and, being present at a much later date at his launch in the Reform Club (to which he and I belong) of the five-volume edition of the *Oxford History of the British Empire* of which he was editor-in-chief, I heard the publisher assert her amazement at receiving all the material ahead of deadline.

For Britons and Americans interested in British culture and political history there have for many years been fewer treats more savoured than an invitation to lecture to his very special seminar at Austin. The text of these lectures, delivered, as Roger himself puts it, 'in a congenial setting of overstuffed armchairs, Persian carpets and generous libations of sherry', forms the basis for chapters in an apparently endless succession of *Adventures with Britannia*, each bearing a flamboyant cover depicting the adventuress herself arriving, brilliantly attired, in an old-fashioned coach. I was to savour this treat myself when, accompanied by Suzy, I spoke about Suez and in the course of the visit to Austin saw thousands of bats fly out simultaneously from under a bridge at a precise time in the evening. We also managed to see LBJ's ranch and San Antonio where Davy Crockett fell. But this was in the future. Now was the time for research in the Middle East.

Travelling in advance of the camera crew I was able to interview many of the people both in Israel and in Egypt who had been involved 30 years earlier. Because peace had at last been established between the two countries it was possible to travel between them overland, changing coaches at the border. I managed to attend celebratory conferences both in Israel and in Egypt, where the phrase 'the triple aggression' was much in use. In Cairo Sir Anthony Nutting, whose promising political career was utterly ruined by his resignation from the post of Minister of State at the Foreign Office in protest at Anthony Eden's acceptance of the French plan of collusion with the Israelis, was for three days once more the hero, treated as a guest of the greatest distinction. He, Michael Foot and I were taken by the Egyptian chairman of the Suez Canal Authority on board a launch for a trip along a major section of the canal. In Jerusalem I learned a great deal about the Israeli side from Shimon Peres and many other politicians and soldiers but above all from Mordechai Bar-On, who was commissioned in the immediate aftermath by David Ben-Gurion to write a history of the affair, including the secret meetings at Sèvres which plotted the Suez operation and the planning and conduct of the actual campaign. The completed work had been kept under wraps for 30 years but was then declassified to enable Bar-On, who was converting himself from soldier to scholar, to publish it in Hebrew. A book in English based upon the materials he had created himself appeared in 1994 under the title of *The Gates of Gaza*, but I owe to his generosity the fact that the essence of his analysis, which involved several major revisions in the hitherto accepted history of the campaign, could be incorporated in my book.

I spent a couple of days at Eilat, Israel's Red Sea port where the state's boundaries reach down like a point of a triangle. Access of Israeli shipping to and from Eilat through the choke point of the Straits of Tiran into the Gulf of Aqaba and the Red Sea proper had been a major issue leading to Israel's participation in the war of 1956, as it was to be also in the war of 1967. I decided, since I was crossing from Eilat into the Egyptian Sinai, to inspect the site at Ras Nasrani, near Sharm el Sheikh, of the gun positions which Nasser intended to use to prevent Israeli ships from passing through the narrow straits. My driver knew where the abandoned remains of Nasser's artillery could be found and delivered me to the spot which, covered by brush, was alongside the beach.

I looked across the stretch of water and noticed the one distant ship which afforded the only hint of the positioning of the narrow Enterprise Channel which alone is deep enough for seagoing vessels to use. I could see that if the guns were of the right calibre and were properly laid, ships passing along this horizon would make easy targets.

I decided to have a swim. The sea, I soon discovered, was very shallow and, as I paddled out, I was nearly abandoning the idea of immersing myself further when the sand beneath my feet abruptly disappeared and I was sent swirling out on a fast current. I did not at first fully realise the implications of this and, much relieved by the comparative coolness of the sea, set about to enjoy my swim. After a while I came to see that there would be serious difficulties in getting back to shore and after several abortive attempts concluded that these added up to an impossibility. I felt very calm and, seeing that it was important that I should not exhaust myself, I lay on my back and waited to see what would turn up. I watched the single ship in the Enterprise Channel. It did not seem to move. The lines of Coleridge came to mind:

As idle as a painted ship
Upon a painted ocean

At school I had committed large stretches of Coleridge to memory, which made it especially vexing that at 61 I could not recall the whole passage. I impulsively thought that, since I was debarred from regaining the shore, my best course was to swim out to the ship. After a short while I concluded that this was a hopeless task and resumed my recumbent posture. I thought of Suzy and the children who might be left without a father if no solution was to present itself and of the irony that when I had at last fully committed myself to writing a book it was fated not to be completed. I looked again at the painted ship. It still seemed to be hanging two-dimensionally and motionless in the Enterprise Channel.

Suddenly I heard a loud noise as of surf breaking on a shore. Using whatever strength I had been building up, I struck out once more until, arriving unexpectedly from the placid sea, a large wave landed me back on the shallow edge of the strait. I got up and walked the considerable distance to my car where I found the driver obviously unaware of my plight. In retrospect I was amused by my adventure and made the great mistake of writing a light-hearted account of it home, where it caused a shock.

The television programme was shot, transmitted and well received, thanks to Peter Hill's production skills. At the outset of 1987 I took three months' unpaid leave from Chatham House and worked full-time in the Public Record Office at Kew and other libraries, including the Bodleian in Oxford and Churchill College in Cambridge. After all the press speculation about what might be withheld I was relieved to discover how much was revealed. I went too to Sweden to make use of the Dag Hammarskjöld archives in Stockholm. I was invited to take the chair at an all-day conference of the RAF Historical Association at which the exchanges with the by now retired RAF officers involved in the Suez operation were immensely helpful.

For 18 months I worked for the first two hours of each day and in the evenings, also at weekends. It was with some pride that together with Suzy, who had played a great role in controlling the logistics of the operation, I delivered the manuscript at the offices of Collins. One great disappointment was that Philip Ziegler, who had received great acclaim for his life of Mountbatten, was no longer there, having quit the publishing business to devote himself to full-time authorship. Still, the work was done, though at the back of my mind I was bothered that the appropriate volume of *Foreign Relations of the United States* had even now not been published and there was relatively little material that had been released on the French side. I had been steered to what there was – including a brilliant volume, *Suez 1956*, by Paul Gaujac and some good political and journalistic books – by the fine French scholar Maurice Vaisse.

There was nothing now to do but to wait for the publisher's reaction. Being new to authorship at this level I was anxious not to appear anxious. Still, nothing happened. I got on to my agent. He was reassuring. They were almost certainly setting it up in print. Then, a short time after, my agent died – I had had no idea that he had been ill. More silence. I approached the publishers directly, they having been in the meantime taken over by Rupert Murdoch. They told me that they no longer wished to publish my book. Their new accountants had told them that given its length – 633 pages – the price would have to be higher than they were prepared to countenance. I would receive the balance of my advance that would normally only come with actual publication and could go straightaway to any other publisher. I drew what comfort I could from being told that the problem was one of accountancy, not of intellectual content. This notwithstanding, it was a severe blow.

I had sufficient confidence in the book – or at any rate in the subject – that I continued to believe that it would somehow appear in print. I was just about to leave for Cyprus with Suzy when we received an invitation for both of us to attend one of the stylish lunch parties at which George Weidenfeld used to celebrate the launching of a new book by one of his favourite authors. I wrote accepting and reminding him, in almost the same breath, of a recent social encounter at which George, in the soft seductive way in which he approached potential authors and others, had reproached me for not having offered him a chance to publish my book on Suez. Now I told him, 'you do have a chance because I've been sacked by Collins'. George rang me and told me to send the manuscript immediately to his senior editor Christopher Falkus. When we returned from Cyprus there was a message to call Falkus. He said, 'Would you do us the honour of allowing us to publish your book?' Next to Suzy's acceptance of me, it was the most beautiful sentence that I had ever heard.

CHAPTER 21

The End — or Almost

As I write this in my 82nd year and look back over the 16 years since my book on Suez was published I realise that this event has made all the difference to my enjoyment of the final stages of life. Beforehand I really had no idea how well the book would be received. I had put a great deal of effort into it and had received much assistance, but in the end writing is a lonely activity of whose quality the writer is in the worst position to be the judge. The change of publisher meant that, whereas my late agent had always been stressing how quickly Collins would be expecting the text, by contrast George Weidenfeld told me that I should take as long as I needed to ensure a 'definitive' version. Though that phrase troubled my historical conscience — since I do not believe that any book can or should be definitive — I was happy to go along with the general idea. One version of a complete manuscript was already in existence but, as I have mentioned, what was missing from my sources were the French documents and the relevant volume of *FRUS — Foreign Relations of the United States*. Having extra time enabled me to integrate material from both these primary sources. The revised book was handed in and I awaited with such patience as I was able to command the verdict of the literary and historical world.

It came in the first instance from Anthony Howard, a political journalist who was also a fine biographer of Dick Crossman, Rab Butler and later Cardinal Basil Hume, in *The Times Literary Supplement*. He wrote that my book 'in its comprehensive command, its overall balance and its narrative sweep easily surpasses all earlier accounts'. The rest of the piece filled out this theme. I could scarcely believe my luck. As the *TLS* has a very high standing in literary journalism this was a wonderful beginning. Tony Howard told me a long time afterwards that, running ahead of the pack, he had begun to wonder if he had not gone too far and was immensely relieved when Roy Jenkins's review appeared in the *Sunday Times*. Lord Jenkins said that my book 'has the quality of making everything that has come before on the infinitely fascinating and convoluted subject of Suez look like a pamphlet written off the top of a partisan's head'. The fact that in my heart I did not entirely agree with the last sentiment in no way diminished my pleasure at seeing it expressed. One point that Jenkins made was especially reassuring: that although my position with *The Economist* in Washington had given me a useful vantage point, 'this is overwhelmingly a book which is based not on chance views or personal insights but on the most meticulous examination of the evidence, about 95% of which has now become available'. Without in any way casting aspersions on journalists' books, which are in my experience a most valuable category, I wanted *Suez* to be acceptable by academic standards. I had to wait quite a bit for the *English Historical Review* but it was worth waiting for. My book, in the opinion of its reviewer, David Reynolds, 'will surely become the standard full-length narrative of the crisis'. I could not have wished for anything better.

Of the 40 reviews in Britain and America of which I had knowledge, all were favourable (with some of the reviewers naturally enough having a quibble or two), with one exception. That was in the *Sunday Express* and it represented almost precisely the reaction that I had from the very beginning thought in my worse fears might be the general one. The article featured in 'our don't buy guide to the newly published books that you would never get round to reading'. *Suez* would, the pseudonymous reviewer said, suddenly appear on all trendy Hampstead coffee tables because it looked important. It was a worthy book, of course but, 'despite all those 650 tedious pages most of Mr Kyle's findings are pretty predictable and old-hat'.

The world evidently did not think so. I was invited to lecture in the United States at the University of Boston and the University of Colorado at Boulder (my old haunt), in France at the Abbey of Royaumont, in Egypt, where I gave five lectures plus a seminar at the American University in Cairo, and in Israel. Godfrey Smith, who, it may be remembered, was the president when I was the secretary of the Oxford Union, wrote in his column in the *Sunday Times* that, of those who had once been prominent in Oxford politics, 'One who had not shown his paces till the other day was a tall, lean, pale, chronically absent-minded yet formidably gifted chap called Keith Kyle. ... He has now published a book, 280,000 words long and four years in the making, called simply *Suez*. It has had a critical ovation.' It had indeed at the eleventh hour established my reputation among the scholarly community whose approbation meant most to me. Whereas when I went up to Oxford 'modern history' began when Charles VIII of France invaded Italy in 1494 and ended on 4 August 1914 (after which everything was politics), the exit date had now been extended 50 years to 1964 (not, I take it, because Harold Wilson had taken office in that year). I was, therefore, technically entitled to call myself a historian.

When the book appeared I had, a few months previously, retired from the Chatham House staff on nearing my 65th birthday but continued to work mainly at home at editing in collaboration with Joel Peters a Chatham House book called *Whither Israel? The Domestic Challenges*, whose contributors were mainly Israeli scholars but to which I also contributed a chapter after a further trip to Israel. It was in part an attempt to rebut the view in some quarters that Chatham House had been since the days of Arnold Toynbee indifferent to or even hostile to the fate of Israel. The whole exercise involved me in intense political discussions on the spot with politicians and intellectuals. It came at a critical moment when the Israeli government had just changed, with the right-wing Likud Party losing narrowly to Labour under Yitzhak Rabin, when the challenge had yet to be fully met of absorbing a huge influx of immigrants from the former Soviet Union, when the ultra-orthodox Sephardic party Shas had just made itself a major player and when proposals for big changes in the electoral system were being enthusiastically debated. 'In most countries you have to apologise for talking politics at a social occasion,' one Israeli told me. 'Here you have to apologise for not talking politics.' By the time of the paperback edition peace had unexpectedly broken out between Israel and the PLO. This called for a new preface by the editors, which I drafted, taking the Oslo Accord into account.

Since Chatham House is a membership organisation which provides an extensive programme for its members, I remain a member and a rather active one, especially but by no means exclusively in the Middle East Programme. In addition I began in 1990 the practice of reviewing books for Chatham House's mainly academic periodical *International Affairs*, which used to come out quarterly but now appears every second month. It is a way of obliging me to keep up to date with the regions — Africa, the Middle East, Ireland, the United States — with which my career has made me familiar.

In 1992 I was in the United States for the anniversary of Columbus's discovery at the World Affairs Conference at Boulder. I delivered a lecture about Suez and took part in various seminars. When I left Britain, the general election was in full swing, I had cast my postal vote and the expectation was that Neil Kinnock's Labour Party was about to put an end to Conservative rule. With two other Brits I was allowed the afternoon off from seminars to watch the results tumbling in. Since I had been on record in Boulder as predicting a Labour victory, the local press inevitably interviewed me when the result became only too clear. 'What will you do now?' they asked. 'I shall apply in the morning for political asylum,' I replied.

I was approached by the University of Ulster with an invitation to become Visiting Professor of History. For the next seven years I flew over twice a term for a week at a time. I lectured on a variety of subjects, most of which were derived from different parts of my career – Suez, American politics, Cyprus, the history of Arab–Israeli relations, the early days of the Northern Ireland Troubles and British fascism. I took a graduate class on the Middle East. One student asked me to account for the oxymoron of contemporary history. I replied, 'That which is history to you, but was contemporary to me.' A good illustration of that was provided by a Baptist minister who was attending the university part-time as an extra-mural student in order to complete a thesis on British policy in the Middle East at the time of the Six Day War. 'I get the impression from the documents,' he said, 'that there was something peculiar about George Brown. Have you any idea what it was?' I had and I told him in some detail.

I was accommodated in the Golf Hotel, which was a snug and friendly place alongside the dunes of the Atlantic seashore at Castlerock close to Coleraine. When the security situation was bad there were not many people in the hotel but they soon returned when things were looking up. Once I found five inebriated judges who had fled from Northern Ireland for a while but were back again to play a few rounds of golf. I used to think that I wished my mother could be alive as she always wished for me to become a professor, though I rather suspected that this was because she associated professorship with absentmindedness.

There was no person I would have more wanted to know of the success of my *Suez* book than A.J.P. Taylor. I knew that his health had been declining and that he was suffering from Parkinson's Disease. I discovered that he had had to retreat into a home and visited him there. I found him seated on a bench, looking very small and very sad. I sat down beside him. He did not recognise me. I was to some extent prepared for this and tried to tell him about my book and about how it begins with an epigraph of his that reads, 'The moral for British governments is clear. Like most respectable people they will make poor criminals and had better stick to respectability. They will not be much good at anything else.' He did not acknowledge his words. He said only, 'I've forgotten all history.' The exchange continued with my running through topics and associations that might produce some response. He said very little but what he did say was uttered with firm diction and his familiar cadence. At one point he said, out of the blue, 'I want to die.' His son Sebastian entered the room. What followed put me in mind of the last scene between Lear and Cordelia. 'They tell me that you are my son,' said my tutor. 'Yes, father, I am.' 'Who was your

20. Honorary D.Litt., University of Ulster.

mother?' 'Margaret.' 'Someone else came the other day who also said he was Margaret's son. She has a lot to answer for.' I had reached my tutor too late. The tragedy of this splendid scholar was well-nigh unbearable.

When A.J.P. had finally left Oxford he had worked for Lord Beaverbrook, whose biography he had written, in setting up and running a library for research into twentieth-century politics. One of the offshoots of this had been a weekly seminar for researchers to read their work in progress and to be open to criticism. The library had not long survived Beaverbrook's death and changes in the ownership of his papers. But Alan's old seminar was kept going by scholars like Kathleen Burk, one of Taylor's biographers, Peter Hennessy, the marvellous historian of our own times, and Peter Catterall, the editor of the Macmillan Diaries, on Wednesday evenings in the London University Senate House. Following the publication of my book, I started attending it fairly regularly. As a result I found myself invited by the Institute of Contemporary History to prepare a paper for their annual conference. I decided that I would not take the lazy path of rehashing some part of my Suez material. Instead I reached back into my personal archive where I still kept in storage the material for my aborted book on East Africa. With fresh additions from the Public Record Office now that 30 years had passed, I was able to produce a paper on 'The Politics of the Independence of Kenya'. A representative of Macmillan's was on hand and he promptly invited me to write a book under the same title for a series, edited by Peter Catterall, entitled 'Contemporary History in Context'. I entered into the task with especial zest in that the series title gave me an excuse to incorporate into my first 65 pages some flavour of the curious history of Kenya between 1895 and the coming of Macmillan and the 'wind of change'.

Thus I was able to find a place for the first East African novel *The Phenomenal Rise of a Rat* – the rodent in question being the first commissioner – which was written by the first newspaper editor. There was also the leading article in the settlers' organ *The East African Standard* on the outbreak of war in August 1914 entitled *The White Man's Burden*, on the lines that acceptance of this burden called for a declaration of neutrality covering African colonies, so that whites should not let themselves down by fighting each other in front of the natives. After that war the white settlers became the first anti-imperialists because they were being asked for the sake of the Empire to extend parity of esteem to Indian settlers. There were bitter polemics between Europeans and Asians, the whites ridiculing arranged marriages and the Asians replying that when white girls married they were already pregnant. I was able to linger on Jomo Kenyatta's splendid journalism when he came to England in 1929 and witnessed a royal procession. There was, naturally, much else to describe that was very tragic, culminating in Mau Mau, on which I was able to make use of long interviews that I had had in 1963 with Bildad Kaggia, who, unlike Kenyatta, was self-confessedly one of the originators of the uprising.

I published the book in 1999. It did not get, and I had not expected, the breadth of coverage I had received for *Suez*, and reactions were slower coming in. All the same, with sometimes, as one should expect, minor reservations, the reception was again distinctly favourable. I had shown that I was capable of writing about something other than Suez, which was not after all, as some people had represented it, a lifetime's obsession. I was also able to prove, what many people had affected to doubt, that I was capable of writing a short book (200 pages, compared with 650 for *Suez*).

Following an article which I published in the *Contemporary Record* for January 1995, which discussed what new material had been revealed about Suez by the releases under the Waldegrave Initiative, a separate publisher and fellow member of the Reform Club, Iradj Bagherzade of I.B.Tauris, asked me if I would prepare a new edition of *Suez* on the expiry of Weidenfeld's copyright. Besides lightly revising the existing text I could have a completely fresh chapter to deal with material which had become available in the last decade. I felt under no necessity to alter the facts or judgements expressed in the original, but the extra chapter allowed me to add much interesting detail. There was some material from Politburo sessions in Moscow, there were naval signals which spelled out precisely how British ships were being placed to respond to the Israeli offensive which was supposed to come as a complete surprise, there were papers left by Lord Monckton and Sir Douglas Dodds-Parker, who both held office under Eden, and there were the weekly reports of the JIC — the Joint Intelligence Committee made famous at the time of the Iraq War. Dodds-Parker's papers were lodged with Magdalen College and are to be reached up the steep steps of the College Founder's Tower. This provided an agreeable excuse for staying in the college which for a total of 17 years was most successfully presided over by the former editor of *Tonight*, Tony Smith.

When I look back now at over 60 years of events and their consequences (over 70 if I take account of my first current-affairs diary), certain things seem paramount. Many of those respects in which I accounted myself at the time to be a rebel — rejection of peer pressure to smoke, breaking free of being a Christian, refusal to accept that early marriage and a family were the inevitable lot of man, readiness to recognise alternative lifestyles as a normal feature of society — now describe the ordinary circumstance of life. Peer pressure of a different — and potentially more sinister — kind, namely drugs, I was never

exposed to, but I am confident that I should have resisted that too. Deference to parents and more distant, totemic figures reaching up through the
peerage to the Crown is infinitely less nowadays than when I was young. The
class system, though symptoms of it are still to be found, is much less dominant. Relationships between the generations are, in my experience, happier
and more relaxed than they were. I wish now that I had known much more
of my father and I think he would have benefited by knowing much more of
me. In some fields such as medical technology and information technology the
changes have been dramatic, though in neither case anything like complete.
Over 50 years ago rationing and currency restrictions pinched our lives to an
extent that is inconceivable nowadays. But at least the currency looked more
robust. A 'fiver' (£5 note) really meant something special. It was printed on
thick paper on a white background. It seemed to me then to resemble the title
deeds of old England. Now it is the scruffiest, least regarded and most often
torn scrap of paper.

As for my country it has occupied the whole of my adult life in adjusting
from being a worldwide imperial power to being one among many members
of a European Union. I can honestly say that the need for such a drastic change
in role was plainly evident to me as an Oxford undergraduate after the end of
the war. I say this not for any desire to claim exceptional farsightedness (there
were many others who felt the same) but simply to underline the conclusion
that immense cultural changes work to a different timescale than the calculations of single minds. And even now, when the switch has in theory (and to
some considerable degree in practice) occurred, there are still in-built resist-
ances. In 2003, for instance, Britain did not take her rightful stand alongside
France and Germany to carve out a European position on the military invasion
of Iraq.

When I was a young man it was Britain's bluff about being a world power
that was being called. As I grew older it was a different kind of bluff, a domestic kind, the kind of bluff that assumed that there existed authentic balances
within the institutions. As I noted when, with only American political experience behind me, I returned to report on the British political scene, this relied
almost solely on a habit of voluntary restraint. Under Thatcher, Major and
Blair the absence of that underpinning has become plain to see since, with
a few exceptions, only the House of Lords and the judges have been able to
present any countervailing power to the 'elected dictatorship' – unless, of
course, one counts brute facts and media headlines.[38]

I have always thought that one should accept the consequences of the positions one has adopted, including the unfortunate ones. As a young man I was

aware that the greater freedom from conventional restraints that I was requiring for myself and therefore for others (some of which were listed in my 1959 *Economist* leader 'Set the people free') would have consequences that were not invariably pleasant. Unfetter all manner of people from customary inhibitions and you are confronted with dozens of fresh conundrums. Yet I do not regret the general thrust of the changes during my lifetime. They seem to have created a world of greater possibilities and opportunities. Among European nations, it is true, the British appear to have reverted to their former reputation up to about 1830 as being the most drunken and disorderly of people. They are the most incarcerated and the most indebted. This represents a major change in instinctive attitudes since my mother would say over some small real or putative sliding into the red, 'Take care or we'll be in Queer Street'.[39]

The current attitude towards sex frankly puzzles me. I had thought when I was young that if the bans on personal conduct were removed and a broader range of behaviour was regarded as normal the hysteria would depart from the subject. In one respect this has happened. Obituary notices in respectable newspapers will speak routinely of a 'partner' being left. Cohabitation, instead of stretching the limits of social acceptance, is well nigh universal. Civil partnerships are an accepted feature of life. Yet I little thought, when I first favoured such developments, that in 40 years' time the mass-circulation papers would more than ever be drenched in stories which constitute flagrant intrusion into private lives. Some changes for the better have refuted my personal scepticism. The abolition of London pea-soupers and the drastic fall in the amount and tolerance of smoking are examples.

The face of Britain has altered. Fifty years ago it was the face of a white European nation, though we now know that some members of the Churchill cabinet were privately disturbed by the small amount of immigration from the Third World that had already occurred. Churchill himself told Sir Hugh Foot over lunch at Chequers that unless immigration were curbed we 'would have a magpie society and this would never do'.[40] Such anxieties were never conveyed to the public at that time. Now we are a racially mixed society – a development which I welcome but which was never consciously endorsed by the host community. In many key service industries – in transportation, for instance, and in hospitals – the face of Britain is liable to be black or brown, and the video that successfully promoted London as the host city of the 2012 Olympics laid great stress on the multicultural character of the city.

In the political sphere readers will certainly have noticed the absence from my story (except tangentially) of the biggest name of the last 25 years: Margaret Thatcher. This reflects the dying out of my close engagement with the political battle, though I remained and remain a close reader of newspapers and periodicals. My time at Chatham House involved me frequently with the Foreign Office but not with Number Ten. When I did meet with the recently created Lady Thatcher shortly after her forced retirement it was in fact the first time I had spoken to her since the short period of rather intense interchange when she was piloting a private member's bill through the Commons just after her election to it. I was presented to her (I noticed that this procedure which I had associated with royalty applies also to her) by a retired diplomat who did not know of this obscure link with the past. 'Oh I know you,' the ex-premier said, 'You were the person who interviewed me over my private member's bill.' This I thought, considering everything that had happened between, was an astonishing display of a politician's memory. Two or three of us went on to talk to her about Saddam Hussein's occupation of Kuwait. 'When Iraqi troops crossed the border,' she said, 'I knew I had to speak to President Reagan. It was no use talking to the Europeans because they believe in CONSENSUS. What we needed at that moment was LEADERSHIP.'

My attitude towards Thatcher's policies over the years was critical but not invariably hostile. After the 1983 election I remained nominally a member of the SDP and when a referendum of all members was held about merger with the Liberals I voted in favour. When David Owen, by then the party leader, refused to accept the result I was flabbergasted. The whole basis of the new party was that it would respond democratically to its members' will. I had respected David up till then but I found this action to be incomprehensible and reading his autobiography does not make it easier to understand.

The 1992 election approached. Hampstead, for all its reputation as a harbour of subversive ideas, had for many elections sent a Conservative to the House. The Tory margins of victory had, however, been steadily on the decline. The opportunity seemed great in this year for turning Hampstead into a Labour seat. I had not forgotten the ugly leftism of the general management committee when last I had been a Labour supporter. But now all had changed. The dominant element in the local party was loyal to Neil Kinnock and John Smith. It wanted to win, had rejoined the mainstream of British progressive opinion and had adopted as its candidate the actress Glenda Jackson, who showed every sign of having made a wholehearted switch to her new profession.

The real battle in Hampstead would be between Mrs Thatcher's Tories and Neil Kinnock's Labour, a party which had resiled from all the stands which had caused my resignation from its ranks. The truth of the matter was that I was vehemently anti-Tory, not that I objected to several of Thatcher's reforms but that I thought that the poll tax, that is a level payment to support local government from everyone regardless of circumstances, was literally mad. There were other issues as well which indicated to me that, whatever were the lady's strengths, she had been in charge for too long, but the poll tax was pre-eminent.

I thought back not only to 1381, which was the first time such an impost had provoked a revolutionary reaction, but also, much more recently, to its introduction in Kenya after the First World War with the object of forcing black Africans into the monetary economy to earn enough to pay their tax. In short, it had hitherto only been resorted to by societies with a primitive administrative system. For twentieth-century Britain it was preposterous.

Although I cast my vote for Glenda I did not rejoin the Labour Party for several years until after Tony Blair had taken over. I was determined, above all, never to apologise for having left the party when I did and would therefore never have rejoined it if I were required to do so. The appeal for new member-ship which came from Gordon Brown was open and unqualified and on that basis I was once more in the ranks of Labour, but now, all ambition spent, was very much an almost silent backbencher.

This is not the place to pursue arguments about current politics in general but I feel I must say a little about the 'War on Terror' and the invasion of Iraq. I happened, just by chance, to be watching the news on BBC News 24 at 2 pm on 9/11 when the second plane was flown into the Twin Towers. When I had heard news about the first, I had recalled a previous occasion when a helicopter had run into a New York skyscraper and thought something similar, though with a larger aircraft, might have happened. Seeing the second collision as it deliberately occurred left no doubt whatever that with the United States under direct attack everything would change. I remained fixed before the set for the rest of the afternoon, watching in real time the dreadful sequence of events that were unfolding. I identified myself with the reaction of Queen and Prime Minister in aligning themselves with the American people. So did diverse people all over the world. I was, however, appalled at the eventual form of the Washington reaction.

Certainly the President needed to speak out robustly and his visit to Ground Zero in New York was well timed and executed. But the proclama-tion of a *war* on terror seemed to me to arouse all the wrong analogies. Terror is a weapons system. It was like declaring war on tanks or submarines. It is also usually fought between states. Admittedly there is also civil war but even then the parties are usually clearly identified. What was required instead was a massive worldwide police operation of unprecedented reach against an appall-ing conspiracy conducted on many fronts, of which international banking would be a salient example. I am not saying that this is not being attempted, but a prime requirement should have been to secure and to hold the maximum amount of willing cooperation from all manner of states. Above all, policies needed to be avoided that threatened to fragment the widest possible coalition.

There was also a technical American implication of asserting that that country was 'at war', of which as a former Washington correspondent I was uncomfortably conscious. Under the constitution the president is in time of war the commander-in-chief. Unlike many of the other provisions which are designed to curb executive powers, there is no provision to define the role of the commander-in-chief, so that George W. Bush might imagine himself clothed with unlimited powers to play as fast and loose with *habeas corpus* as did Abraham Lincoln during the American Civil War.

The intervention in Afghanistan was justified because the government was playing host to Osama bin Laden and his terror apparatus. But any knowledge of Afghan history should have told us what a major and long-term task the rebuilding of the Afghan state and society would be. This would be fully suffi-cient to occupy the resources and energies of the United States and its allies for many years to come. Further, when a situation becomes as fluid as the collapse of organised government by the Taliban, it is essential that the whole country be rapidly prepared for reconstruction. Neither of these conditions was met in Afghanistan, where the British were sent to help in the reconstruction of Helmand Province some three and a half years after the Taliban's overthrow. The amount of opposition that the revived Taliban was then able to put up came as a great surprise. The basic reason for this loss of momentum in dealing with Afghanistan came from the decision to undertake an additional military action against Saddam Hussein. This was the supreme folly.

One expression much overused in judging the rightness of political deci-sions is that 20/20 vision requires the benefit of hindsight. The implication is always that it had been impossible to show foresight. Sometimes that is true and the rebuke to armchair critics is fully justified. But not in the case of Iraq. Almost every argument that was used in 1991 against an advance on Bagh-dad once the Iraqis had been thrown out of Kuwait applied in the situation of 2002–3. As James A. Baker III, the elder Bush's Secretary of State at the time of the first Gulf War, put it, 'If Saddam were captured and his regime toppled, American forces would still have been confronted with the spectre of a military occupation of indefinite duration to pacify a country and sustain a government in power. The ensuing urban warfare would surely have resulted in more casualties to American GIs than the war itself. ... And as much as Saddam's neighbours wanted to see him gone, they feared Iraq would fragment in unpredictable ways that would play into the hands of the mullahs in Iran.' The Israelis never made the mistake of occupying a large city. After the complete victory of the Six Day War they never went on to Cairo or Damascus or Amman. Of course in 2003 Americans' notions of themselves as liberators clouded much of their thinking. But nevertheless most people who had some knowledge of the Middle East foresaw perfectly clearly the dismal consequences the United States and Britain would face as they moved into 2007.

In the course of my researches in the Public Record Office (now renamed the National Archives) I found papers recording a meeting in Washington shortly after Britain had joined the EEC between Henry Kissinger, then Secretary of State, and Sir Alec Douglas-Home, the former Prime Minister who had reverted to being the Foreign Secretary under Ted Heath. Sir Alec patiently explained that in future when the United States wanted British advice it would have to wait until policy had been coordinated with the European partners. Kissinger exploded that this would change everything, since Washington had been accustomed to treating Britain as almost the equivalent of a major US government department. It was a pity that over Iraq Britain did not think first of attempting a European position on Iraq in collaboration with France and Germany, backing Dr Hans Blix, the UN expert on weapons of mass destruction, instead of crudely clearing him out of the way a few weeks before he would have finished his work.

But I must not go on. In my ninth decade I can only sit back and splutter in the privacy of my study about the excessive subordination of British policy to the mistaken policies of the United States. As for that subordination it dates from the fiasco of Suez, and so I did get the opportunity of my being called out of the shadows in 2006 on the occasion of the 50th anniversary of Suez to point out some parallels between Britain in 1956 and the United States (with Britain going along) in 2003. Regime change as an aim, pre-emptive self-defence as a strategic doctrine, cherry-picking of raw intelligence data as an unfortunate practice by democratic rulers are three examples. However Iraq finally works out, it is proving to be a disaster for Messrs. Bush and Blair, supporting the adage that the main lesson from history is that people do not learn the lessons of history, except when they learn the wrong ones, as Eden did over Munich at Suez.

As finally I look back on my long life, in a sense I have to confront something of a paradox. It has been on balance a very happy life. It has seemed to me that a large proportion of people have to spend their time doing boring or unpleasant tasks. For almost the whole time I have been able to avoid this, for which I am profoundly grateful. During my retirement I have had pleasurable

21. With Suzy outside Chatham House in 1990.

things to occupy my mind. Suzy and I have travelled abroad a good deal and have taken care to enjoy our friendships, which are more vital to us as time moves on. Yet, as readers will have noticed, of my three ambitions, to be a peacemaker, to be a politician and to be an academic, only the last was realised and only then in the very last phase of my active life. Sometimes I surprise myself at my approaching the end of the story without feeling any really great disappointments. Partly it is because I have had to accept the consequences of ME and the stroke. More deeply I am bound to ask myself whether in respect of the first two professions at least my absentmindedness would not have let me down in some dramatic fashion. As a journalist I was able to cope with it to a considerable extent, though not always, as I have shown. In my stubborn way I refused to believe that I could not overcome it as an MP. I was determined that if individual constituents were ever to rely on me I would not let them down. But I did realise nevertheless that I would stand in need of an exceptionally understanding private secretary.

Fortunately there is something in my make-up which does not dwell on disappointments and enables me, thanks to a happy home and a ration of by now relatively modest intellectual tasks, to move agreeably towards the inevitable conclusion of this tale.

Postscript by Suzy Kyle

I would like to thank Dr Lester Crook of I.B.Tauris for his enthusiasm and support.

My husband wrote this book from memory, having never kept a diary. He finished it on 1 February 2007. We chose the photographs together the day before I rushed him to hospital, where he died on 21 February.

25 Oppidans Road, Primrose Hill, London NW3 3AG

Notes

1. Lord Radnor's judgement of his own family's lack of interest in the Muniment Room has subsequently been refuted spectacularly by his elder son Jacob ('Jake'), now himself the Earl of Radnor. He has published a delightful, sumptuously presented family history, *A Huguenot Family. Des Bouverie, Bouverie, Pleydell-Bouverie 1536–1889* (Winchester: Foxbury Press, 2001).
2. (By Suzy Kyle): My husband's last words were in fact an eloquent account of James I selling knighthoods to pay for his Irish wars. Our sons and I were with him in the hospital where he died shortly afterwards.
3. (By Suzy Kyle): My husband's obituary in the *Guardian* by Godfrey Smith started off: 'Even among the torrent of ex-servicemen returning to Oxford from the war, Keith Kyle stood out. Six feet three, lean, vague, aquiline, scholarly, he looked like some benign bird of paradise that had wandered into the cloisters. An improbable former infantry captain, he came up to read history under A.J.P. Taylor in 1947, and quickly made his name as a precocious Union speaker. He delivered his speeches – cogent, fluent and learned – without a note. He composed his own budget for fun each year just before the chancellor delivered his.'
4. Now the District of Columbia has an elected mayor (since 1974) and three votes in the electoral college for the presidency (since 1964). It has no senator and only a non-voting delegate in the House of Representatives.
5. In British terminology a piece of legislation is a 'bill' until it has been enacted. In America it is an 'act' throughout.
6. 'Choice for Virginia', *The Economist*, 7 January 1956, p 39.
7. 'The Organisation Men. Kennedy's Convention', *Time & Tide*, 23 July 1960, pp 850–1.
8. 'Open Minds and Open Skies', *Time & Tide*, 24 September 1960, pp 1143–4.
9. 'Disarmament: Is Khrushchev's Proposal "Unthinkable?"', *The New Republic*, 2 January 1961, pp 11–15.
10. 'Special Report: The Lord Chancellor. An office that might scandalise Americans', *The London American*, 26 May–1 June 1961, p 4.
11. The next occasion was in 2001 when Vice-President Gore was required to

291

announce his defeat in electoral votes (though he had a popular majority) by George W. Bush.

12. 'President Kennedy and his first Congress', *Time & Tide*, 27 January 1961, p 124.

13. Richard Lindley, *Panorama. Fifty Years of Pride and Paranoia* (Politico's, 2002), p 196.

14. *Reynolds News*, 19 November 1961.

15. 'More about the Common Market: The Political Challenge Facing Britain', *Sunday Times*, 24 June 1962.

16. 'European Report: Commonwealth Food Still the Stumbling Block', *Sunday Times*, 22 July 1962.

17. Richard Posnett, *The Scent of Eucalyptus. A Journal of Colonial and Foreign Service* (The Radcliffe Press, 2001).

18. 'Adoula controls all Congo except for Katanga', *Sunday Times*, 28 October 1962.

19. 'Kenya election', BBC General Overseas Service, May 1963.

20. 'Dr Nkrumah's New Man', *The Spectator*, 4 September 1964.

21. In 1455 and 1461.

22. 'How to Get Chosen', *The Economist*, 2 May 1959, pp 404–5.

23. 'Britain and the German Problem', *The Listener*, 4 May 1967, pp 575–7.

24. 'Morality and Conscience in Politics', *The Listener*, 18 May 1967, pp 639–40, 667.

25. 'Britain's Part in World Affairs', *The Listener*, 15 June 1967, pp 775–7

26. 'The Middle East Crisis: A Personal View', *The Listener*, 1 June 1967, pp 703–5.

27. The Rev Hugh Hanna (1821–92) was a Presbyterian minister thus described in *Punch*: 'What's faction's flame or hatred's gall / What's riot, blooded row or brawl / Roaring Hanna / To one who boasts an inward call / Roaring Hanna.' A large bronze statue of Roaring Hanna in Carlisle Circus, Belfast, was destroyed by explosives in 1970.

28. 'Ulster' and 'the Province' are used here as equivalents of 'Northern Ireland'. It should be remembered, though, that the actual Irish Province of Ulster has nine counties, three of which are within the Irish Republic.

29. 'BBC man "knew in advance"', *Jewish Chronicle*, 21 February 1969.

30. Much was made at the time of the fact that Yusuf Sayigh insisted on taking part from a different studio from the rest of us. Being a member of the PLO he was subject to its discipline, which at the time forbade Palestinians appearing in public with Jews. But, as a decent human being, he came across afterwards and engaged in cordial conversation with the others.

31. 'Israel rejects Kyle allegations', *Jewish Chronicle*, 9 May 1969. Hyam Corney, 'Kyle given a verbal hammering,' *Jewish Chronicle*, 18 July 1969.

32. Marion Gain, *Personal Reminiscences of Chatham House 1957–1969* (1986), p 7.

33. 'Conflict and Cohesion', *New Europe*, June 1973, pp 18–19, 32.

34. 'The European Parliament', *The World Today*, December 1972.

35. The detailed story and background of Yao's polemic have subsequently been brilliantly narrated in the third volume of Roderick MacFarquhar's great work *The Origins of the Cultural Revolution* (OUP & Columbia UP, 1997).

36. Tony Newton received 20,559 votes to my 19,469 and 12,004 for the Liberal, Richard Holme. The majority was down from 2,001 to 1,090 and the swing in my favour 0.7 per cent. Would I have benefited enough from the fall in the Liberal vote if it had not been known that I was ill? No one will ever know.

37. Ivor Crewe and Anthony King, *SDP. The Birth, Life and Death of the Social Democratic Party* (OUP, 1995), pp 468–9.

38. See Simon Jenkins, *Thatcher & Sons. A Revolution in Three Acts* (Allen Lane, 2006).

39. A phase, popular at the time of my youth, for being in disreputable debt.

40. Quoted in Peter Hennessy, *Having It So Good. Britain in the Fifties* (Allen Lane, 2006), p 224.

Index